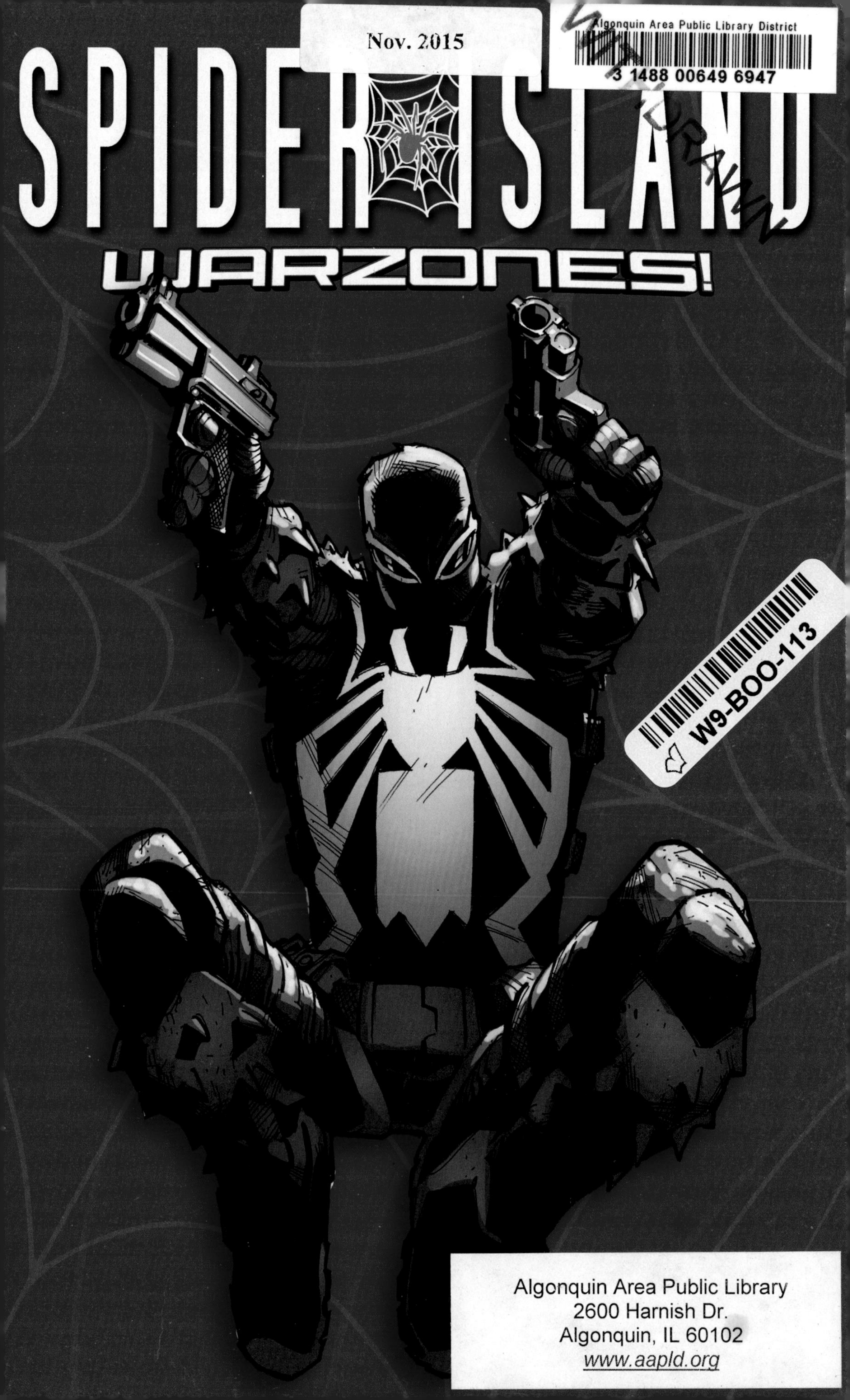
SPIDER-ISLAND
WARZONES!

THE MULTIVERSE WAS DESTROYED!
HEROES OF EARTH-616 AND EARTH-1610 WERE POWERLESS TO SAVE IT!
NOW, ALL THAT REMAINS...IS **BATTLEWORLD**:
A MASSIVE, PATCHWORK PLANET COMPOSED OF THE FRAGMENTS OF WORLDS THAT NO LONGER EXIST, MAINTAINED BY THE IRON WILL OF ITS GOD AND MASTER, VICTOR VON DOOM!
EACH REGION IS A DOMAIN UNTO ITSELF!

SPIDER-ISLAND
WARZONES!

Writer: **CHRISTOS GAGE**
Artist: **PACO DIAZ**
Colorist: **FRANK D'ARMATA**

Letterers: **VC's TRAVIS LANHAM** (#1-3 & #5) & **CLAYTON COWLES** (#4)
Cover Art: **HUMBERTO RAMOS & EDGAR DELGADO**

"MAYDAY PARKER: SPIDER-WOMAN"

Script, plot and pencils: **TOM DEFALCO & RON FRENZ**
Finished art: **SAL BUSCEMA**
Colorist: **ANDREW CROSSLEY** | Letterer: **VC's TRAVIS LANHAM**

Assistant Editor: **DEVIN LEWIS** | Editor: **NICK LOWE**

Collection Editor: SARAH BRUNSTAD
Associate Managing Editor: ALEX STARBUCK
Editors, Special Projects: JENNIFER GRÜNWALD & MARK D. BEAZLEY
Senior Editor, Special Projects: JEFF YOUNGQUIST
SVP Print, Sales & Marketing: DAVID GABRIEL
Book Designer: ADAM DEL RE

Editor in Chief: AXEL ALONSO
Chief Creative Officer: JOE QUESADA
Publisher: DAN BUCKLEY
Executive Producer: ALAN FINE

SPIDER-ISLAND: WARZONES! Contains material originally published in magazine form as SPIDER-ISLAND #1-5. First printing 2015. ISBN# 978-0-7851-9885-7. Published by MARVEL WORLDWIDE, INC., a subsidiary of MARVEL ENTERTAINMENT, LLC. OFFICE OF PUBLICATION: 135 West 50th Street, New York, NY 10020. **Printed in Canada.** ALAN FINE, President, Marvel Entertainment; DAN BUCKLEY, President, TV, Publishing and Brand Management; JOE QUESADA, Chief Creative Officer; TOM BREVOORT, SVP of Publishing; DAVID BOGART, SVP of Operations & Procurement, Publishing; C.B. CEBULSKI, VP of International Development & Brand Management; DAVID GABRIEL, SVP Print, Sales & Marketing; JIM O'KEEFE, VP of Operations & Logistics; DAN CARR, Executive Director of Publishing Technology; SUSAN CRESPI, Editorial Operations Manager; ALEX MORALES, Publishing Operations Manager; STAN LEE, Chairman Emeritus. For information regarding advertising in Marvel Comics or on Marvel.com, please contact Jonathan Rheingold, VP of Custom Solutions & Ad Sales, at jrheingold@marvel.com. For Marvel subscription inquiries, please call 800-217-9158. **Manufactured between 9/18/2015 and 10/26/2015 by SOLISCO PRINTERS, SCOTT, QC, CANADA.**

10 9 8 7 6 5 4 3 2 1

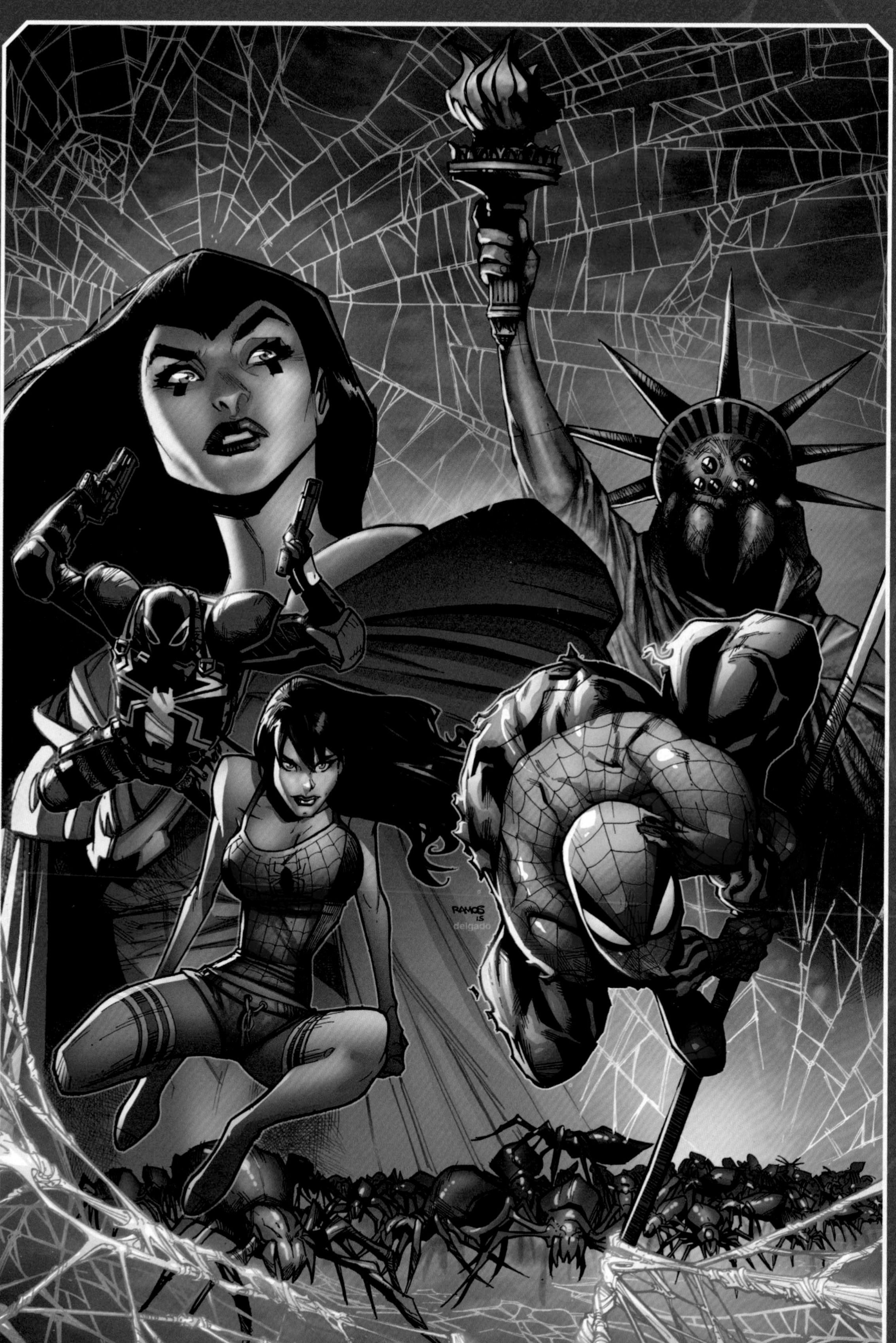
RAMOS 15
delgado

PART ONE: **ALTERED STATES**

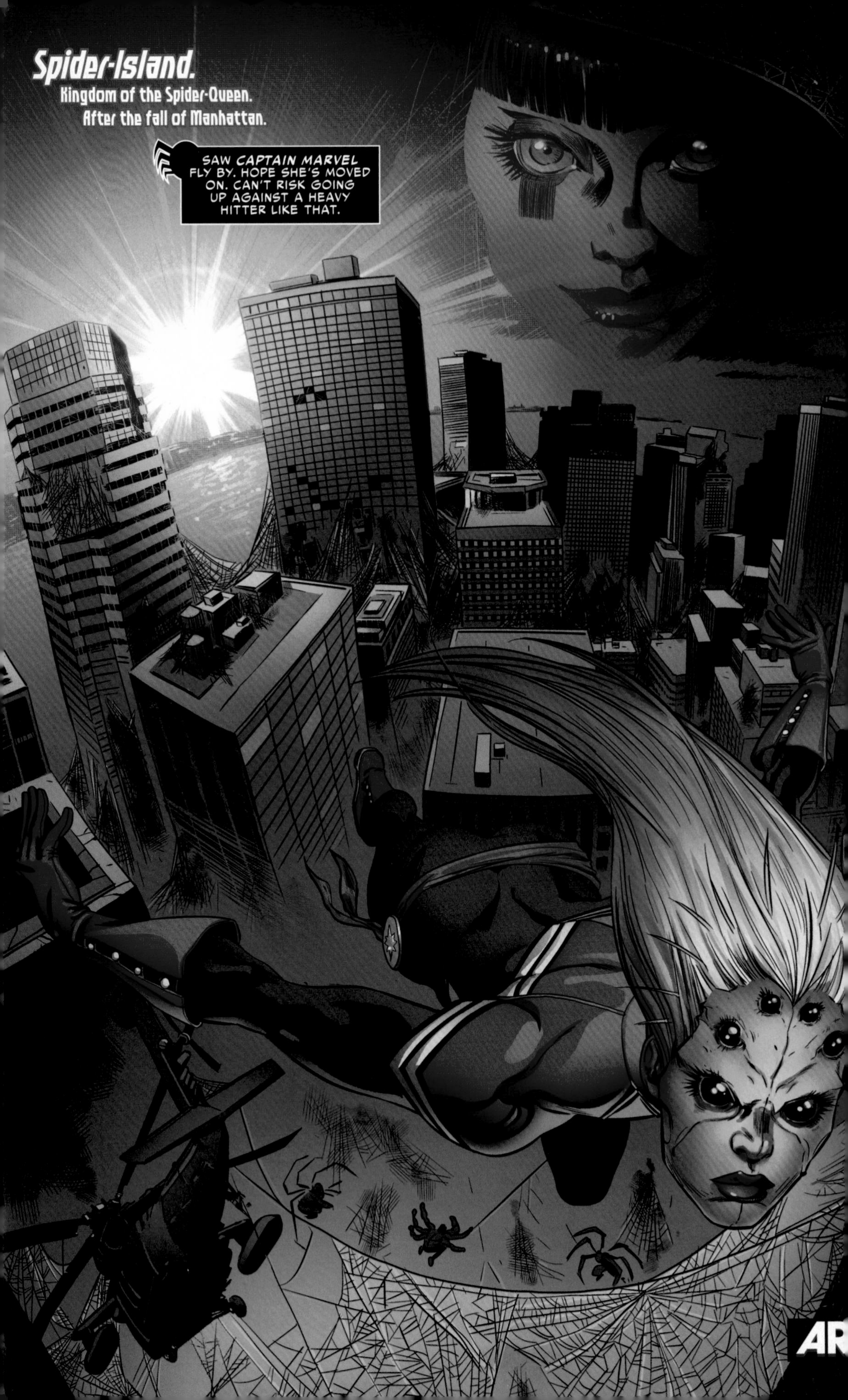
Spider-Island.
Kingdom of the Spider-Queen.
After the fall of Manhattan.
SAW CAPTAIN MARVEL FLY BY. HOPE SHE'S MOVED ON. CAN'T RISK GOING UP AGAINST A HEAVY HITTER LIKE THAT.

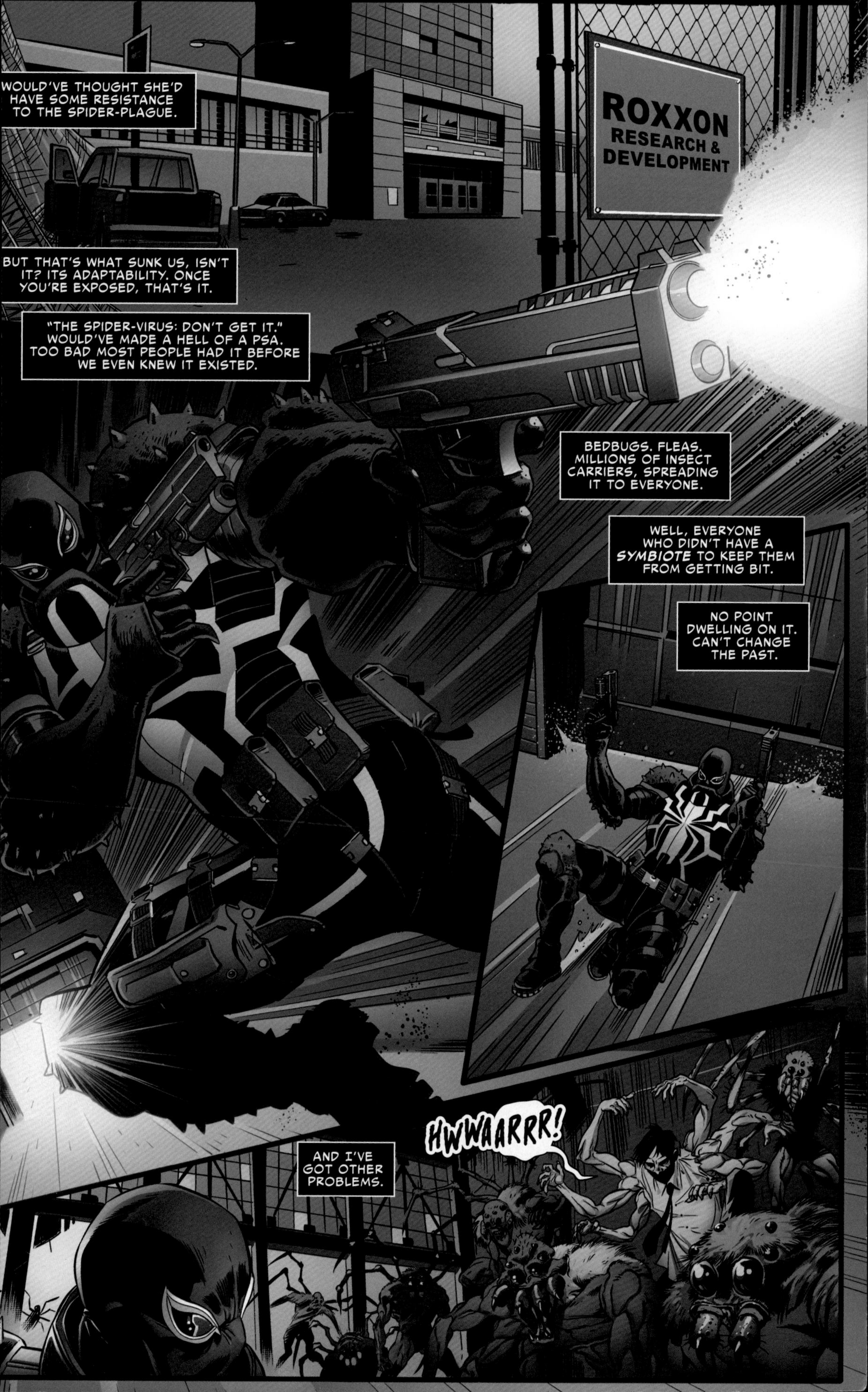
ROXXON RESEARCH & DEVELOPMENT
WOULD'VE THOUGHT SHE'D HAVE SOME RESISTANCE TO THE SPIDER-PLAGUE.
BUT THAT'S WHAT SUNK US, ISN'T IT? ITS ADAPTABILITY. ONCE YOU'RE EXPOSED, THAT'S IT.
"THE SPIDER-VIRUS: DON'T GET IT." WOULD'VE MADE A HELL OF A PSA. TOO BAD MOST PEOPLE HAD IT BEFORE WE EVEN KNEW IT EXISTED.
BEDBUGS. FLEAS. MILLIONS OF INSECT CARRIERS, SPREADING IT TO EVERYONE.
WELL, EVERYONE WHO DIDN'T HAVE A *SYMBIOTE* TO KEEP THEM FROM GETTING BIT.
NO POINT DWELLING ON IT. CAN'T CHANGE THE PAST.
HWWAARRR!
AND I'VE GOT OTHER PROBLEMS.

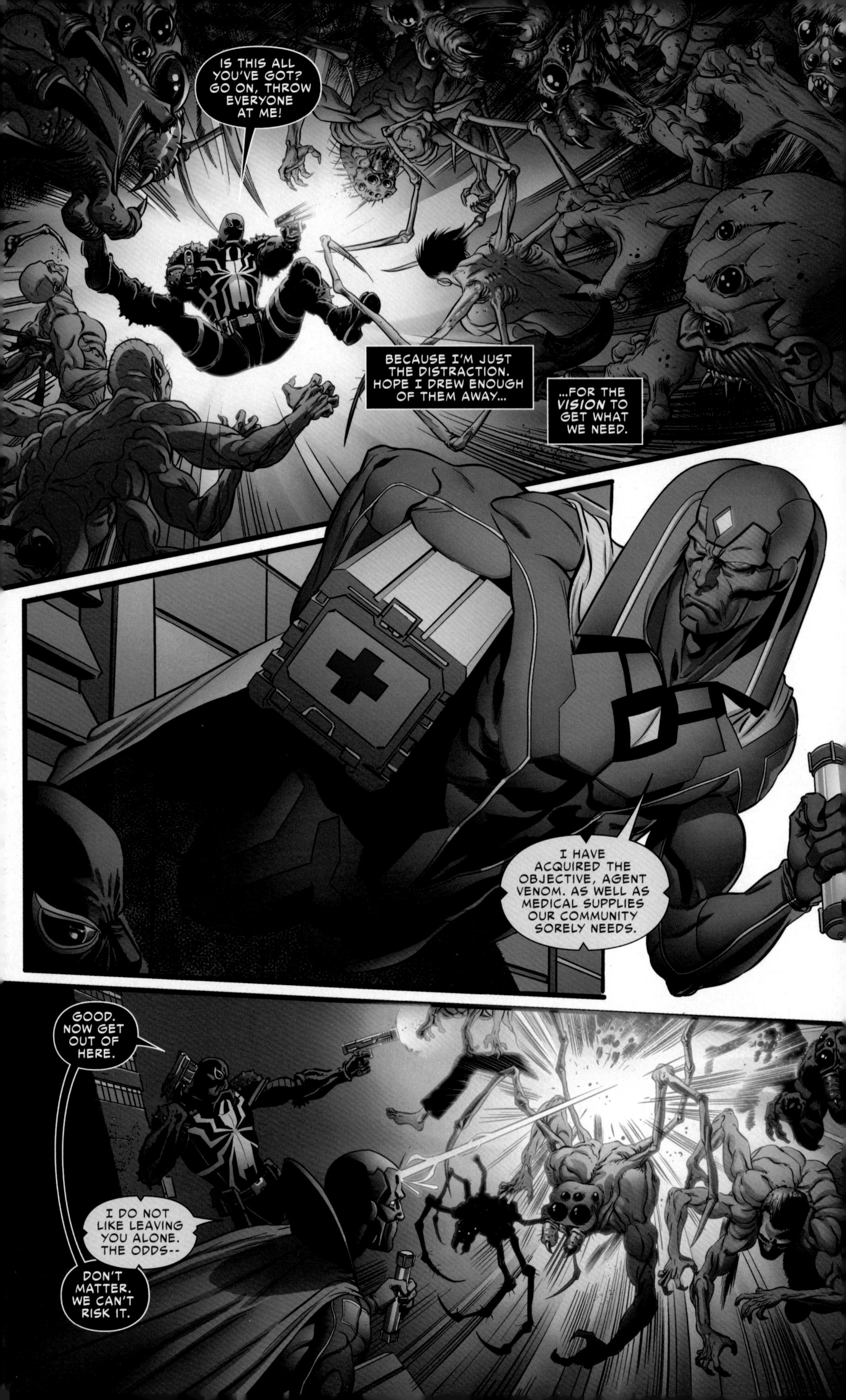
IS THIS ALL YOU'VE GOT? GO ON, THROW EVERYONE AT ME!
BECAUSE I'M JUST THE DISTRACTION. HOPE I DREW ENOUGH OF THEM AWAY...
...FOR THE VISION TO GET WHAT WE NEED.
I HAVE ACQUIRED THE OBJECTIVE, AGENT VENOM. AS WELL AS MEDICAL SUPPLIES OUR COMMUNITY SORELY NEEDS.
GOOD. NOW GET OUT OF HERE.
I DO NOT LIKE LEAVING YOU ALONE. THE ODDS--
DON'T MATTER. WE CAN'T RISK IT.

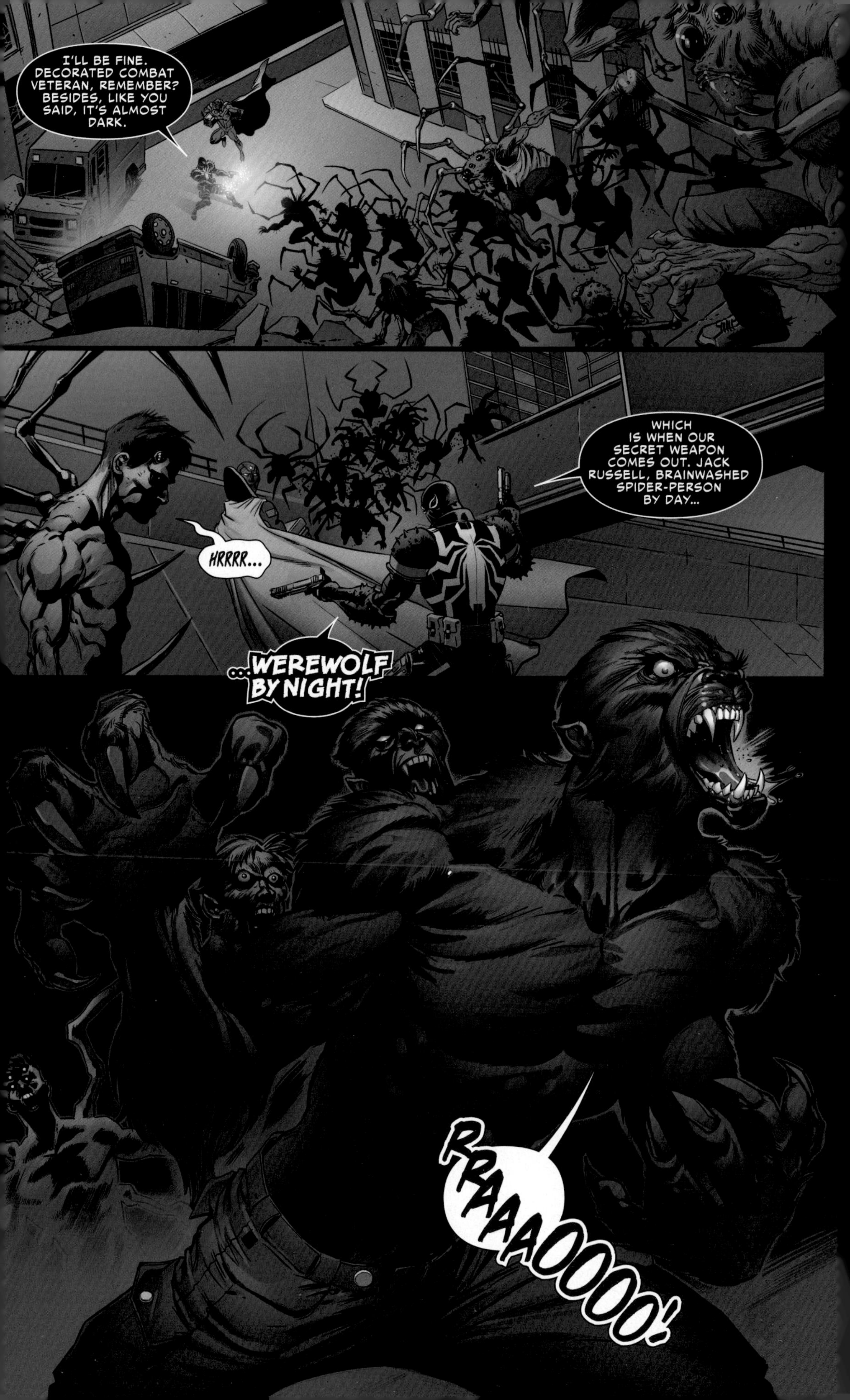

I'LL BE FINE. DECORATED COMBAT VETERAN, REMEMBER? BESIDES, LIKE YOU SAID, IT'S ALMOST DARK.
WHICH IS WHEN OUR SECRET WEAPON COMES OUT. JACK RUSSELL, BRAINWASHED SPIDER-PERSON BY DAY...
HRRRR...
...WEREWOLF BY NIGHT!
RRAAAOOOO!

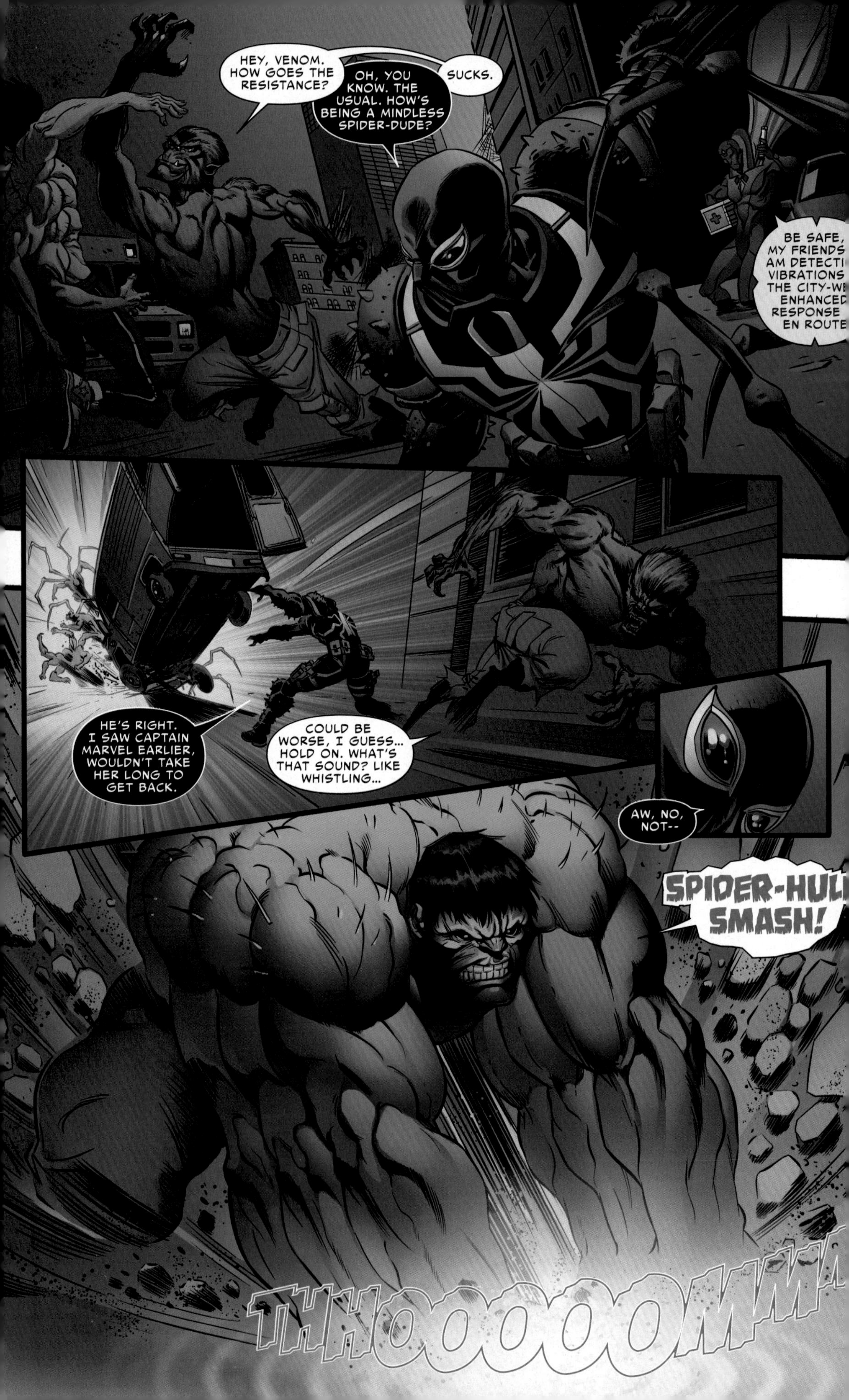
HEY, VENOM. HOW GOES THE RESISTANCE?
OH, YOU KNOW. THE USUAL. HOW'S BEING A MINDLESS SPIDER-DUDE?
SUCKS.
BE SAFE, MY FRIENDS AM DETECTI VIBRATIONS THE CITY-W ENHANCED RESPONSE EN ROUTE
HE'S RIGHT. I SAW CAPTAIN MARVEL EARLIER, WOULDN'T TAKE HER LONG TO GET BACK.
COULD BE WORSE, I GUESS... HOLD ON. WHAT'S THAT SOUND? LIKE WHISTLING...
AW, NO, NOT--
SPIDER-HUL SMASH!
THOOOOOMM

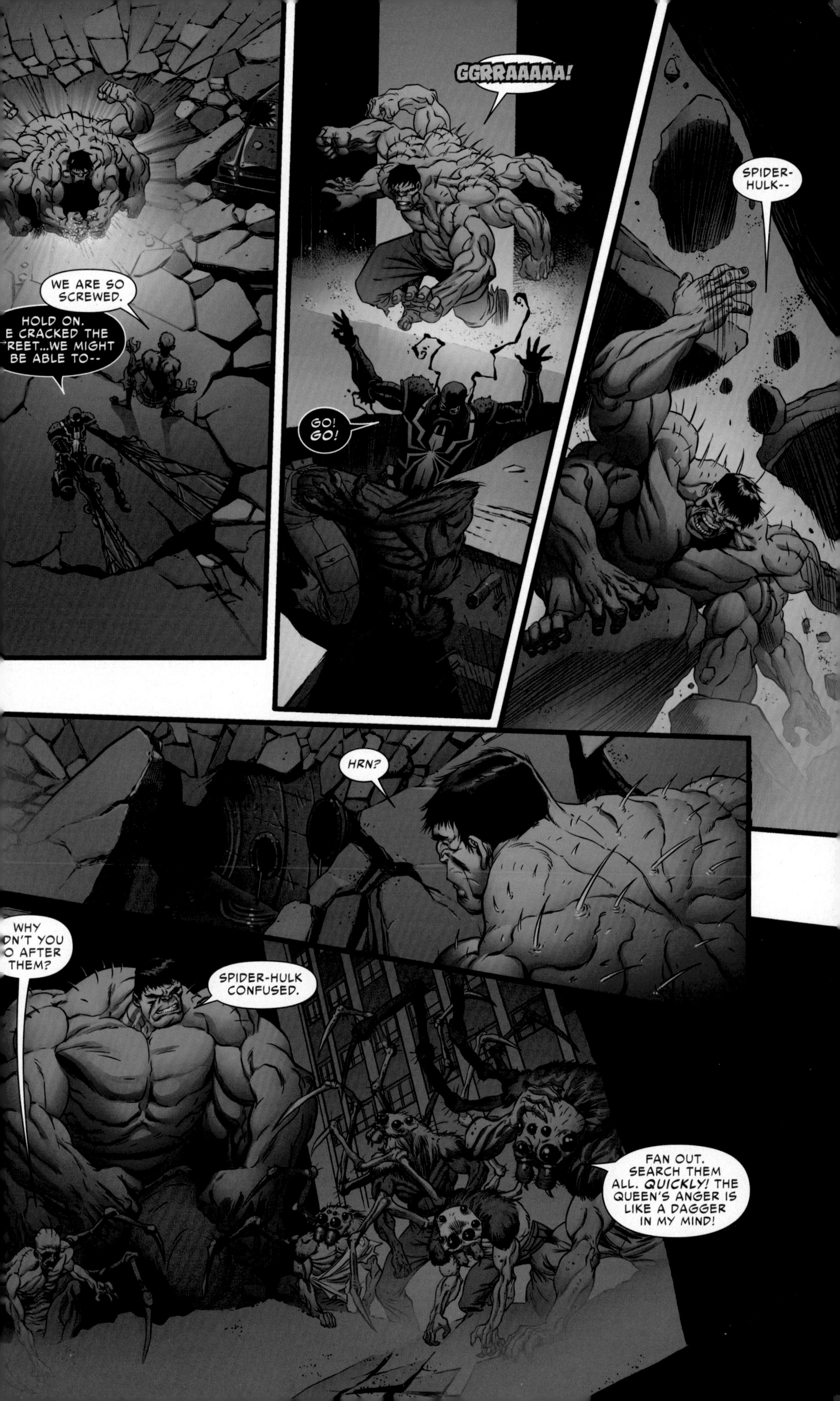

WE ARE SO SCREWED.
HOLD ON. E CRACKED THE REET...WE MIGHT BE ABLE TO--
GGRRAAAAA!
GO! GO!
SPIDER-HULK--
HRN?
WHY N'T YOU O AFTER THEM?
SPIDER-HULK CONFUSED.
FAN OUT. SEARCH THEM ALL. QUICKLY! THE QUEEN'S ANGER IS LIKE A DAGGER IN MY MIND!

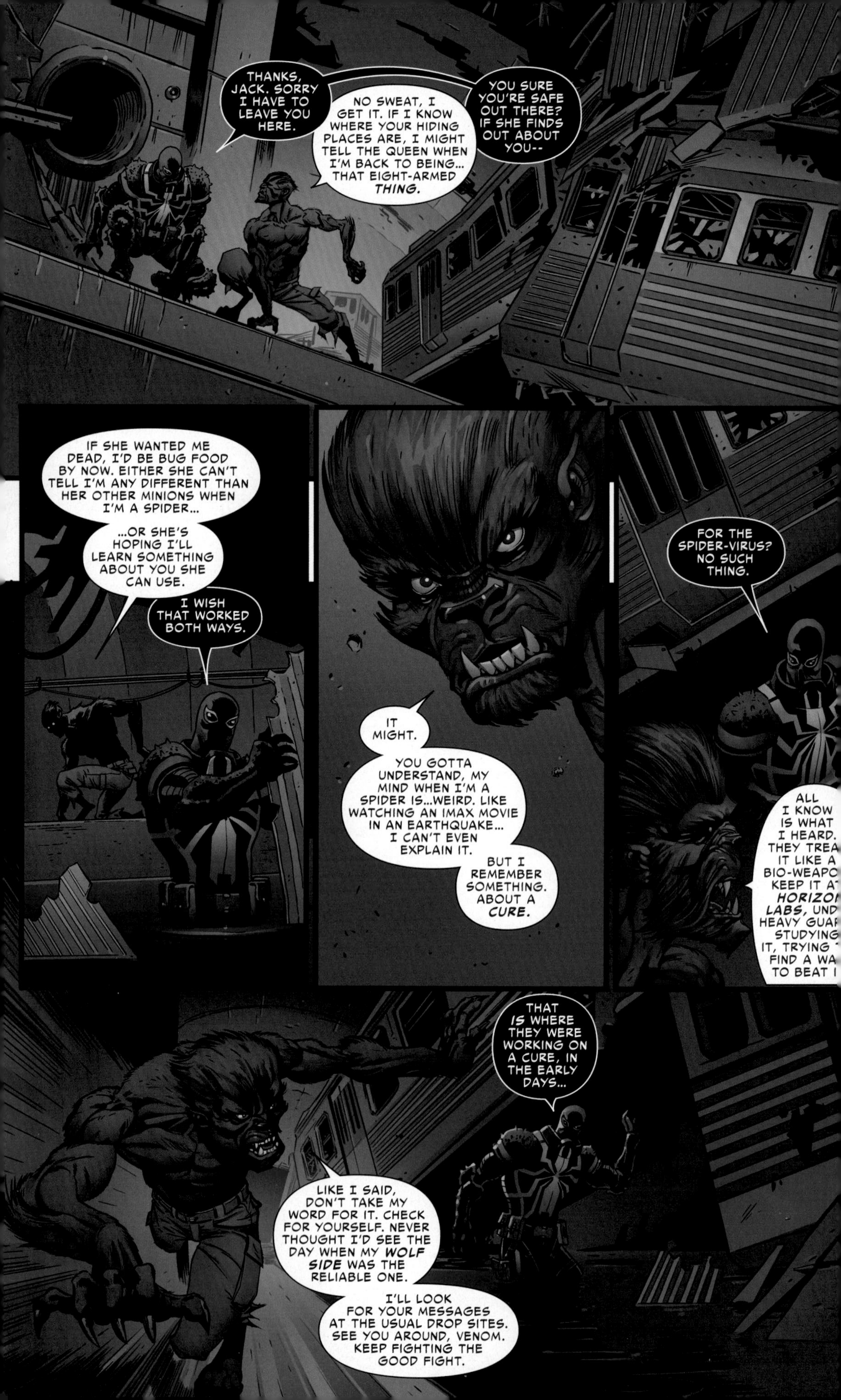
THANKS, JACK. SORRY I HAVE TO LEAVE YOU HERE.
NO SWEAT, I GET IT. IF I KNOW WHERE YOUR HIDING PLACES ARE, I MIGHT TELL THE QUEEN WHEN I'M BACK TO BEING... THAT EIGHT-ARMED THING.
YOU SURE YOU'RE SAFE OUT THERE? IF SHE FINDS OUT ABOUT YOU--
IF SHE WANTED ME DEAD, I'D BE BUG FOOD BY NOW. EITHER SHE CAN'T TELL I'M ANY DIFFERENT THAN HER OTHER MINIONS WHEN I'M A SPIDER...
...OR SHE'S HOPING I'LL LEARN SOMETHING ABOUT YOU SHE CAN USE.
I WISH THAT WORKED BOTH WAYS.
IT MIGHT.
YOU GOTTA UNDERSTAND, MY MIND WHEN I'M A SPIDER IS...WEIRD. LIKE WATCHING AN IMAX MOVIE IN AN EARTHQUAKE... I CAN'T EVEN EXPLAIN IT.
BUT I REMEMBER SOMETHING. ABOUT A CURE.
FOR THE SPIDER-VIRUS? NO SUCH THING.
ALL I KNOW IS WHAT I HEARD. THEY TREA IT LIKE A BIO-WEAPO KEEP IT A HORIZO LABS, UND HEAVY GUAR STUDYING IT, TRYING FIND A WA TO BEAT I
THAT IS WHERE THEY WERE WORKING ON A CURE, IN THE EARLY DAYS...
LIKE I SAID, DON'T TAKE MY WORD FOR IT. CHECK FOR YOURSELF. NEVER THOUGHT I'D SEE THE DAY WHEN MY WOLF SIDE WAS THE RELIABLE ONE.
I'LL LOOK FOR YOUR MESSAGES AT THE USUAL DROP SITES. SEE YOU AROUND, VENOM. KEEP FIGHTING THE GOOD FIGHT.

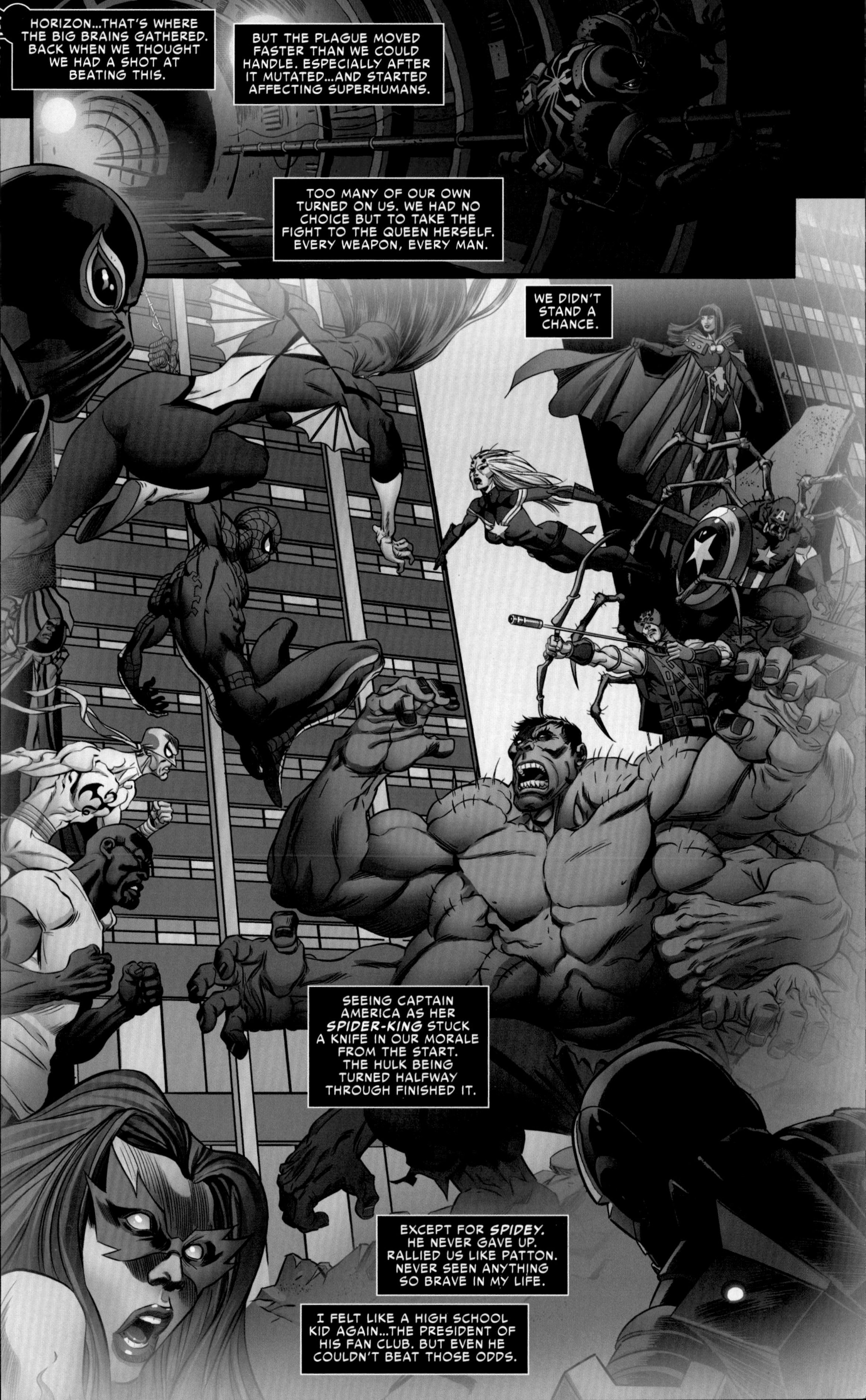
HORIZON...THAT'S WHERE THE BIG BRAINS GATHERED. BACK WHEN WE THOUGHT WE HAD A SHOT AT BEATING THIS.
BUT THE PLAGUE MOVED FASTER THAN WE COULD HANDLE. ESPECIALLY AFTER IT MUTATED...AND STARTED AFFECTING SUPERHUMANS.
TOO MANY OF OUR OWN TURNED ON US. WE HAD NO CHOICE BUT TO TAKE THE FIGHT TO THE QUEEN HERSELF. EVERY WEAPON, EVERY MAN.
WE DIDN'T STAND A CHANCE.
SEEING CAPTAIN AMERICA AS HER SPIDER-KING STUCK A KNIFE IN OUR MORALE FROM THE START. THE HULK BEING TURNED HALFWAY THROUGH FINISHED IT.
EXCEPT FOR SPIDEY. HE NEVER GAVE UP. RALLIED US LIKE PATTON. NEVER SEEN ANYTHING SO BRAVE IN MY LIFE.
I FELT LIKE A HIGH SCHOOL KID AGAIN...THE PRESIDENT OF HIS FAN CLUB. BUT EVEN HE COULDN'T BEAT THOSE ODDS.

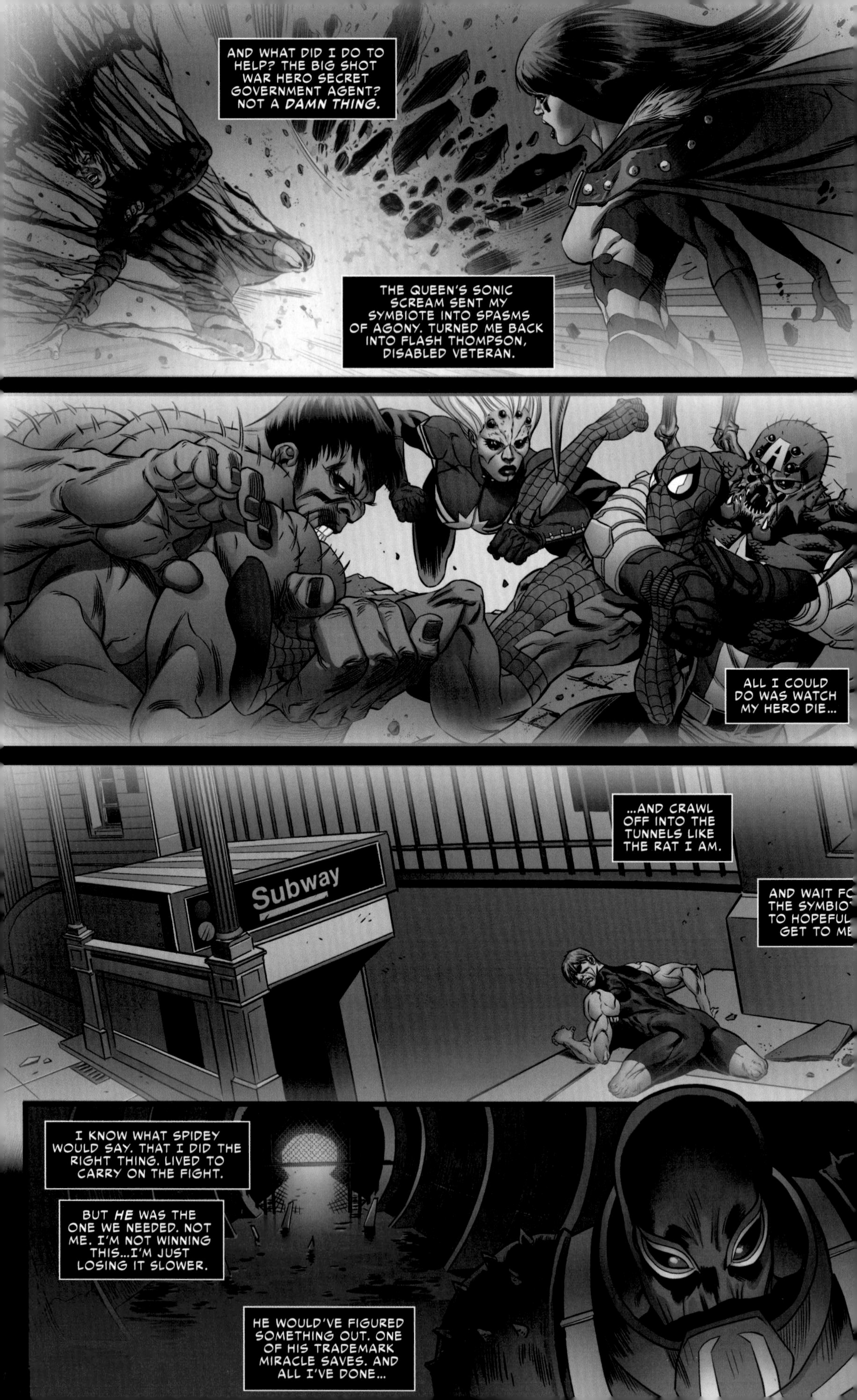
AND WHAT DID I DO TO HELP? THE BIG SHOT WAR HERO SECRET GOVERNMENT AGENT? NOT A *DAMN THING.*
THE QUEEN'S SONIC SCREAM SENT MY SYMBIOTE INTO SPASMS OF AGONY. TURNED ME BACK INTO FLASH THOMPSON, DISABLED VETERAN.
ALL I COULD DO WAS WATCH MY HERO DIE...
...AND CRAWL OFF INTO THE TUNNELS LIKE THE RAT I AM.
Subway
I KNOW WHAT SPIDEY WOULD SAY. THAT I DID THE RIGHT THING. LIVED TO CARRY ON THE FIGHT.
BUT *HE* WAS THE ONE WE NEEDED. NOT ME. I'M NOT WINNING THIS...I'M JUST LOSING IT SLOWER.
HE WOULD'VE FIGURED SOMETHING OUT. ONE OF HIS TRADEMARK MIRACLE SAVES. AND ALL I'VE DONE...

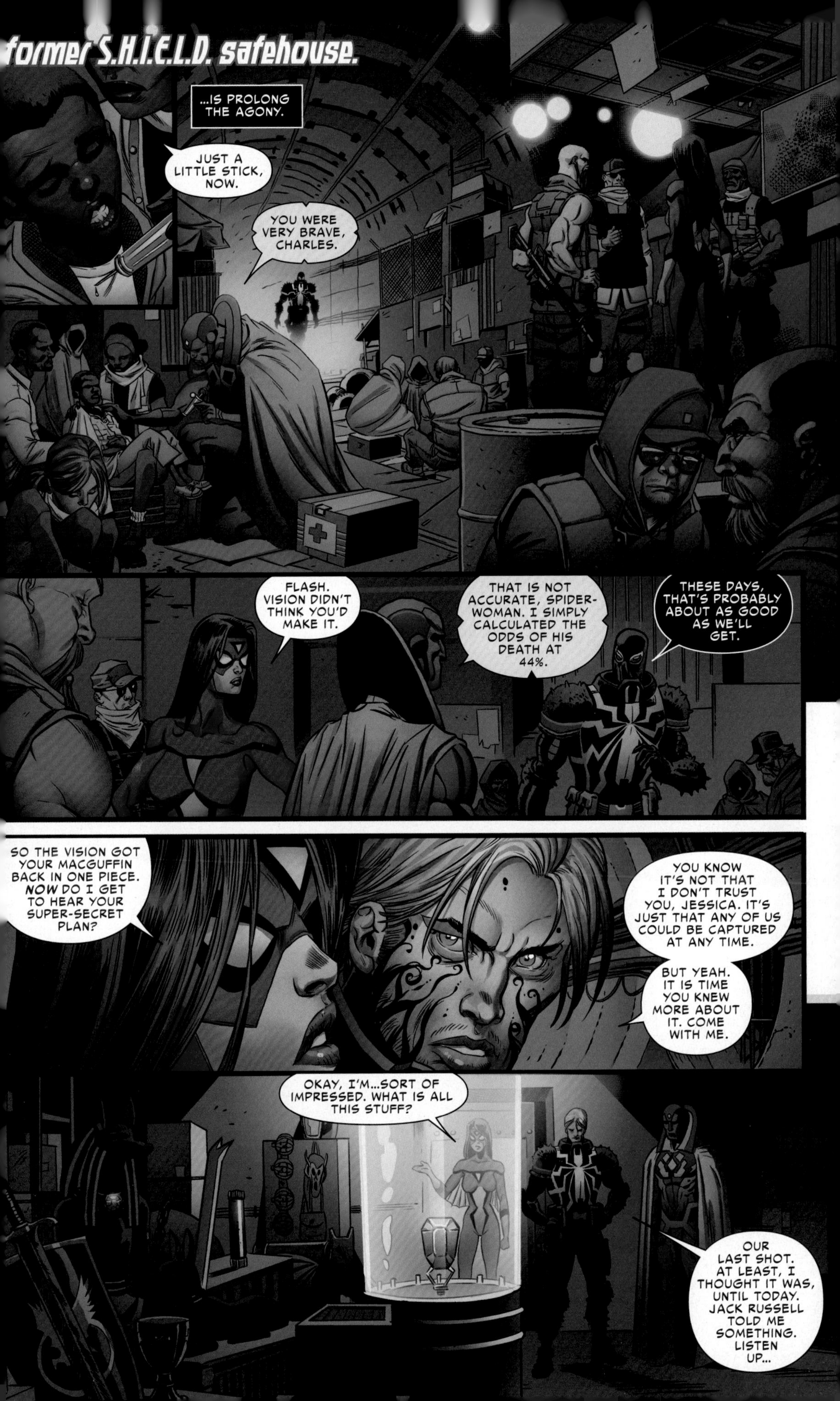

former S.H.I.E.L.D. safehouse.
...IS PROLONG THE AGONY.
JUST A LITTLE STICK, NOW.
YOU WERE VERY BRAVE, CHARLES.
FLASH. VISION DIDN'T THINK YOU'D MAKE IT.
THAT IS NOT ACCURATE, SPIDER-WOMAN. I SIMPLY CALCULATED THE ODDS OF HIS DEATH AT 44%.
THESE DAYS, THAT'S PROBABLY ABOUT AS GOOD AS WE'LL GET.
SO THE VISION GOT YOUR MACGUFFIN BACK IN ONE PIECE. NOW DO I GET TO HEAR YOUR SUPER-SECRET PLAN?
YOU KNOW IT'S NOT THAT I DON'T TRUST YOU, JESSICA. IT'S JUST THAT ANY OF US COULD BE CAPTURED AT ANY TIME.
BUT YEAH. IT IS TIME YOU KNEW MORE ABOUT IT. COME WITH ME.
OKAY, I'M...SORT OF IMPRESSED. WHAT IS ALL THIS STUFF?
OUR LAST SHOT. AT LEAST, I THOUGHT IT WAS, UNTIL TODAY. JACK RUSSELL TOLD ME SOMETHING. LISTEN UP...

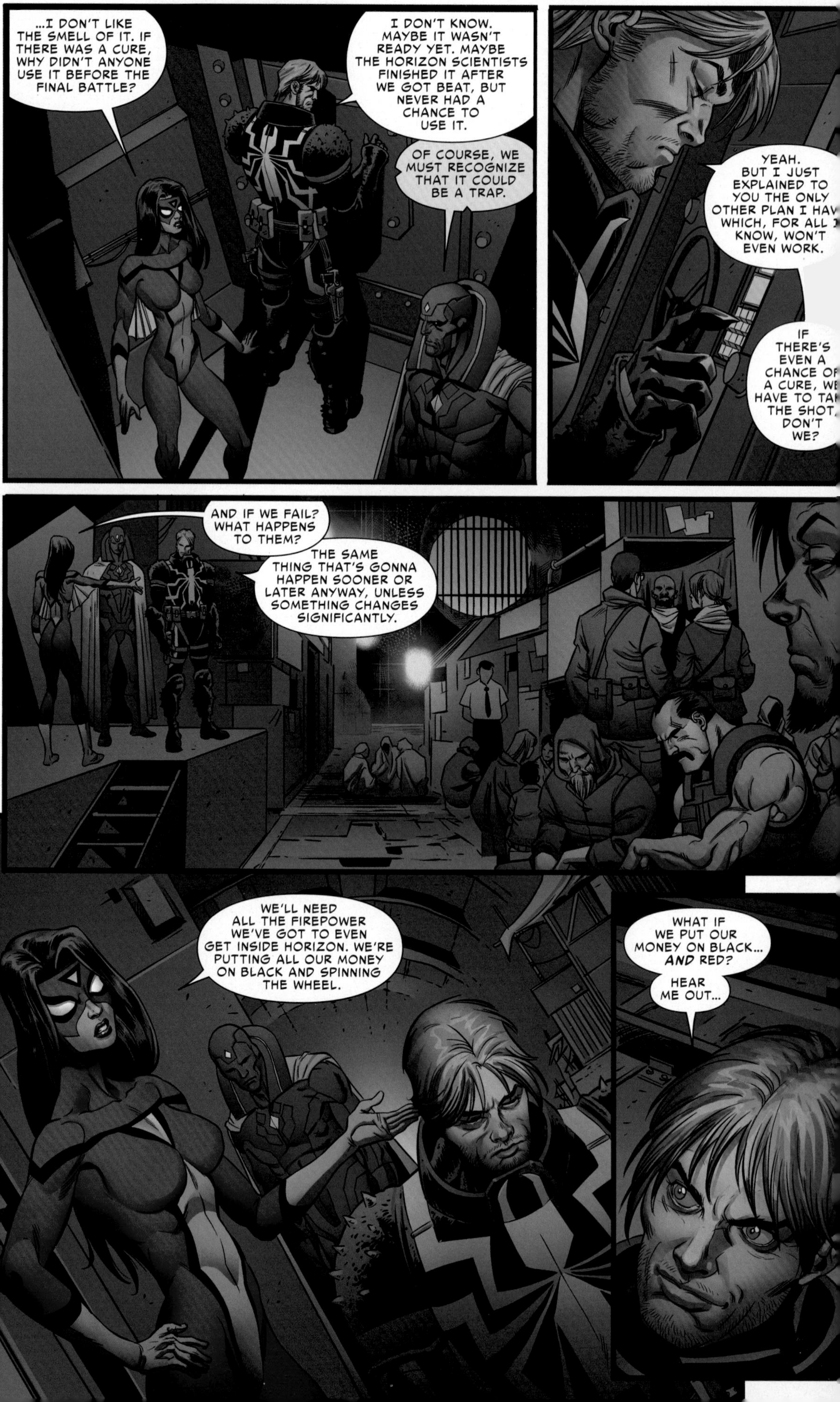

...I DON'T LIKE THE SMELL OF IT. IF THERE WAS A CURE, WHY DIDN'T ANYONE USE IT BEFORE THE FINAL BATTLE?
I DON'T KNOW. MAYBE IT WASN'T READY YET. MAYBE THE HORIZON SCIENTISTS FINISHED IT AFTER WE GOT BEAT, BUT NEVER HAD A CHANCE TO USE IT.
OF COURSE, WE MUST RECOGNIZE THAT IT COULD BE A TRAP.
YEAH. BUT I JUST EXPLAINED TO YOU THE ONLY OTHER PLAN I HAV WHICH, FOR ALL KNOW, WON'T EVEN WORK.
IF THERE'S EVEN A CHANCE OF A CURE, WE HAVE TO TA THE SHOT. DON'T WE?
AND IF WE FAIL? WHAT HAPPENS TO THEM?
THE SAME THING THAT'S GONNA HAPPEN SOONER OR LATER ANYWAY, UNLESS SOMETHING CHANGES SIGNIFICANTLY.
WE'LL NEED ALL THE FIREPOWER WE'VE GOT TO EVEN GET INSIDE HORIZON. WE'RE PUTTING ALL OUR MONEY ON BLACK AND SPINNING THE WHEEL.
WHAT IF WE PUT OUR MONEY ON BLACK... AND RED?
HEAR ME OUT...

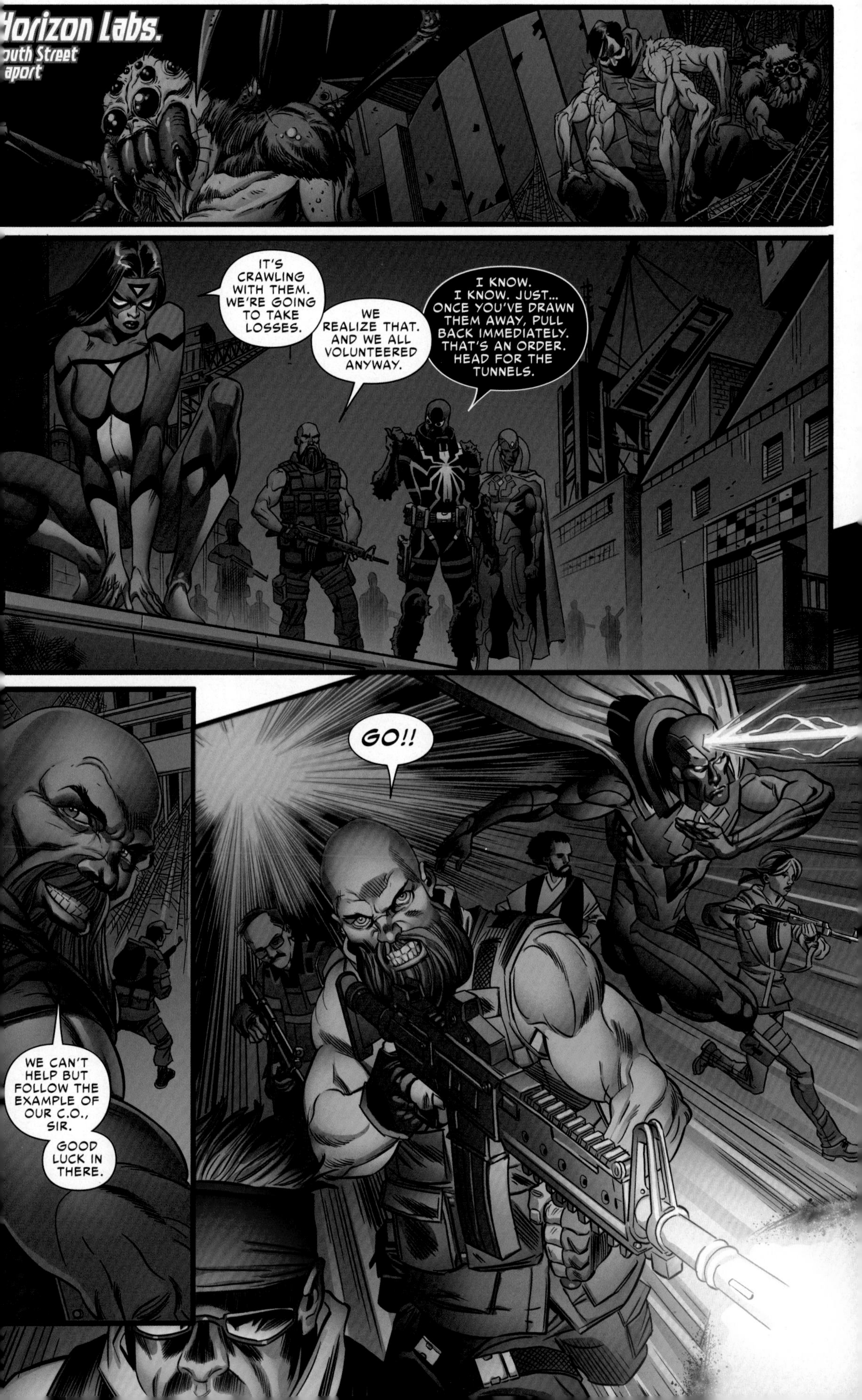

Horizon Labs.
South Street
Seaport
IT'S CRAWLING WITH THEM. WE'RE GOING TO TAKE LOSSES.
WE REALIZE THAT. AND WE ALL VOLUNTEERED ANYWAY.
I KNOW. I KNOW. JUST... ONCE YOU'VE DRAWN THEM AWAY, PULL BACK IMMEDIATELY. THAT'S AN ORDER. HEAD FOR THE TUNNELS.
WE CAN'T HELP BUT FOLLOW THE EXAMPLE OF OUR C.O., SIR.
GOOD LUCK IN THERE.
GO!!

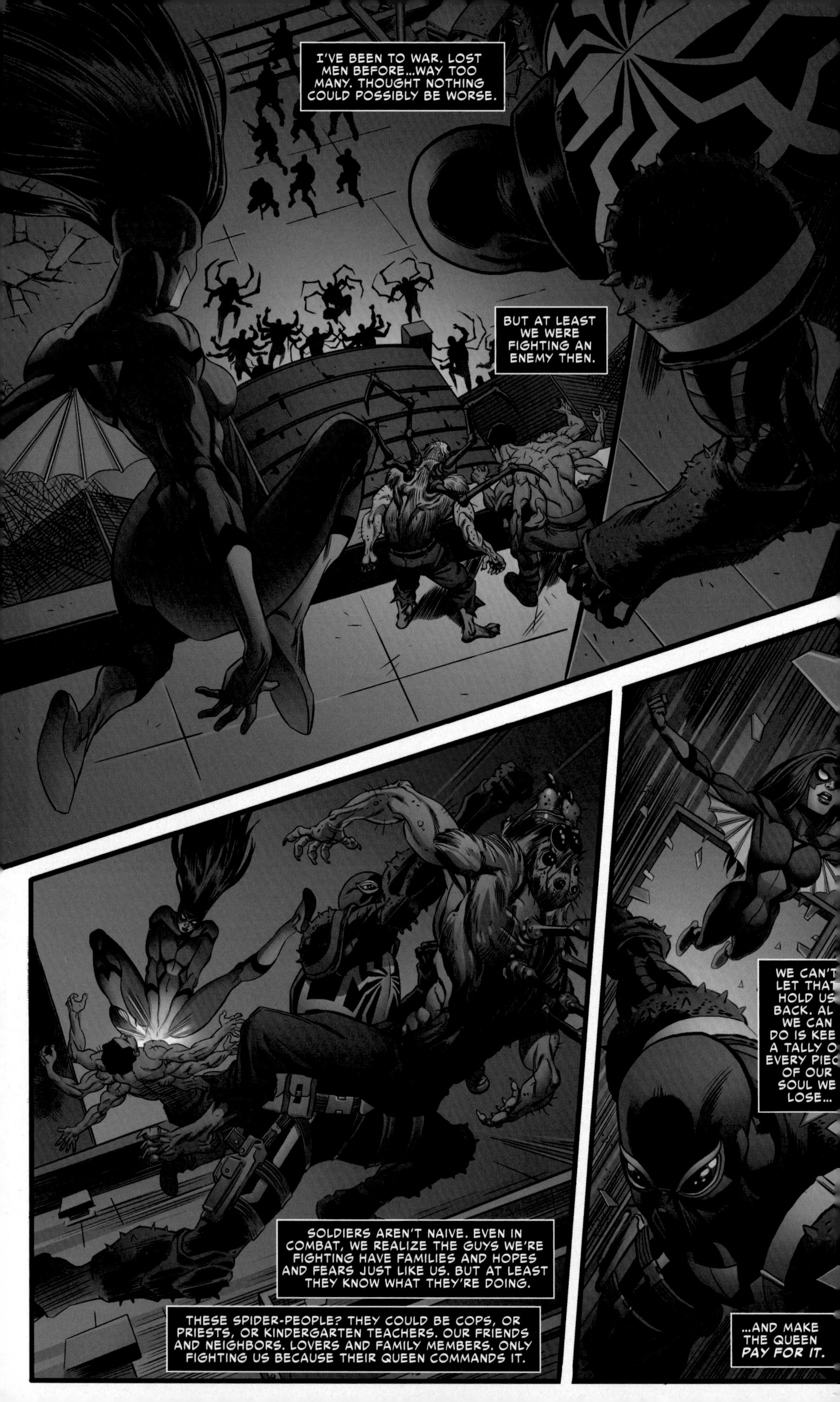
I'VE BEEN TO WAR. LOST MEN BEFORE...WAY TOO MANY. THOUGHT NOTHING COULD POSSIBLY BE WORSE.
BUT AT LEAST WE WERE FIGHTING AN ENEMY THEN.
SOLDIERS AREN'T NAIVE. EVEN IN COMBAT, WE REALIZE THE GUYS WE'RE FIGHTING HAVE FAMILIES AND HOPES AND FEARS JUST LIKE US. BUT AT LEAST THEY KNOW WHAT THEY'RE DOING.
THESE SPIDER-PEOPLE? THEY COULD BE COPS, OR PRIESTS, OR KINDERGARTEN TEACHERS. OUR FRIENDS AND NEIGHBORS. LOVERS AND FAMILY MEMBERS. ONLY FIGHTING US BECAUSE THEIR QUEEN COMMANDS IT.
WE CAN'T LET THAT HOLD US BACK. AL WE CAN DO IS KEE A TALLY O EVERY PIEC OF OUR SOUL WE LOSE...
...AND MAKE THE QUEEN *PAY FOR IT.*

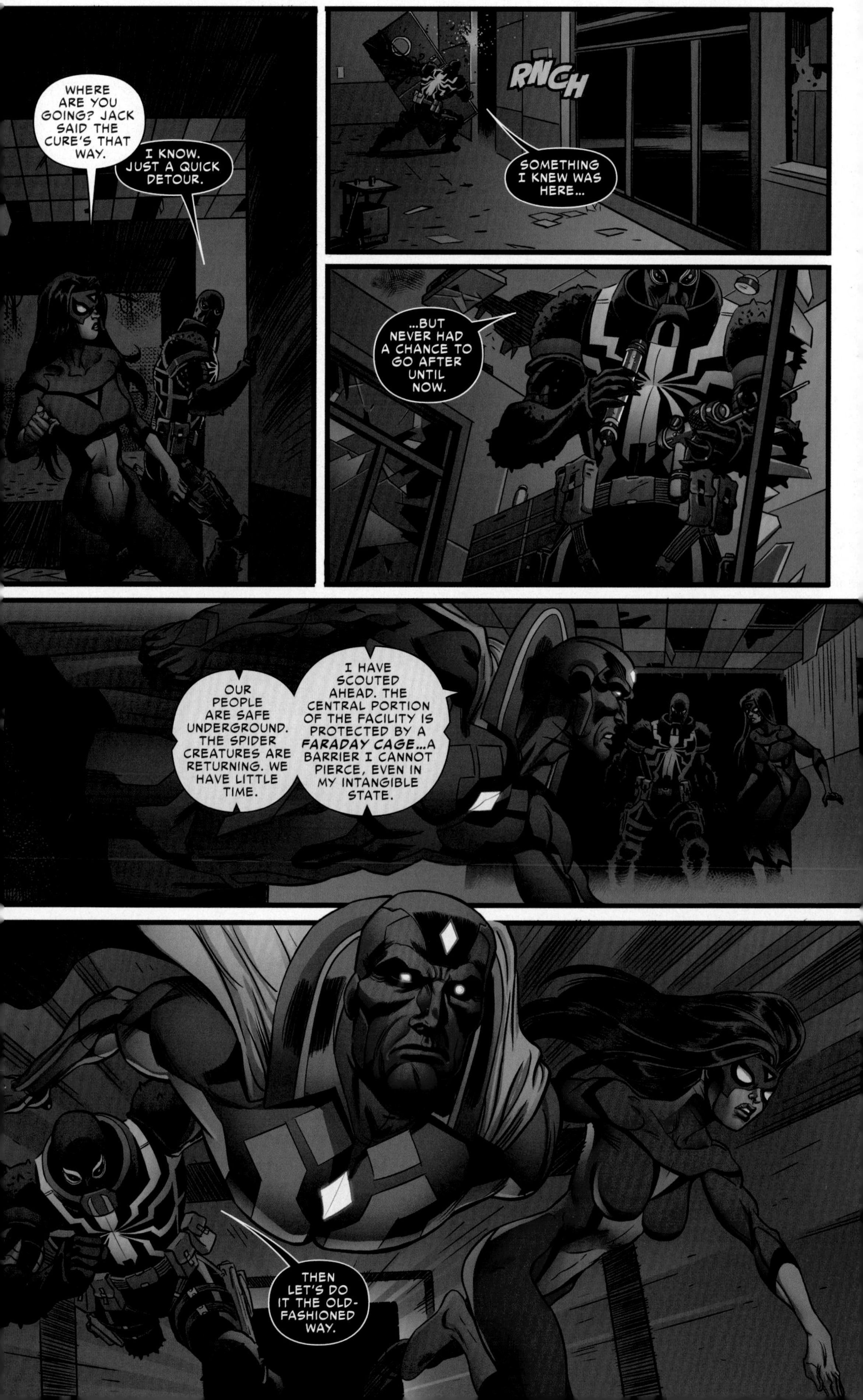

WHERE ARE YOU GOING? JACK SAID THE CURE'S THAT WAY.
I KNOW. JUST A QUICK DETOUR.
RNCH
SOMETHING I KNEW WAS HERE...
...BUT NEVER HAD A CHANCE TO GO AFTER UNTIL NOW.
OUR PEOPLE ARE SAFE UNDERGROUND. THE SPIDER CREATURES ARE RETURNING. WE HAVE LITTLE TIME.
I HAVE SCOUTED AHEAD. THE CENTRAL PORTION OF THE FACILITY IS PROTECTED BY A FARADAY CAGE...A BARRIER I CANNOT PIERCE, EVEN IN MY INTANGIBLE STATE.
THEN LET'S DO IT THE OLD-FASHIONED WAY.

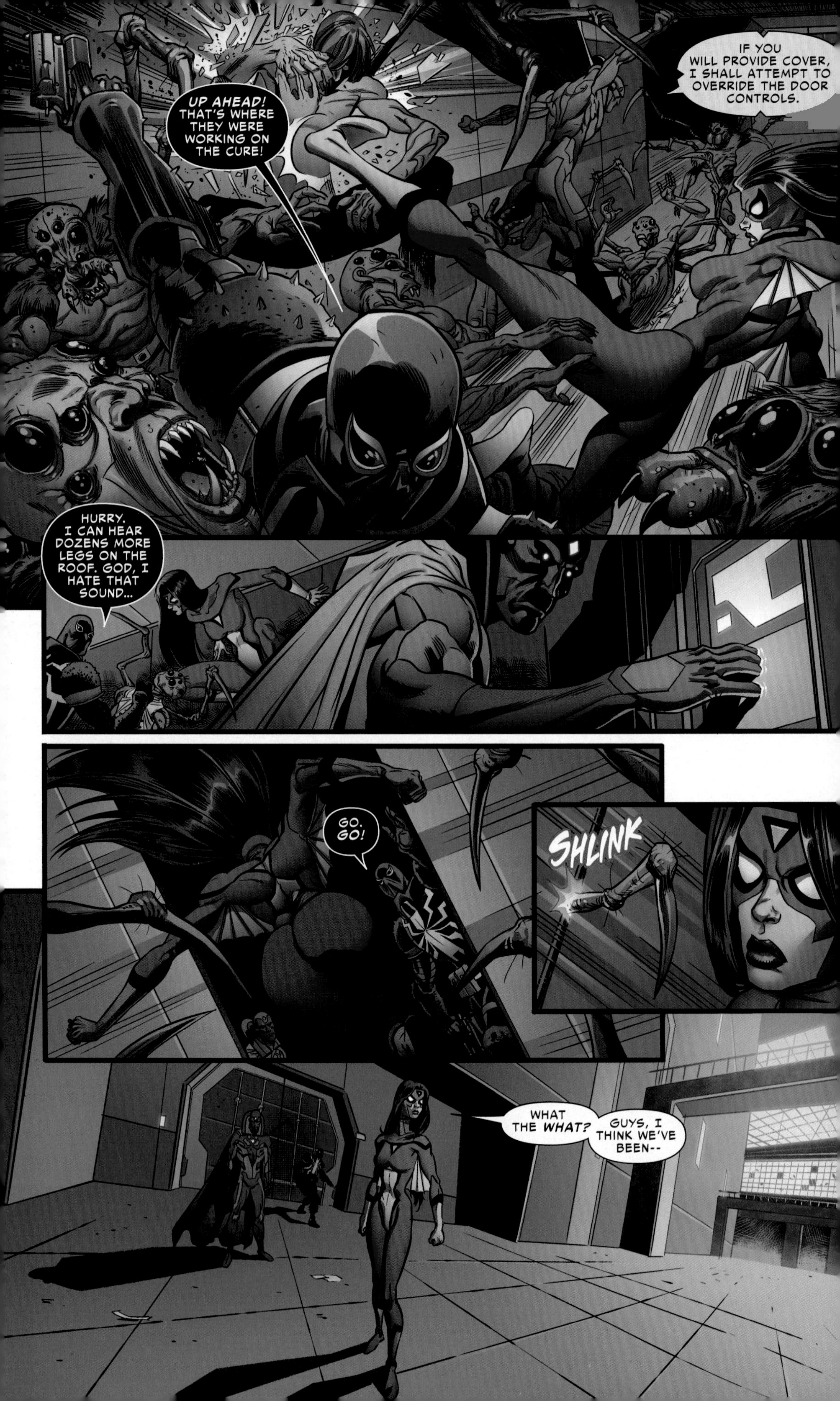
UP AHEAD! THAT'S WHERE THEY WERE WORKING ON THE CURE!
IF YOU WILL PROVIDE COVER, I SHALL ATTEMPT TO OVERRIDE THE DOOR CONTROLS.
HURRY. I CAN HEAR DOZENS MORE LEGS ON THE ROOF. GOD, I HATE THAT SOUND...
GO. GO!
SHLINK
WHAT THE WHAT?
GUYS, I THINK WE'VE BEEN--

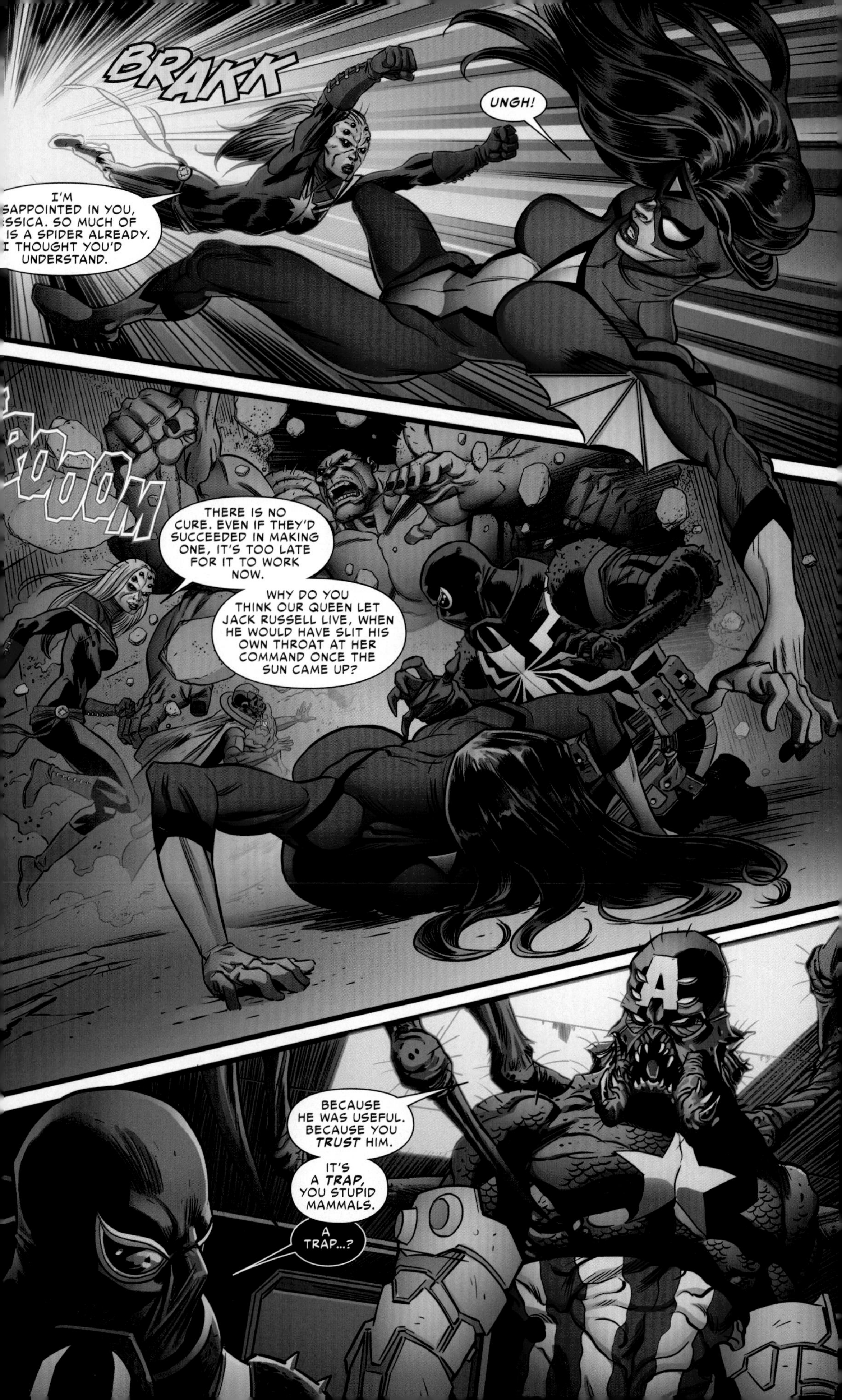
BRAKK
UNGH!
I'M
SAPPOINTED IN YOU,
SSICA. SO MUCH OF
IS A SPIDER ALREADY.
I THOUGHT YOU'D
UNDERSTAND.
OOOOM
THERE IS NO CURE. EVEN IF THEY'D SUCCEEDED IN MAKING ONE, IT'S TOO LATE FOR IT TO WORK NOW.
WHY DO YOU THINK OUR QUEEN LET JACK RUSSELL LIVE, WHEN HE WOULD HAVE SLIT HIS OWN THROAT AT HER COMMAND ONCE THE SUN CAME UP?
BECAUSE HE WAS USEFUL. BECAUSE YOU TRUST HIM.
IT'S A TRAP, YOU STUPID MAMMALS.
A TRAP...?

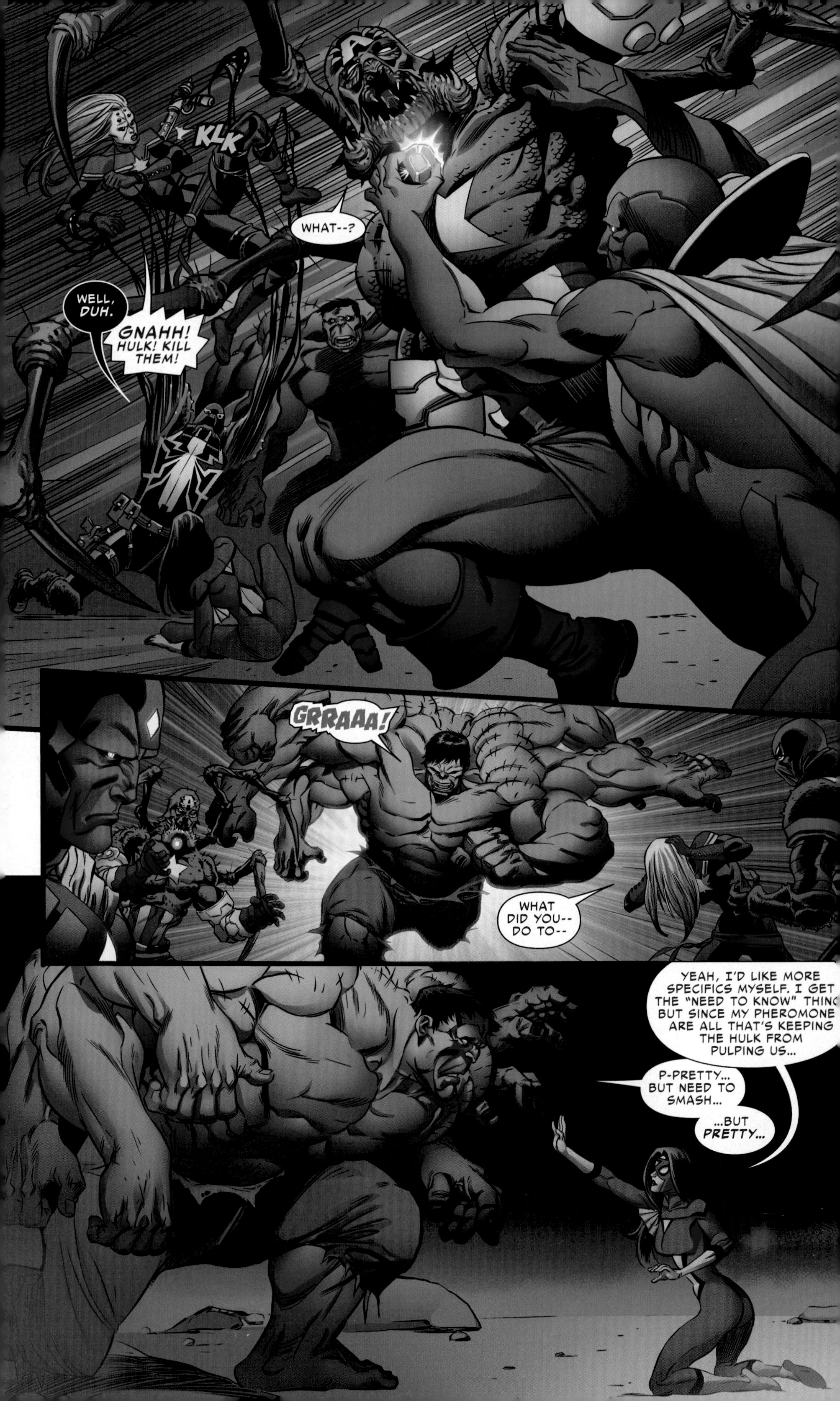
KLK
WHAT--?
WELL, DUH.
GNAHH! HULK! KILL THEM!
GRRAAA!
WHAT DID YOU-- DO TO--
YEAH, I'D LIKE MORE SPECIFICS MYSELF. I GET THE "NEED TO KNOW" THING BUT SINCE MY PHEROMONE ARE ALL THAT'S KEEPING THE HULK FROM PULPING US...
P-PRETTY... BUT NEED TO SMASH...
...BUT PRETTY...

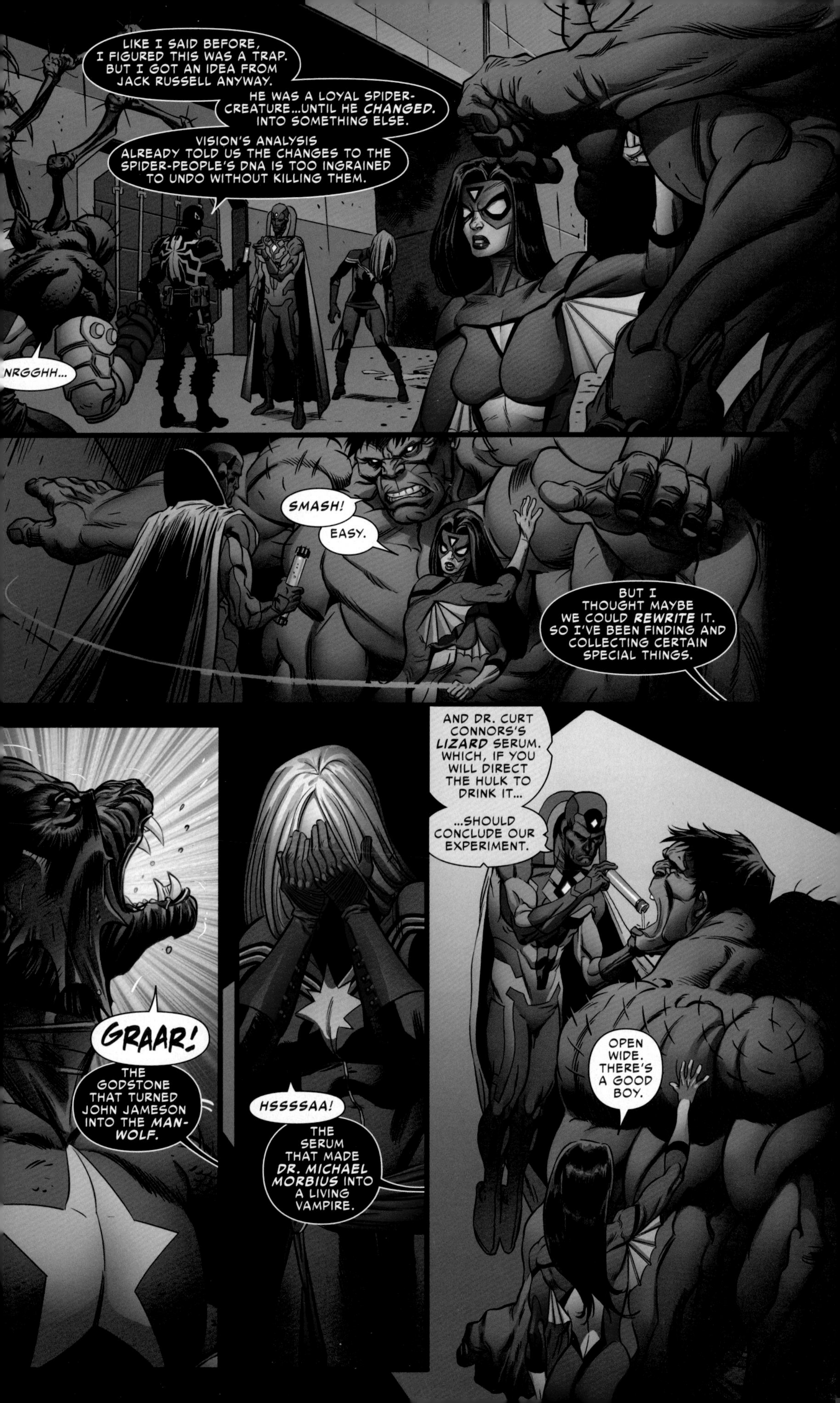
LIKE I SAID BEFORE, I FIGURED THIS WAS A TRAP. BUT I GOT AN IDEA FROM JACK RUSSELL ANYWAY.
HE WAS A LOYAL SPIDER-CREATURE...UNTIL HE CHANGED. INTO SOMETHING ELSE.
VISION'S ANALYSIS ALREADY TOLD US THE CHANGES TO THE SPIDER-PEOPLE'S DNA IS TOO INGRAINED TO UNDO WITHOUT KILLING THEM.
NRGGHH...
SMASH!
EASY.
BUT I THOUGHT MAYBE WE COULD REWRITE IT. SO I'VE BEEN FINDING AND COLLECTING CERTAIN SPECIAL THINGS.
GRAAR!
THE GODSTONE THAT TURNED JOHN JAMESON INTO THE MAN-WOLF.
HSSSSAA!
THE SERUM THAT MADE DR. MICHAEL MORBIUS INTO A LIVING VAMPIRE.
AND DR. CURT CONNORS'S LIZARD SERUM. WHICH, IF YOU WILL DIRECT THE HULK TO DRINK IT...
...SHOULD CONCLUDE OUR EXPERIMENT.
OPEN WIDE. THERE'S A GOOD BOY.

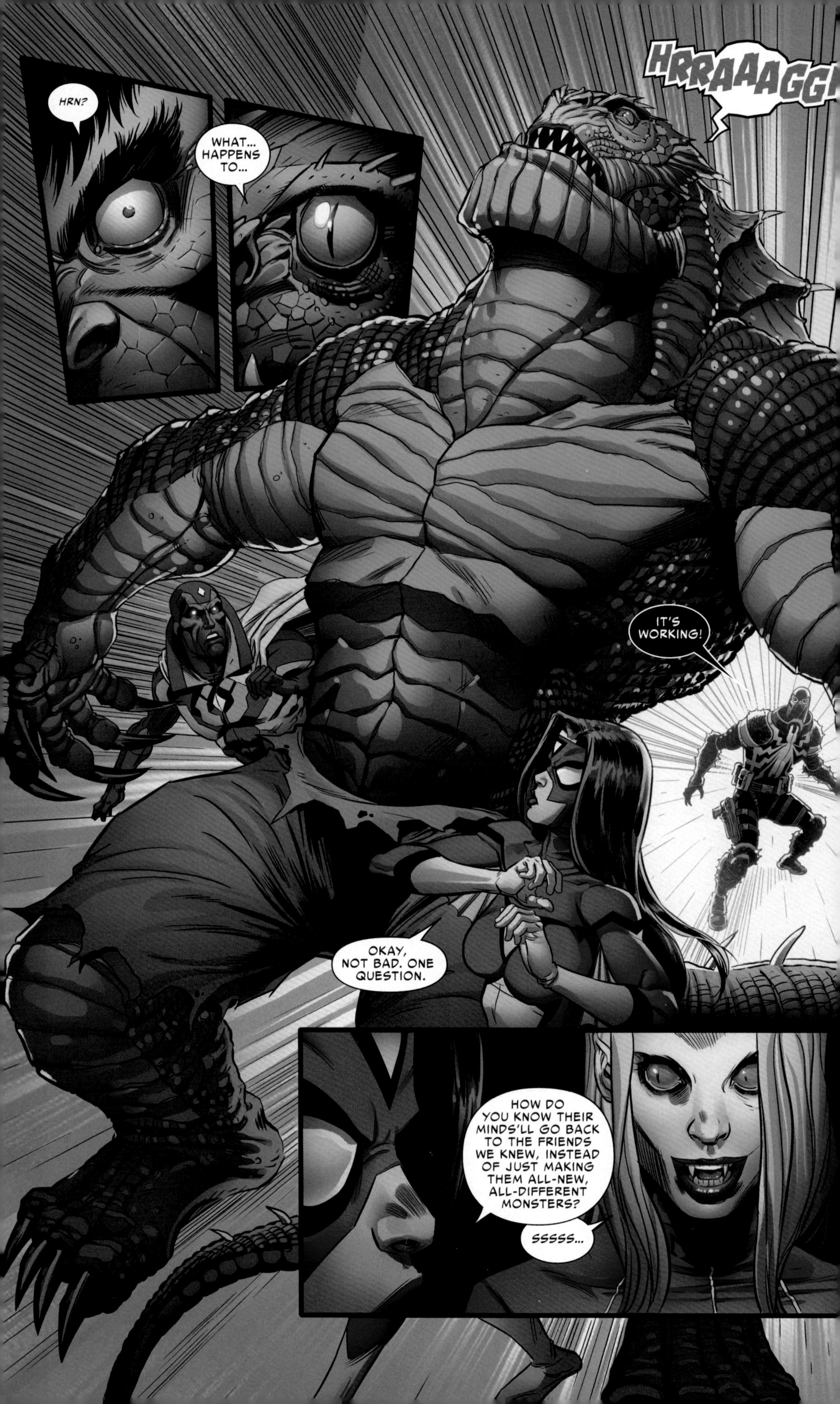
HRN?
WHAT... HAPPENS TO...
HRRAAAGG!
IT'S WORKING!
OKAY, NOT BAD. ONE QUESTION.
HOW DO YOU KNOW THEIR MINDS'LL GO BACK TO THE FRIENDS WE KNEW, INSTEAD OF JUST MAKING THEM ALL-NEW, ALL-DIFFERENT MONSTERS?
SSSSS...

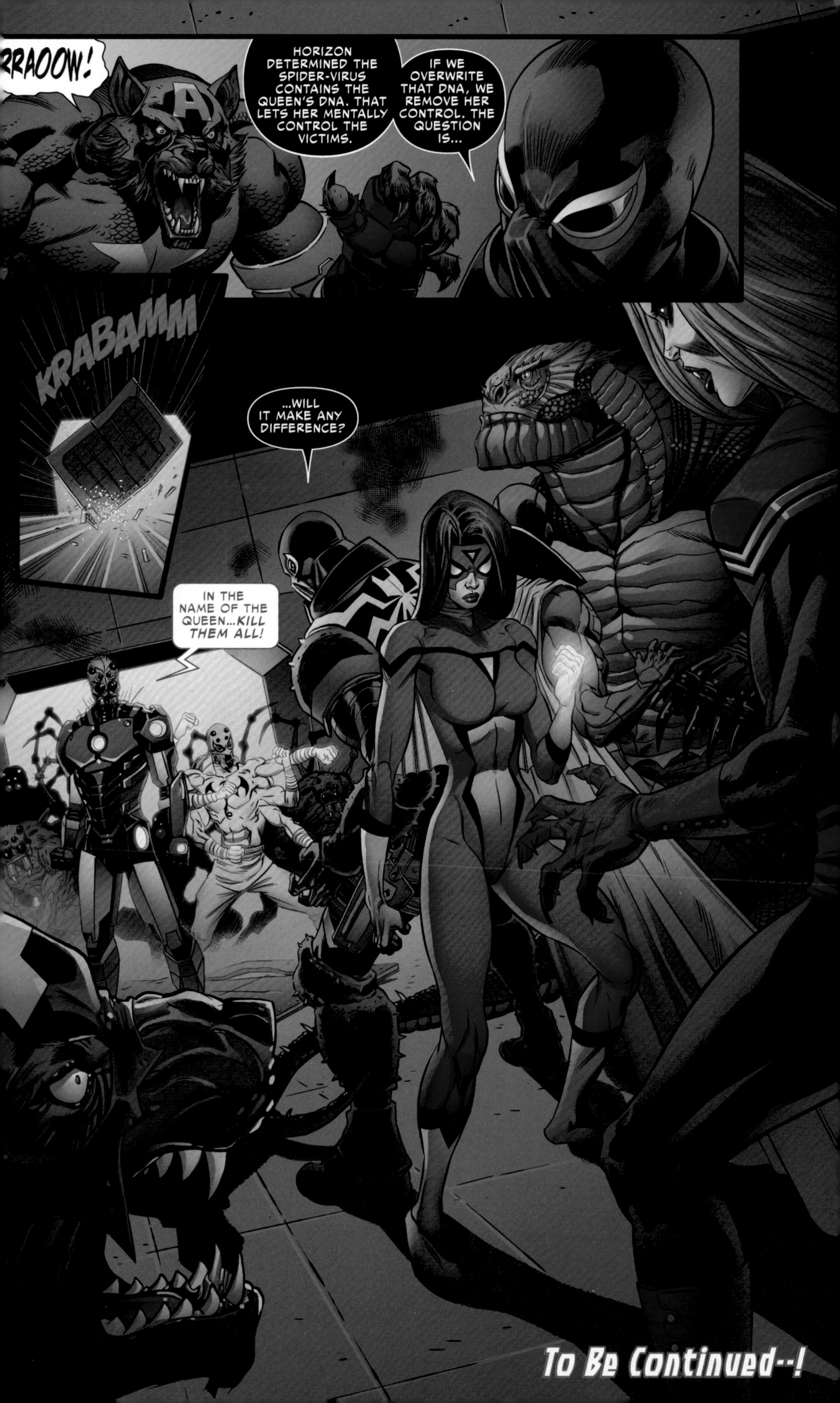

RRAOOW!
HORIZON DETERMINED THE SPIDER-VIRUS CONTAINS THE QUEEN'S DNA. THAT LETS HER MENTALLY CONTROL THE VICTIMS.
IF WE OVERWRITE THAT DNA, WE REMOVE HER CONTROL. THE QUESTION IS...
KRABAMM
...WILL IT MAKE ANY DIFFERENCE?
IN THE NAME OF THE QUEEN...KILL THEM ALL!
To Be Continued--!

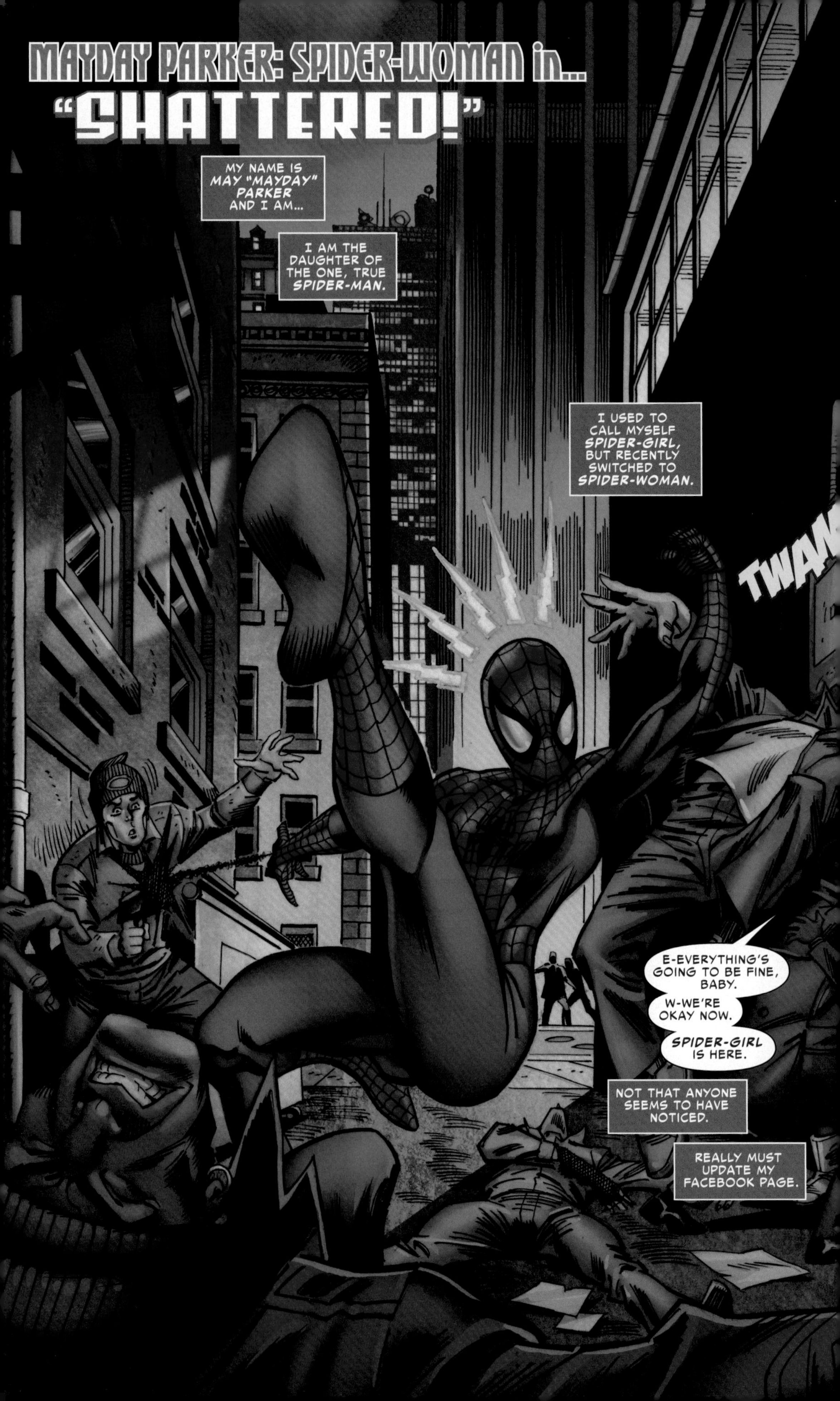
MAYDAY PARKER: SPIDER-WOMAN in...
"SHATTERED!"
MY NAME IS MAY "MAYDAY" PARKER AND I AM...
I AM THE DAUGHTER OF THE ONE, TRUE SPIDER-MAN.
I USED TO CALL MYSELF SPIDER-GIRL, BUT RECENTLY SWITCHED TO SPIDER-WOMAN.
TWAM
E-EVERYTHING'S GOING TO BE FINE, BABY.
W-WE'RE OKAY NOW.
SPIDER-GIRL IS HERE.
NOT THAT ANYONE SEEMS TO HAVE NOTICED.
REALLY MUST UPDATE MY FACEBOOK PAGE.

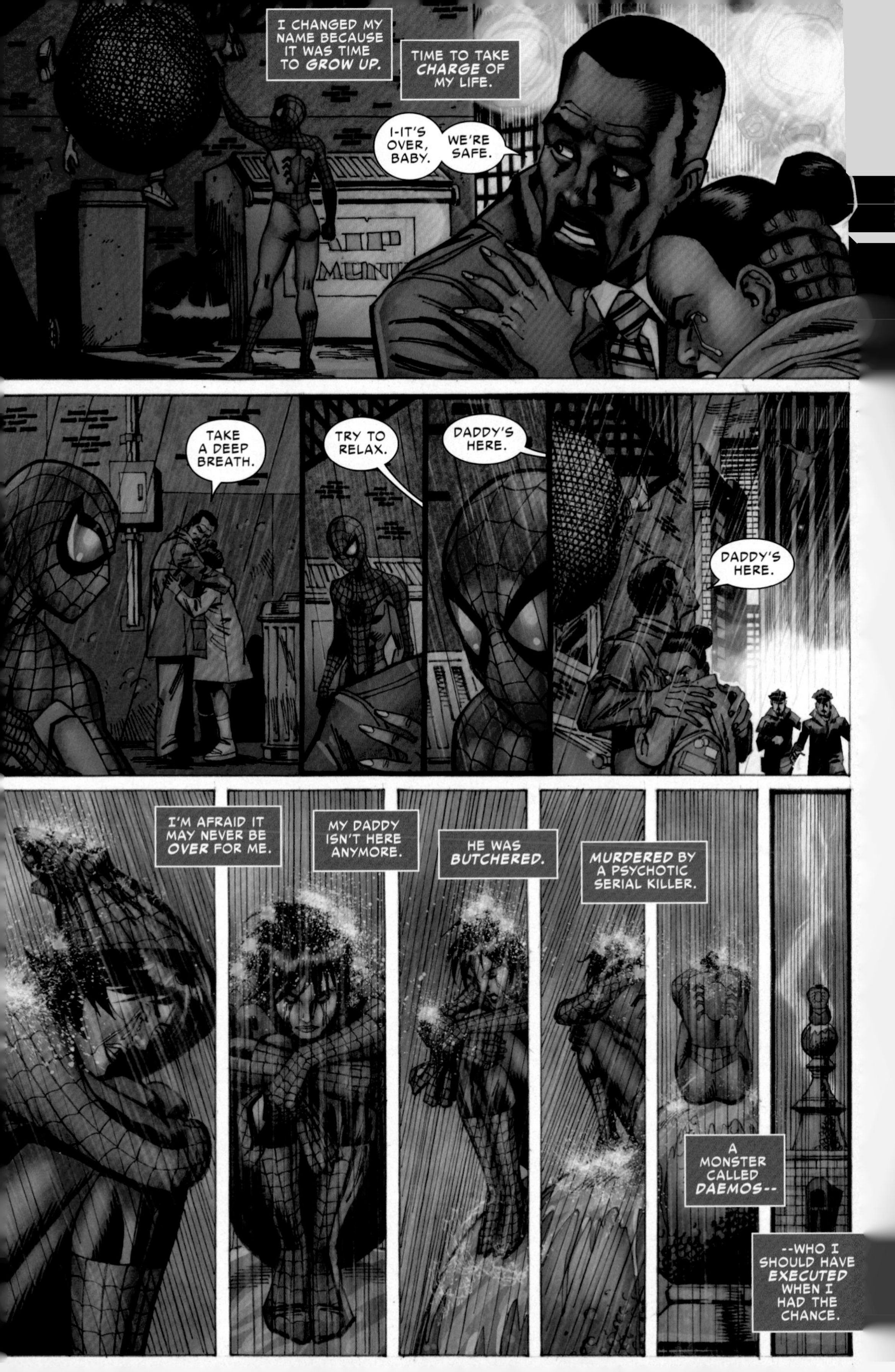
I CHANGED MY NAME BECAUSE IT WAS TIME TO GROW UP.
TIME TO TAKE CHARGE OF MY LIFE.
I-IT'S OVER, BABY.
WE'RE SAFE.
TAKE A DEEP BREATH.
TRY TO RELAX.
DADDY'S HERE.
DADDY'S HERE.
I'M AFRAID IT MAY NEVER BE OVER FOR ME.
MY DADDY ISN'T HERE ANYMORE.
HE WAS BUTCHERED.
MURDERED BY A PSYCHOTIC SERIAL KILLER.
A MONSTER CALLED DAEMOS--
--WHO I SHOULD HAVE EXECUTED WHEN I HAD THE CHANCE.

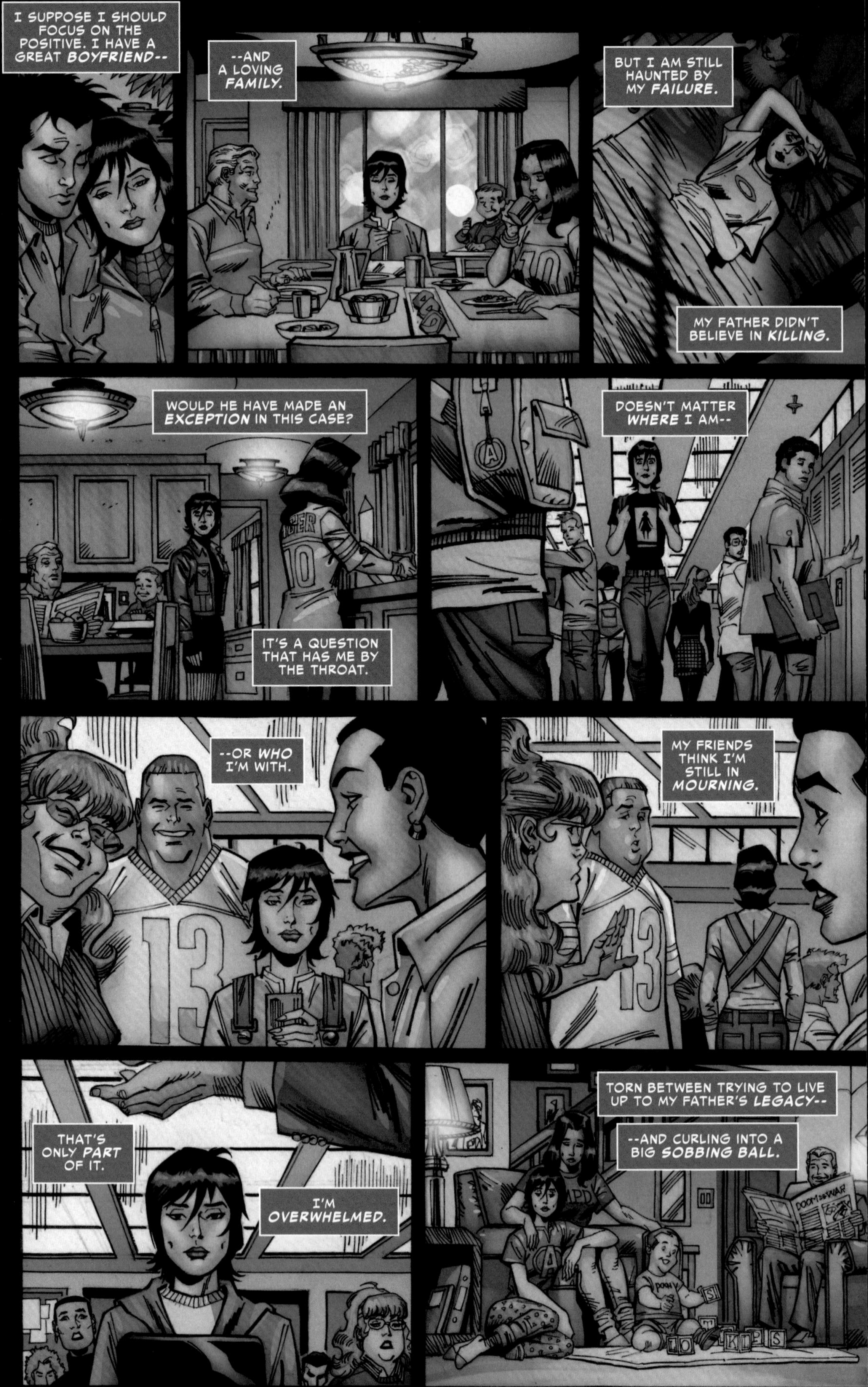
I SUPPOSE I SHOULD FOCUS ON THE POSITIVE. I HAVE A GREAT BOYFRIEND--
--AND A LOVING FAMILY.
BUT I AM STILL HAUNTED BY MY FAILURE.
MY FATHER DIDN'T BELIEVE IN KILLING.
WOULD HE HAVE MADE AN EXCEPTION IN THIS CASE?
IT'S A QUESTION THAT HAS ME BY THE THROAT.
DOESN'T MATTER WHERE I AM--
--OR WHO I'M WITH.
MY FRIENDS THINK I'M STILL IN MOURNING.
THAT'S ONLY PART OF IT.
I'M OVERWHELMED.
TORN BETWEEN TRYING TO LIVE UP TO MY FATHER'S LEGACY--
--AND CURLING INTO A BIG SOBBING BALL.

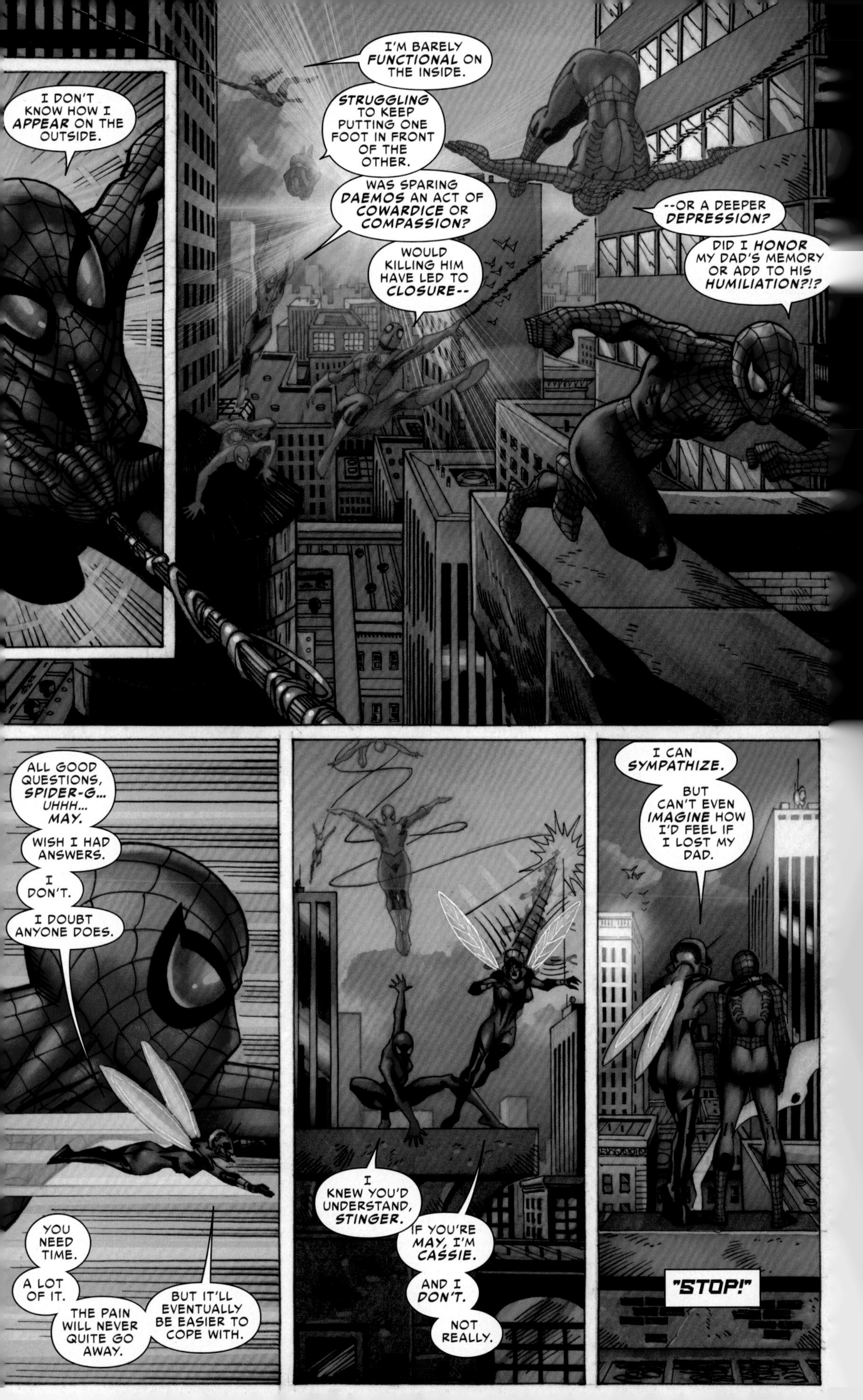
I DON'T KNOW HOW I APPEAR ON THE OUTSIDE.
I'M BARELY FUNCTIONAL ON THE INSIDE.
STRUGGLING TO KEEP PUTTING ONE FOOT IN FRONT OF THE OTHER.
WAS SPARING DAEMOS AN ACT OF COWARDICE OR COMPASSION?
WOULD KILLING HIM HAVE LED TO CLOSURE--
--OR A DEEPER DEPRESSION?
DID I HONOR MY DAD'S MEMORY OR ADD TO HIS HUMILIATION?!?
ALL GOOD QUESTIONS, SPIDER-G... UHHH... MAY.
WISH I HAD ANSWERS.
I DON'T.
I DOUBT ANYONE DOES.
YOU NEED TIME.
A LOT OF IT.
THE PAIN WILL NEVER QUITE GO AWAY.
BUT IT'LL EVENTUALLY BE EASIER TO COPE WITH.
I KNEW YOU'D UNDERSTAND, STINGER.
IF YOU'RE MAY, I'M CASSIE.
AND I DON'T.
NOT REALLY.
I CAN SYMPATHIZE.
BUT CAN'T EVEN IMAGINE HOW I'D FEEL IF I LOST MY DAD.
"STOP!"

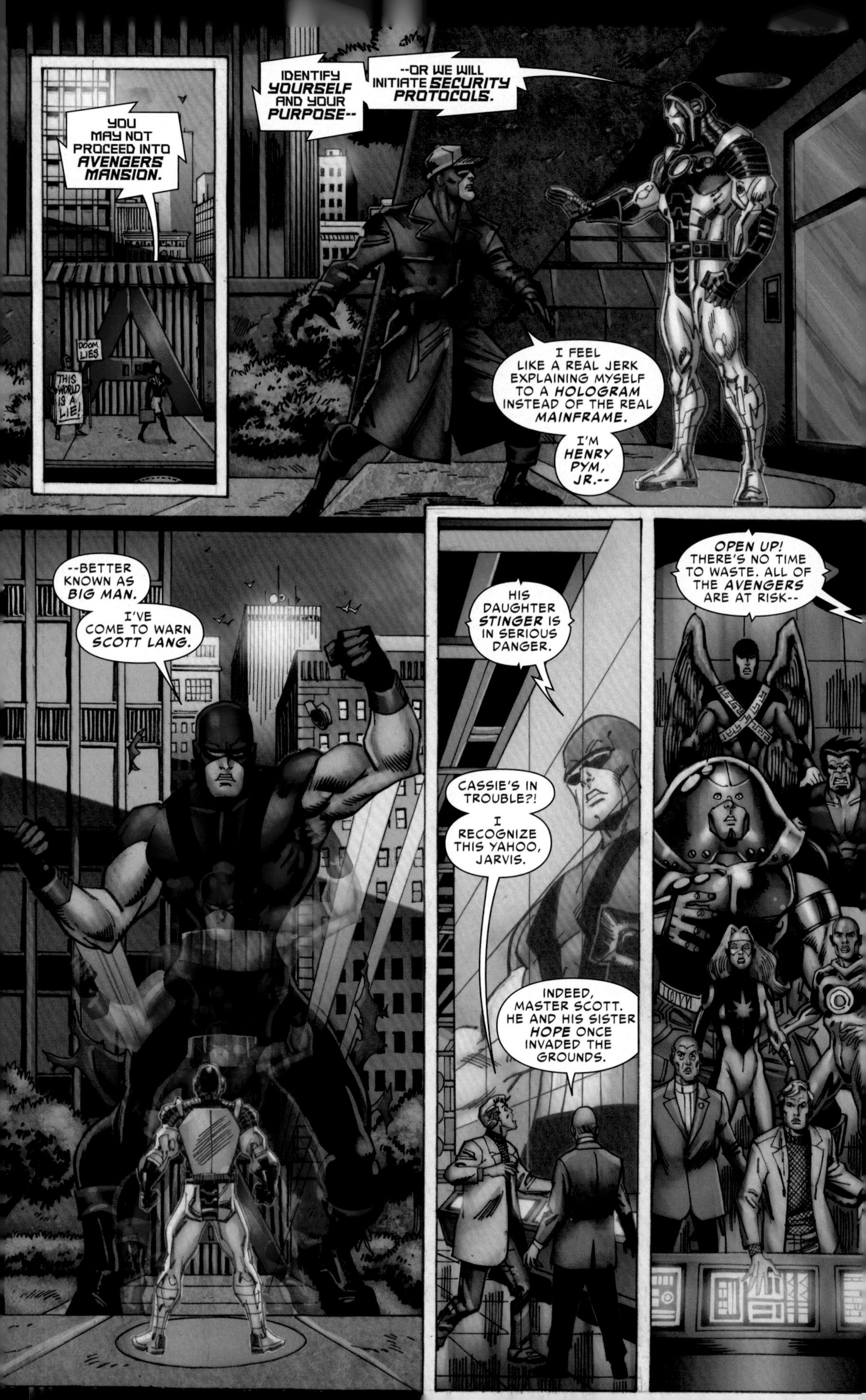

YOU MAY NOT PROCEED INTO AVENGERS MANSION.
DOOM LIES
THIS WORLD IS A LIE!
IDENTIFY YOURSELF AND YOUR PURPOSE--
--OR WE WILL INITIATE SECURITY PROTOCOLS.
I FEEL LIKE A REAL JERK EXPLAINING MYSELF TO A HOLOGRAM INSTEAD OF THE REAL MAINFRAME.
I'M HENRY PYM, JR.--
--BETTER KNOWN AS BIG MAN.
I'VE COME TO WARN SCOTT LANG.
HIS DAUGHTER STINGER IS IN SERIOUS DANGER.
CASSIE'S IN TROUBLE?!
I RECOGNIZE THIS YAHOO, JARVIS.
INDEED, MASTER SCOTT. HE AND HIS SISTER HOPE ONCE INVADED THE GROUNDS.
OPEN UP! THERE'S NO TIME TO WASTE. ALL OF THE AVENGERS ARE AT RISK--

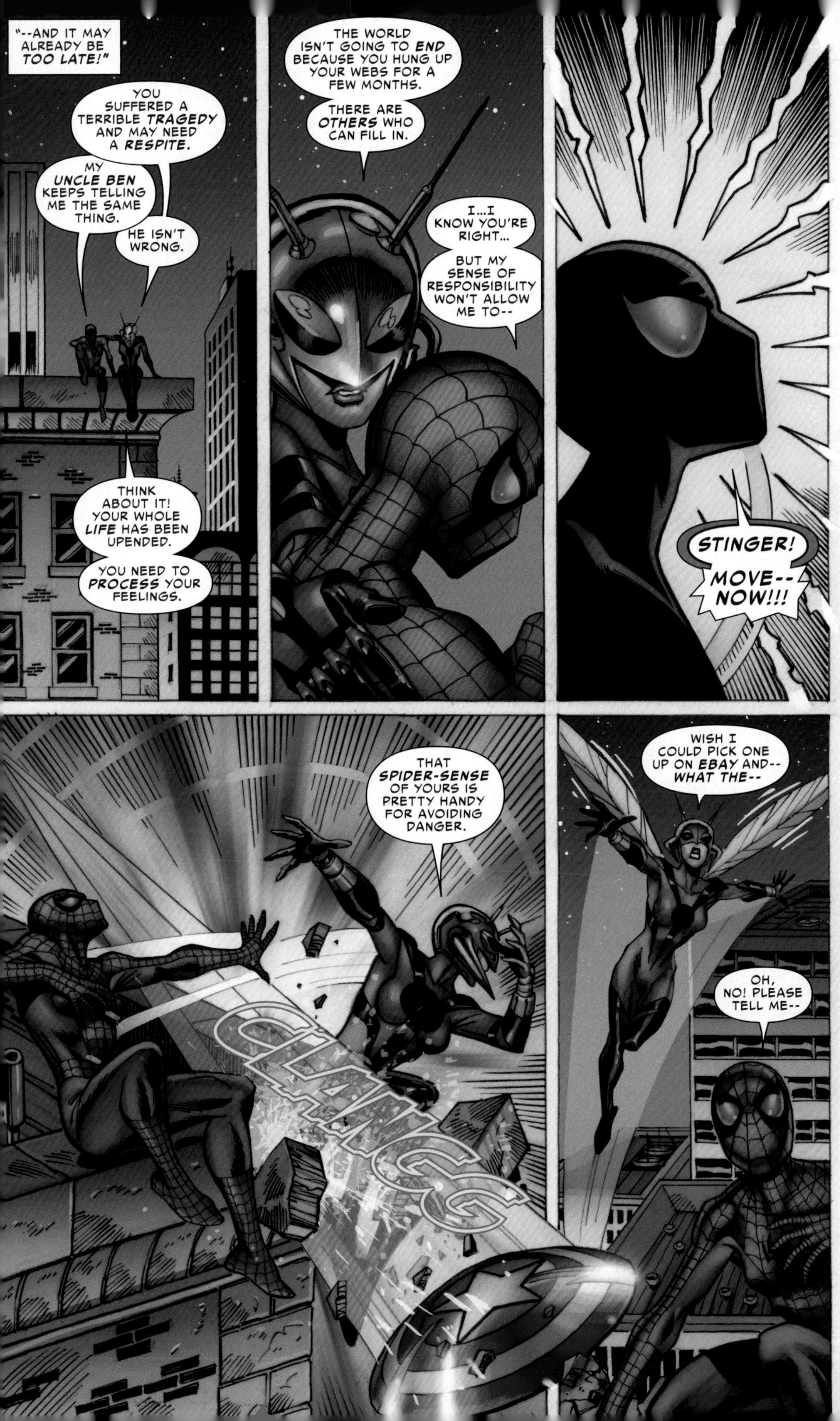
"--AND IT MAY ALREADY BE TOO LATE!"
YOU SUFFERED A TERRIBLE TRAGEDY AND MAY NEED A RESPITE.
MY UNCLE BEN KEEPS TELLING ME THE SAME THING.
HE ISN'T WRONG.
THINK ABOUT IT! YOUR WHOLE LIFE HAS BEEN UPENDED.
YOU NEED TO PROCESS YOUR FEELINGS.
THE WORLD ISN'T GOING TO END BECAUSE YOU HUNG UP YOUR WEBS FOR A FEW MONTHS.
THERE ARE OTHERS WHO CAN FILL IN.
I...I KNOW YOU'RE RIGHT...
BUT MY SENSE OF RESPONSIBILITY WON'T ALLOW ME TO--
STINGER!
MOVE-- NOW!!!
THAT SPIDER-SENSE OF YOURS IS PRETTY HANDY FOR AVOIDING DANGER.
CHUNG
WISH I COULD PICK ONE UP ON EBAY AND-- WHAT THE--
OH, NO! PLEASE TELL ME--

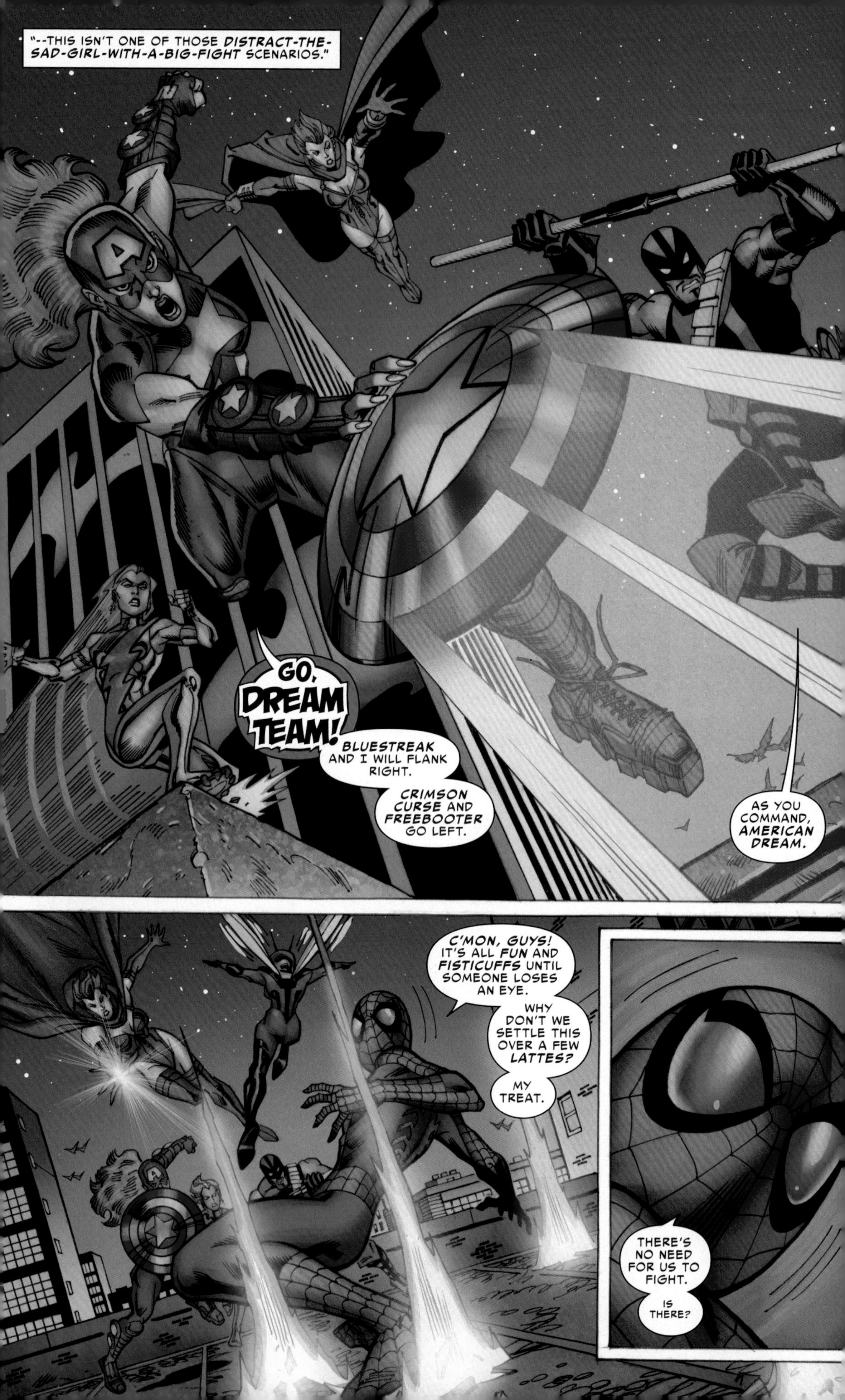
"--THIS ISN'T ONE OF THOSE DISTRACT-THE-SAD-GIRL-WITH-A-BIG-FIGHT SCENARIOS."
GO, DREAM TEAM!
BLUESTREAK AND I WILL FLANK RIGHT.
CRIMSON CURSE AND FREEBOOTER GO LEFT.
AS YOU COMMAND, AMERICAN DREAM.
C'MON, GUYS! IT'S ALL FUN AND FISTICUFFS UNTIL SOMEONE LOSES AN EYE.
WHY DON'T WE SETTLE THIS OVER A FEW LATTES?
MY TREAT.
THERE'S NO NEED FOR US TO FIGHT.
IS THERE?

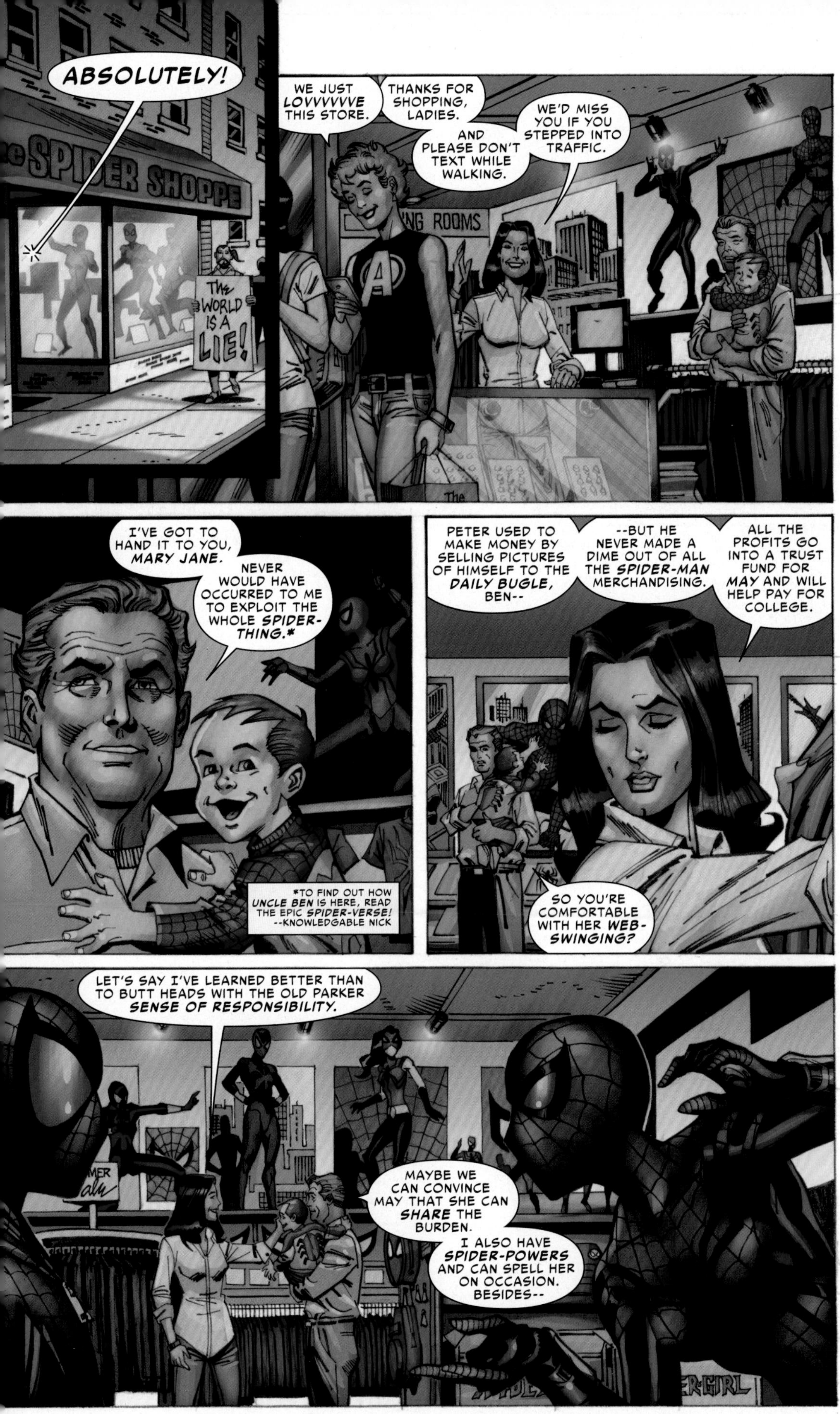

ABSOLUTELY!
The SPIDER SHOPPE
THE WORLD IS A LIE!
WE JUST LOVVVVVVVE THIS STORE.
THANKS FOR SHOPPING, LADIES.
AND PLEASE DON'T TEXT WHILE WALKING.
WE'D MISS YOU IF YOU STEPPED INTO TRAFFIC.
I'VE GOT TO HAND IT TO YOU, MARY JANE.
NEVER WOULD HAVE OCCURRED TO ME TO EXPLOIT THE WHOLE SPIDER-THING.*
*TO FIND OUT HOW UNCLE BEN IS HERE, READ THE EPIC SPIDER-VERSE! --KNOWLEDGABLE NICK
PETER USED TO MAKE MONEY BY SELLING PICTURES OF HIMSELF TO THE DAILY BUGLE, BEN--
--BUT HE NEVER MADE A DIME OUT OF ALL THE SPIDER-MAN MERCHANDISING.
ALL THE PROFITS GO INTO A TRUST FUND FOR MAY AND WILL HELP PAY FOR COLLEGE.
SO YOU'RE COMFORTABLE WITH HER WEB-SWINGING?
LET'S SAY I'VE LEARNED BETTER THAN TO BUTT HEADS WITH THE OLD PARKER SENSE OF RESPONSIBILITY.
MAYBE WE CAN CONVINCE MAY THAT SHE CAN SHARE THE BURDEN.
I ALSO HAVE SPIDER-POWERS AND CAN SPELL HER ON OCCASION. BESIDES--

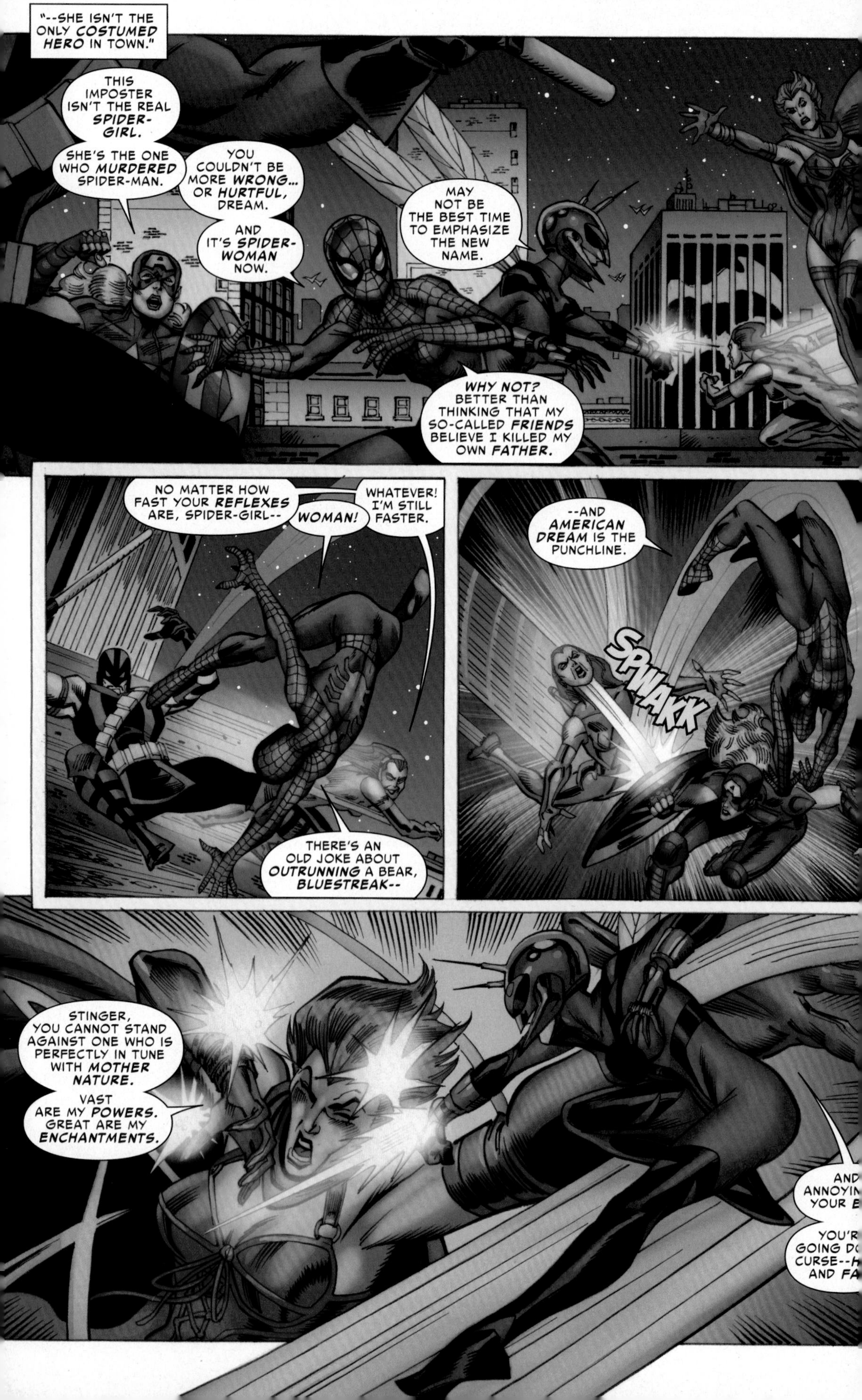
"--SHE ISN'T THE ONLY COSTUMED HERO IN TOWN."
THIS IMPOSTER ISN'T THE REAL SPIDER-GIRL.
SHE'S THE ONE WHO MURDERED SPIDER-MAN.
YOU COULDN'T BE MORE WRONG... OR HURTFUL, DREAM.
AND IT'S SPIDER-WOMAN NOW.
MAY NOT BE THE BEST TIME TO EMPHASIZE THE NEW NAME.
WHY NOT? BETTER THAN THINKING THAT MY SO-CALLED FRIENDS BELIEVE I KILLED MY OWN FATHER.
NO MATTER HOW FAST YOUR REFLEXES ARE, SPIDER-GIRL--
WOMAN!
WHATEVER! I'M STILL FASTER.
THERE'S AN OLD JOKE ABOUT OUTRUNNING A BEAR, BLUESTREAK--
--AND AMERICAN DREAM IS THE PUNCHLINE.
SPWAKK
STINGER, YOU CANNOT STAND AGAINST ONE WHO IS PERFECTLY IN TUNE WITH MOTHER NATURE.
VAST ARE MY POWERS. GREAT ARE MY ENCHANTMENTS.
AND ANNOYIN YOUR
YOU'R GOING D CURSE--H AND FA

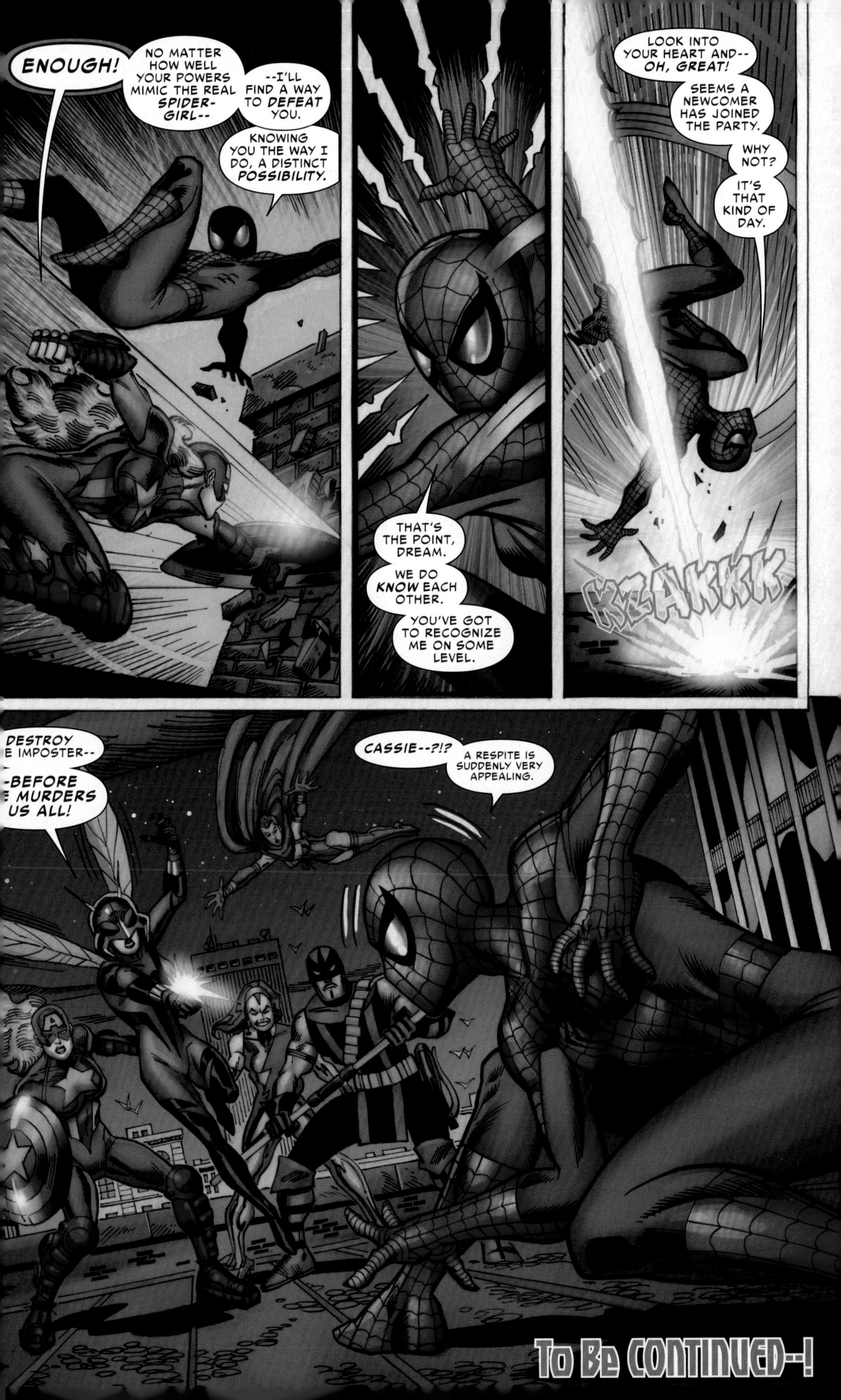

ENOUGH!
NO MATTER HOW WELL YOUR POWERS MIMIC THE REAL SPIDER-GIRL--
--I'LL FIND A WAY TO DEFEAT YOU.
KNOWING YOU THE WAY I DO, A DISTINCT POSSIBILITY.
THAT'S THE POINT, DREAM.
WE DO KNOW EACH OTHER.
YOU'VE GOT TO RECOGNIZE ME ON SOME LEVEL.
LOOK INTO YOUR HEART AND-- OH, GREAT!
SEEMS A NEWCOMER HAS JOINED THE PARTY.
WHY NOT?
IT'S THAT KIND OF DAY.
KRAKKK
DESTROY E IMPOSTER--
-BEFORE E MURDERS US ALL!
CASSIE--?!?
A RESPITE IS SUDDENLY VERY APPEALING.
To Be CONTINUED--!

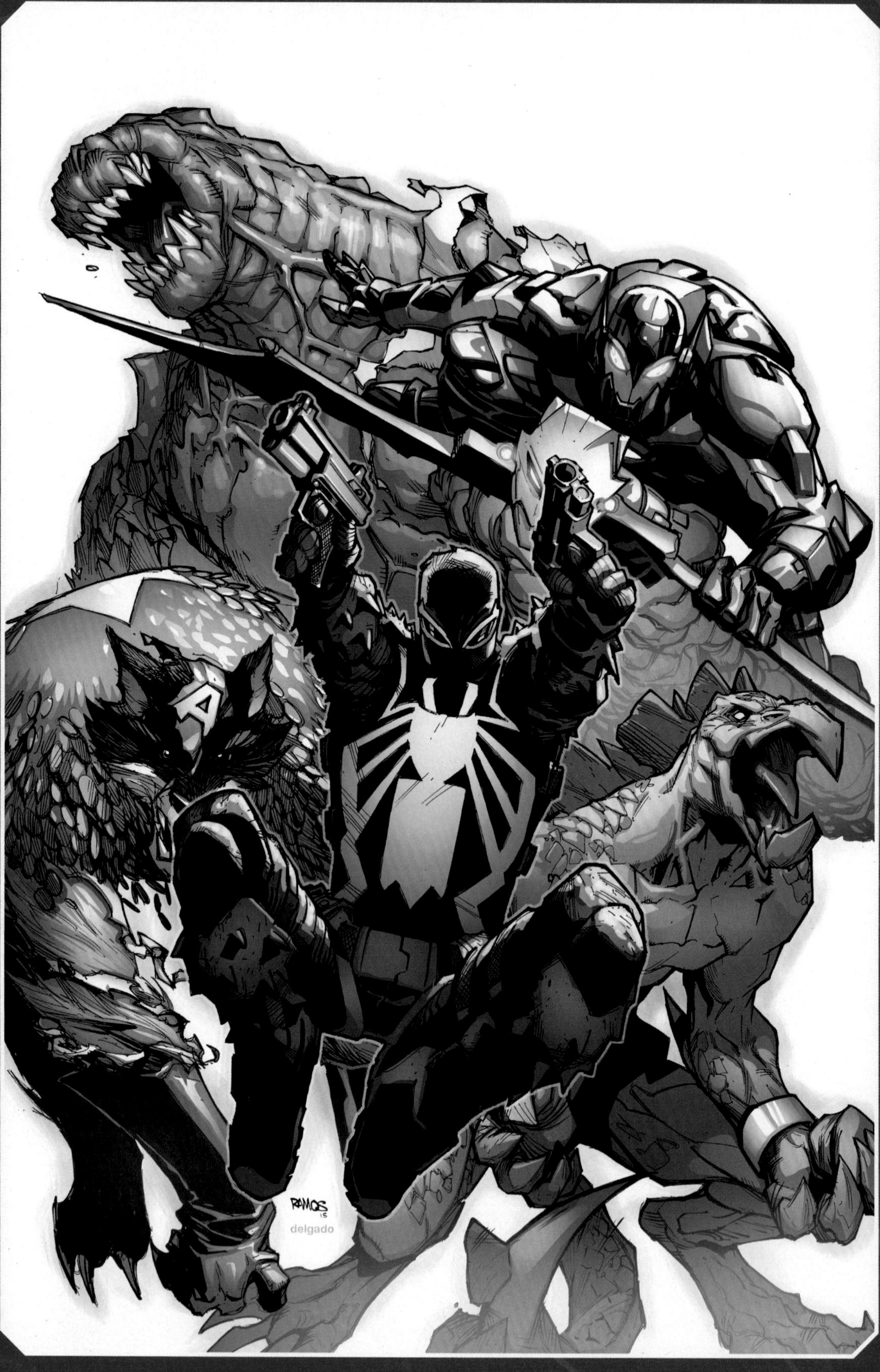
RAMOS 15
delgado

PART TWO: **YOU SAY YOU WANT EVOLUTION**

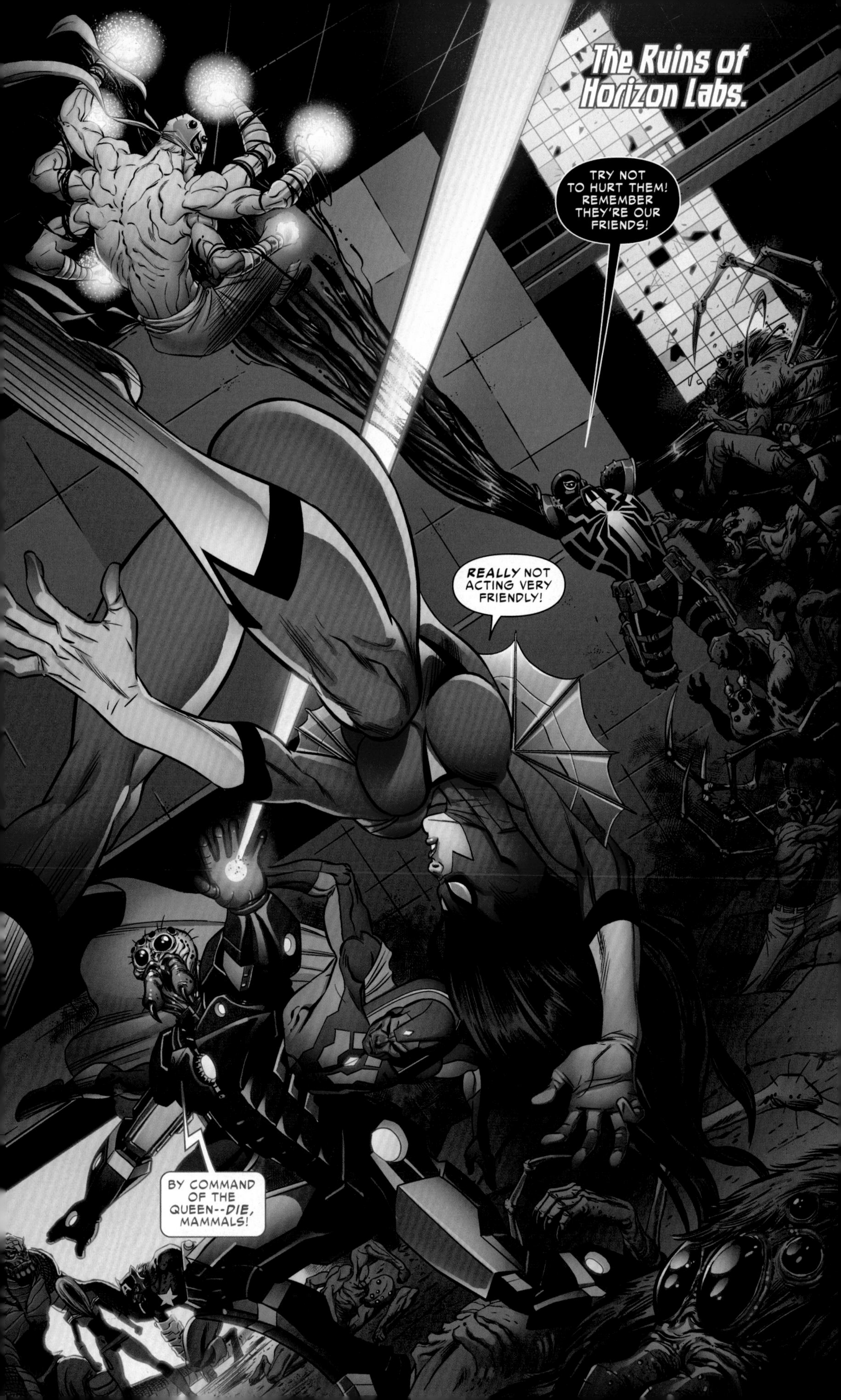
The Ruins of Horizon Labs.
TRY NOT TO HURT THEM! REMEMBER THEY'RE OUR FRIENDS!
REALLY NOT ACTING VERY FRIENDLY!
BY COMMAND OF THE QUEEN--DIE, MAMMALS!

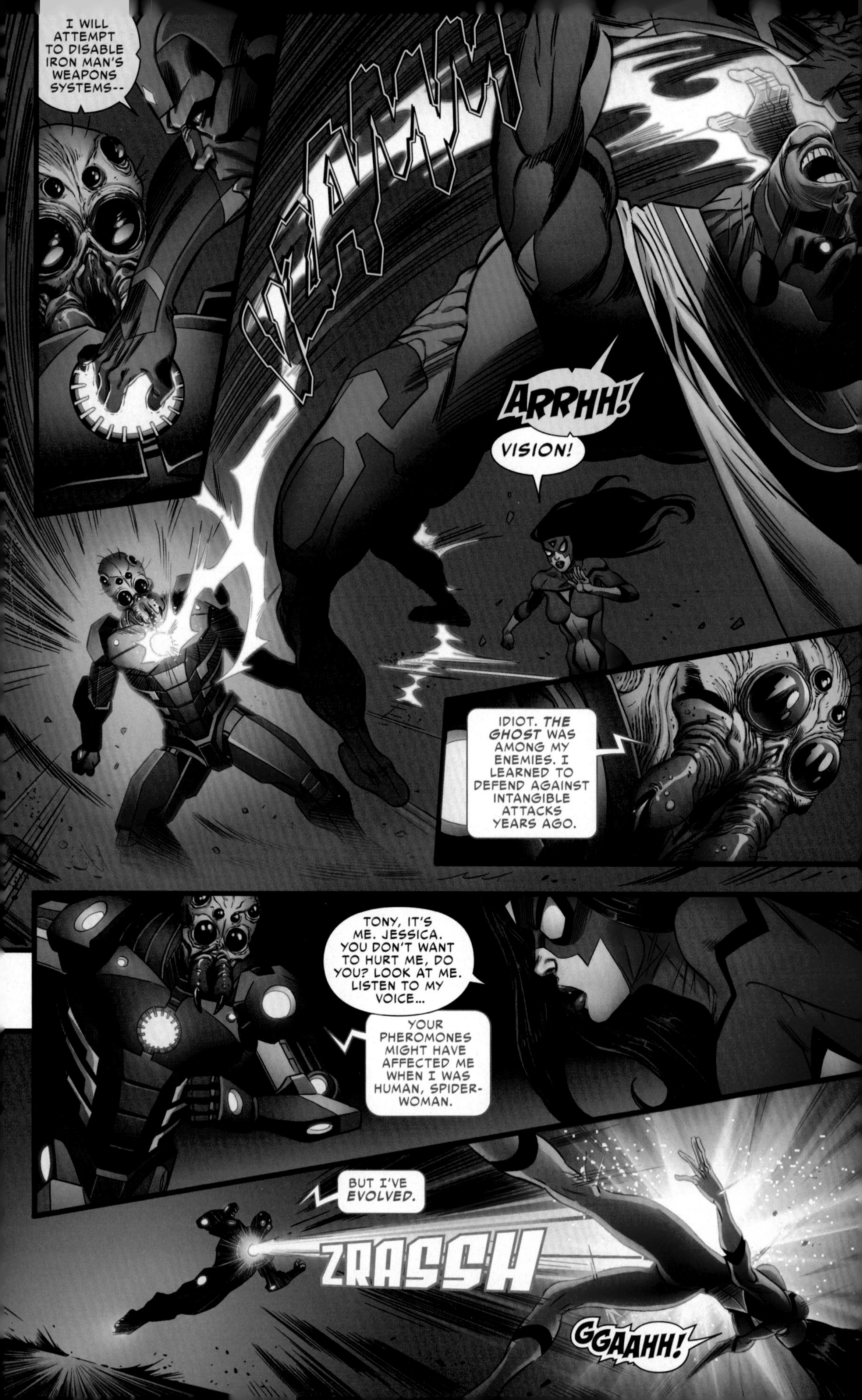
I WILL ATTEMPT TO DISABLE IRON MAN'S WEAPONS SYSTEMS--
ARRHH!
VISION!
IDIOT. *THE GHOST* WAS AMONG MY ENEMIES. I LEARNED TO DEFEND AGAINST INTANGIBLE ATTACKS YEARS AGO.
TONY, IT'S ME. JESSICA. YOU DON'T WANT TO HURT ME, DO YOU? LOOK AT ME. LISTEN TO MY VOICE...
YOUR PHEROMONES MIGHT HAVE AFFECTED ME WHEN I WAS HUMAN, SPIDER-WOMAN.
BUT I'VE *EVOLVED.*
ZRASSH
GGAAHH!

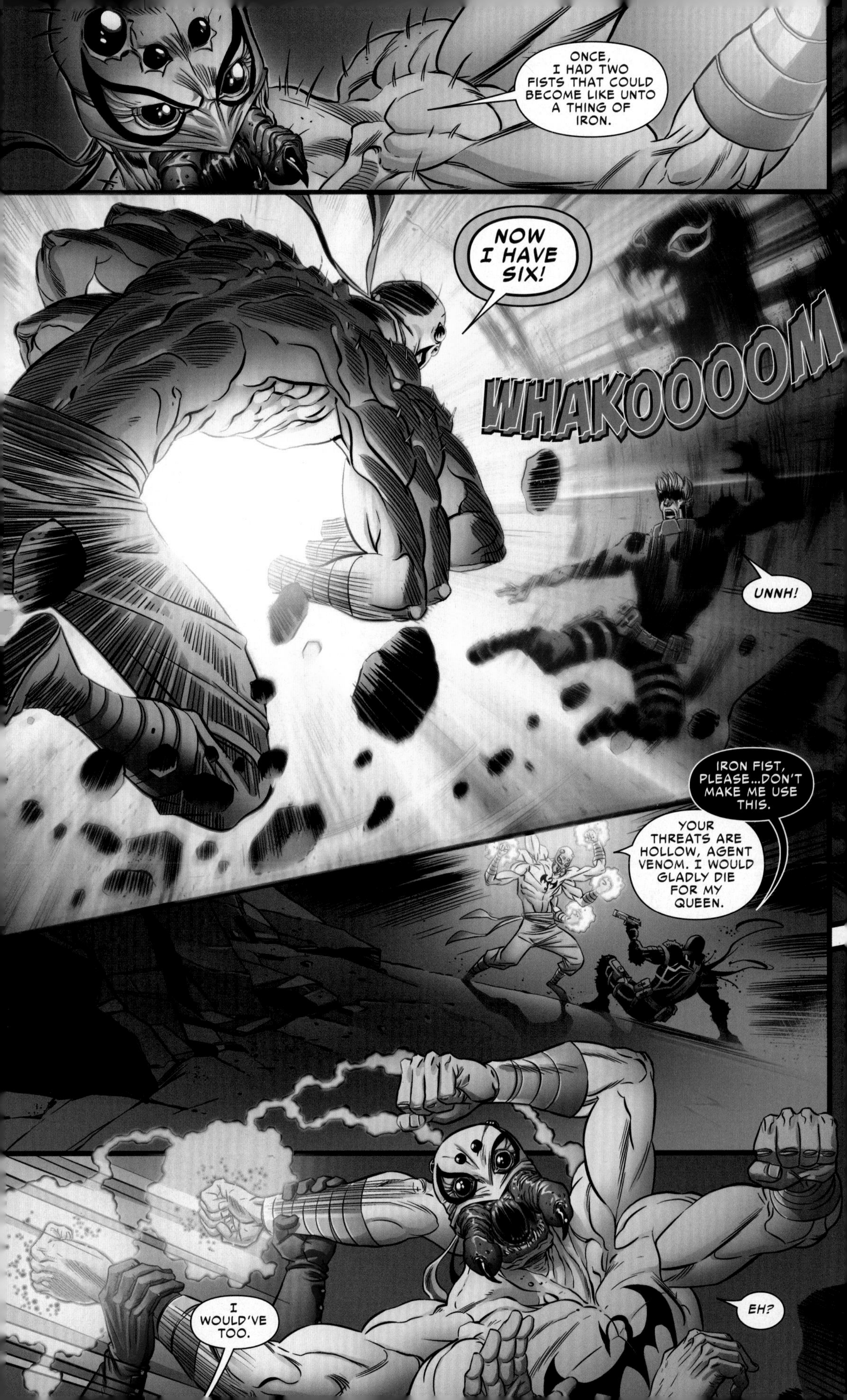
ONCE, I HAD TWO FISTS THAT COULD BECOME LIKE UNTO A THING OF IRON.
NOW I HAVE SIX!
WHAKOOOOOM
UNNH!
IRON FIST, PLEASE...DON'T MAKE ME USE THIS.
YOUR THREATS ARE HOLLOW, AGENT VENOM. I WOULD GLADLY DIE FOR MY QUEEN.
I WOULD'VE TOO.
EH?

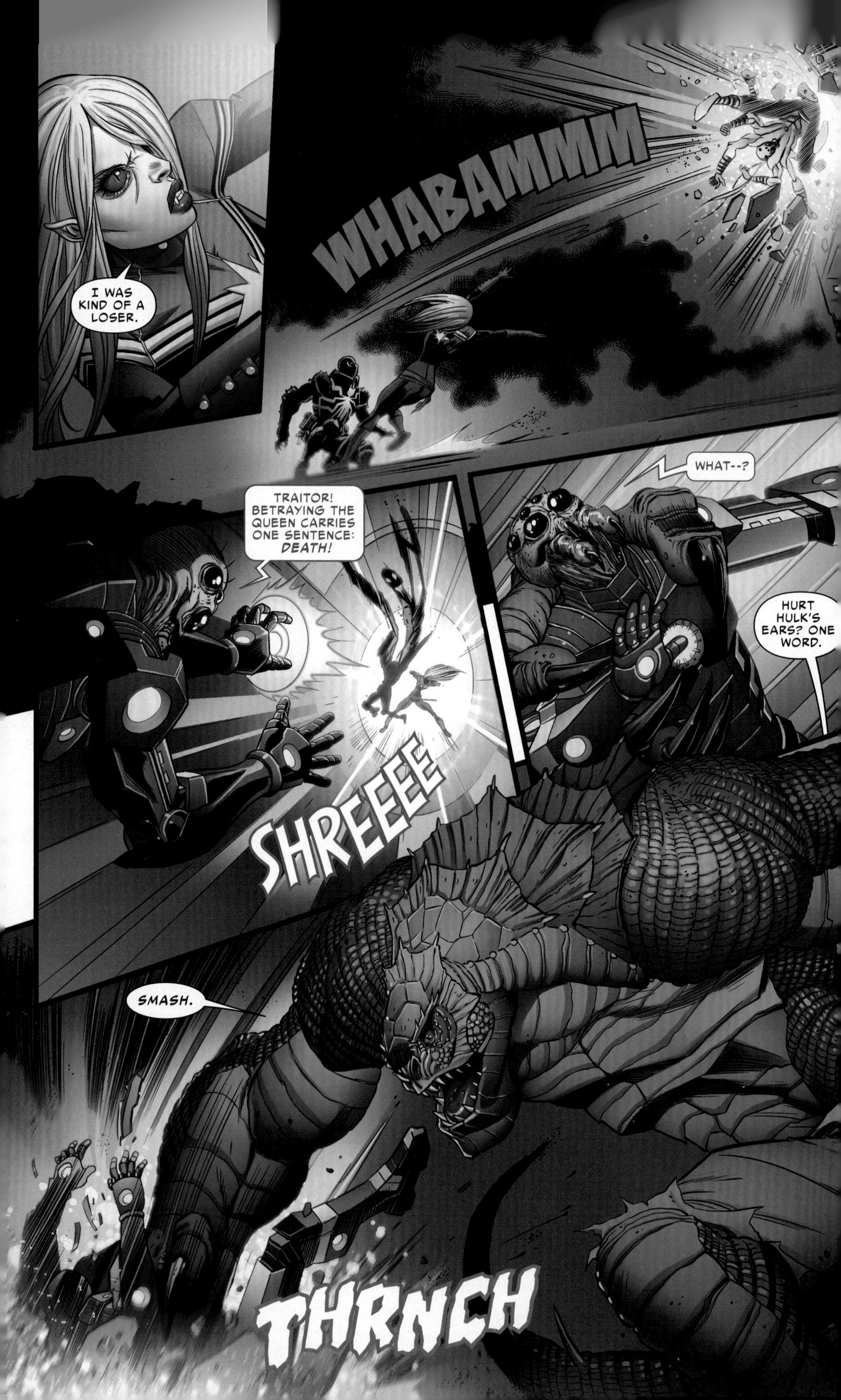
I WAS KIND OF A LOSER.
WHABAMMM
TRAITOR! BETRAYING THE QUEEN CARRIES ONE SENTENCE: DEATH!
SHREEEE
WHAT--?
HURT HULK'S EARS? ONE WORD.
SMASH.
THRNCH

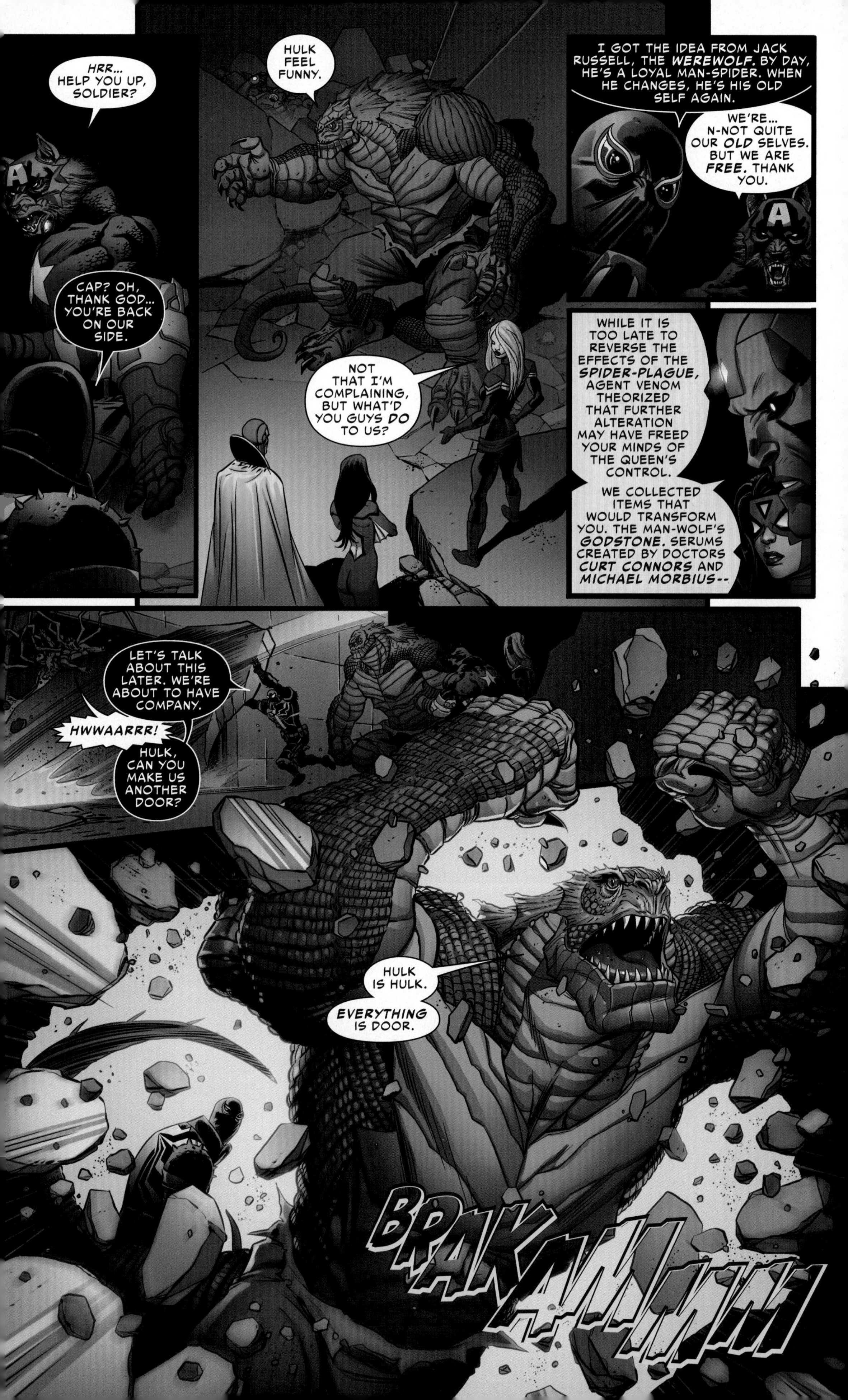
HRR... HELP YOU UP, SOLDIER?
CAP? OH, THANK GOD... YOU'RE BACK ON OUR SIDE.
HULK FEEL FUNNY.
NOT THAT I'M COMPLAINING, BUT WHAT'D YOU GUYS DO TO US?
I GOT THE IDEA FROM JACK RUSSELL, THE WEREWOLF. BY DAY, HE'S A LOYAL MAN-SPIDER. WHEN HE CHANGES, HE'S HIS OLD SELF AGAIN.
WE'RE... N-NOT QUITE OUR OLD SELVES. BUT WE ARE FREE. THANK YOU.
WHILE IT IS TOO LATE TO REVERSE THE EFFECTS OF THE SPIDER-PLAGUE, AGENT VENOM THEORIZED THAT FURTHER ALTERATION MAY HAVE FREED YOUR MINDS OF THE QUEEN'S CONTROL.
WE COLLECTED ITEMS THAT WOULD TRANSFORM YOU. THE MAN-WOLF'S GODSTONE. SERUMS CREATED BY DOCTORS CURT CONNORS AND MICHAEL MORBIUS--
LET'S TALK ABOUT THIS LATER. WE'RE ABOUT TO HAVE COMPANY.
HWWAARRR!
HULK, CAN YOU MAKE US ANOTHER DOOR?
HULK IS HULK.
EVERYTHING IS DOOR.
BRAKAMMMM

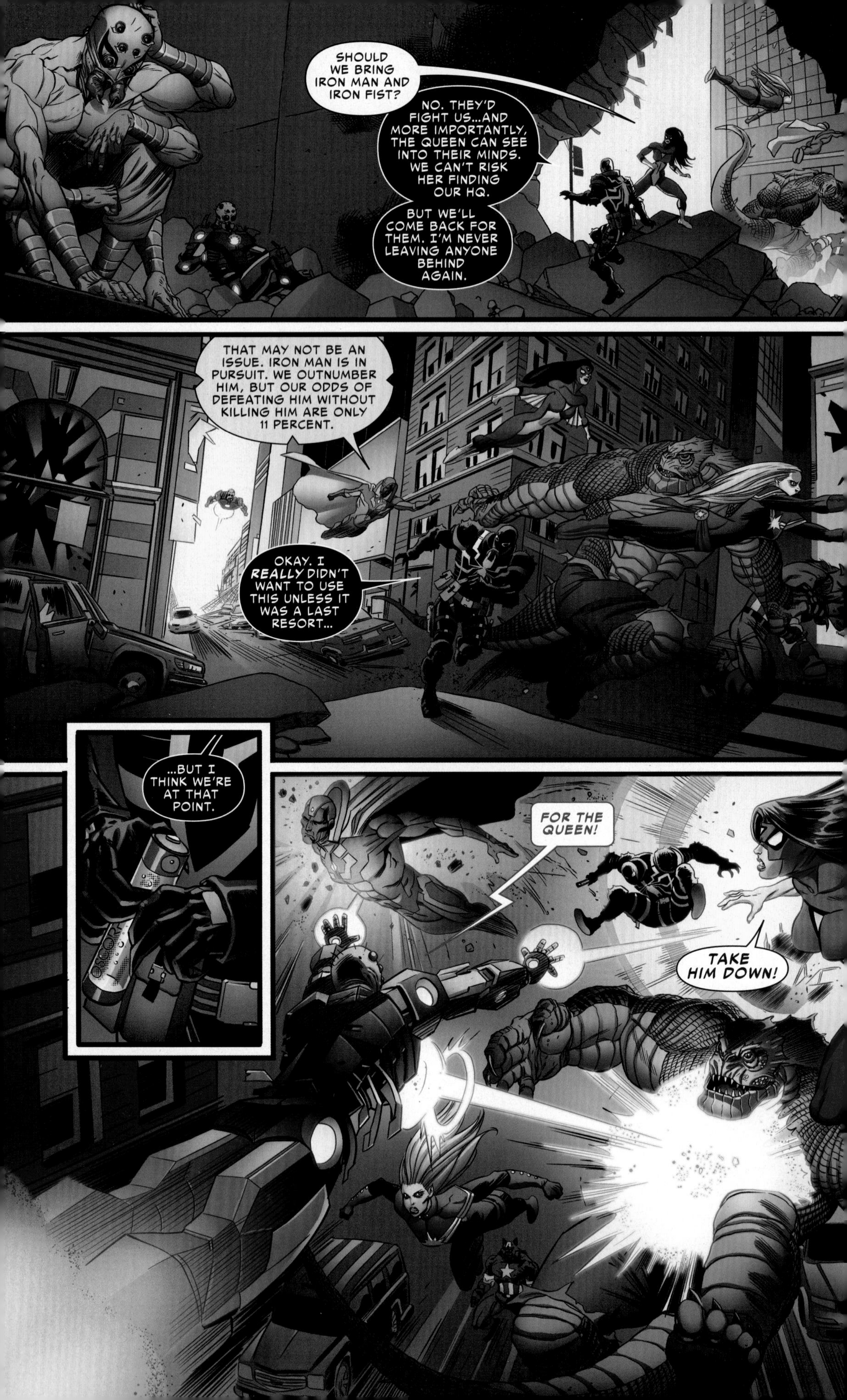
SHOULD WE BRING IRON MAN AND IRON FIST?
NO. THEY'D FIGHT US...AND MORE IMPORTANTLY, THE QUEEN CAN SEE INTO THEIR MINDS. WE CAN'T RISK HER FINDING OUR HQ.
BUT WE'LL COME BACK FOR THEM. I'M NEVER LEAVING ANYONE BEHIND AGAIN.
THAT MAY NOT BE AN ISSUE. IRON MAN IS IN PURSUIT. WE OUTNUMBER HIM, BUT OUR ODDS OF DEFEATING HIM WITHOUT KILLING HIM ARE ONLY 11 PERCENT.
OKAY. I *REALLY* DIDN'T WANT TO USE THIS UNLESS IT WAS A LAST RESORT...
...BUT I THINK WE'RE AT THAT POINT.
FOR THE QUEEN!
TAKE HIM DOWN!

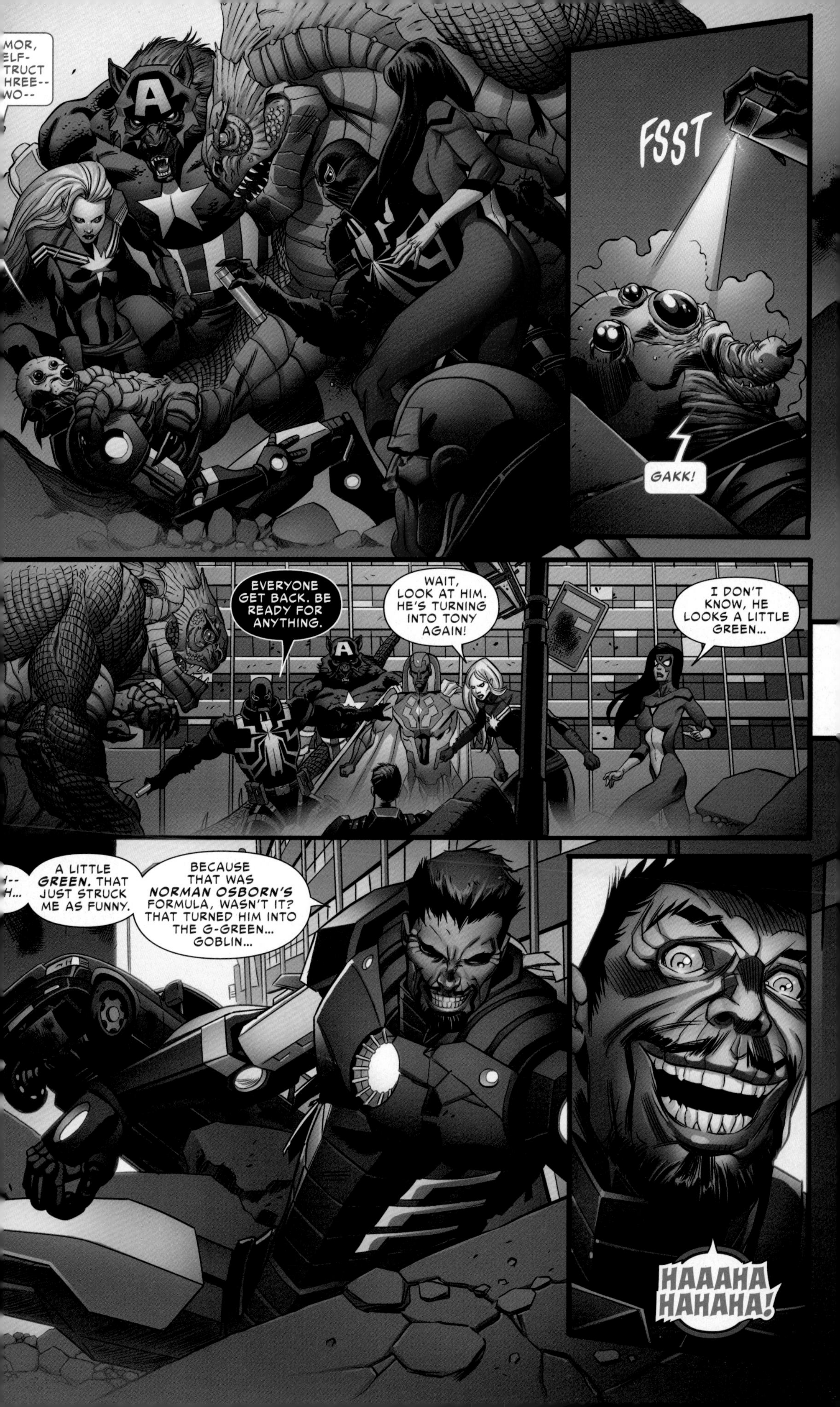

MOR, ELF- TRUCT HREE-- WO--
FSST
GAKK!
EVERYONE GET BACK. BE READY FOR ANYTHING.
WAIT, LOOK AT HIM. HE'S TURNING INTO TONY AGAIN!
I DON'T KNOW, HE LOOKS A LITTLE GREEN...
A LITTLE GREEN. THAT JUST STRUCK ME AS FUNNY.
BECAUSE THAT WAS NORMAN OSBORN'S FORMULA, WASN'T IT? THAT TURNED HIM INTO THE G-GREEN... GOBLIN...
HAAAHA HAHAHA!

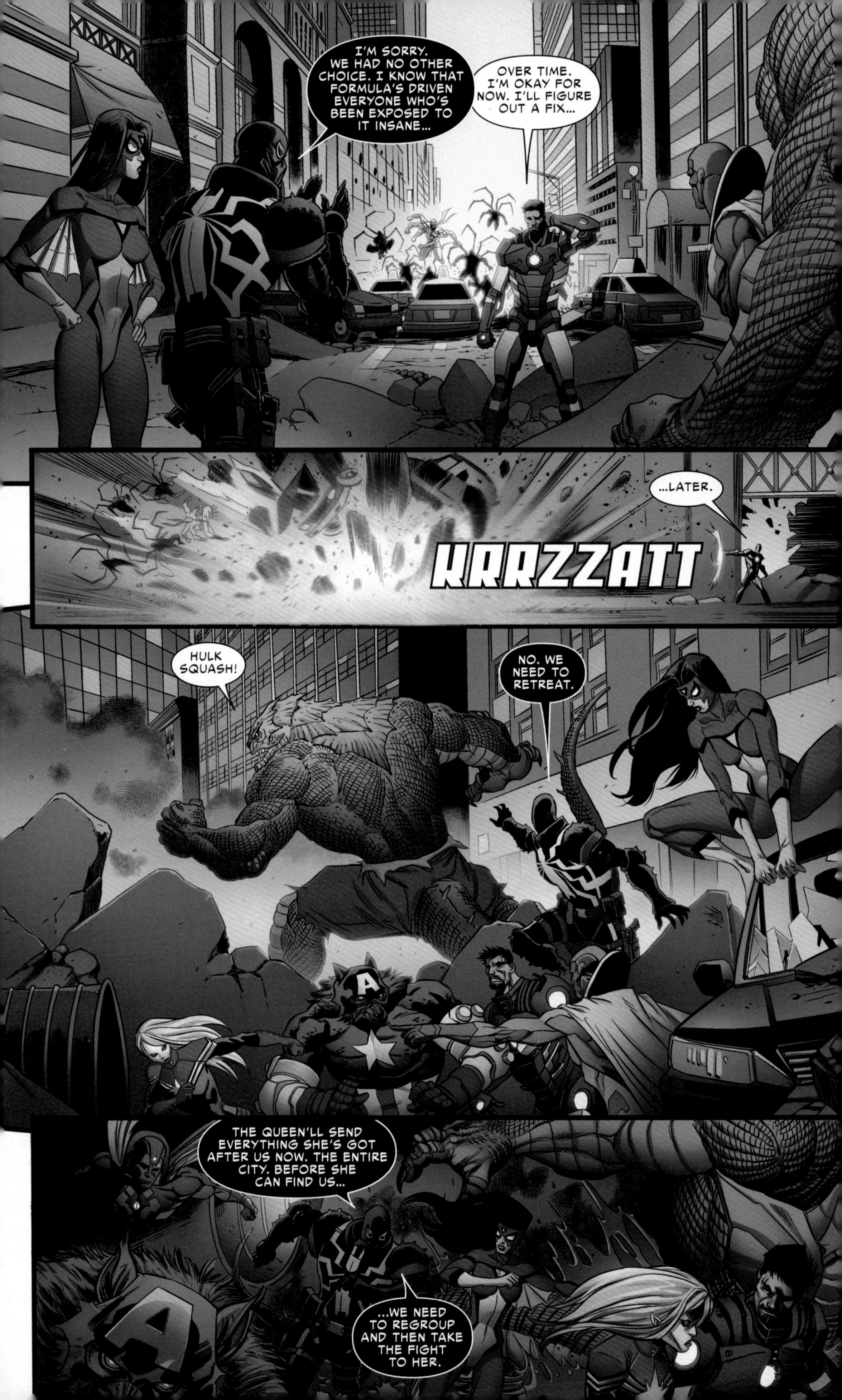
I'M SORRY. WE HAD NO OTHER CHOICE. I KNOW THAT FORMULA'S DRIVEN EVERYONE WHO'S BEEN EXPOSED TO IT INSANE...
OVER TIME. I'M OKAY FOR NOW. I'LL FIGURE OUT A FIX...
...LATER.
KRRZZATT
HULK SQUASH!
NO. WE NEED TO RETREAT.
THE QUEEN'LL SEND EVERYTHING SHE'S GOT AFTER US NOW. THE ENTIRE CITY. BEFORE SHE CAN FIND US...
...WE NEED TO REGROUP AND THEN TAKE THE FIGHT TO HER.

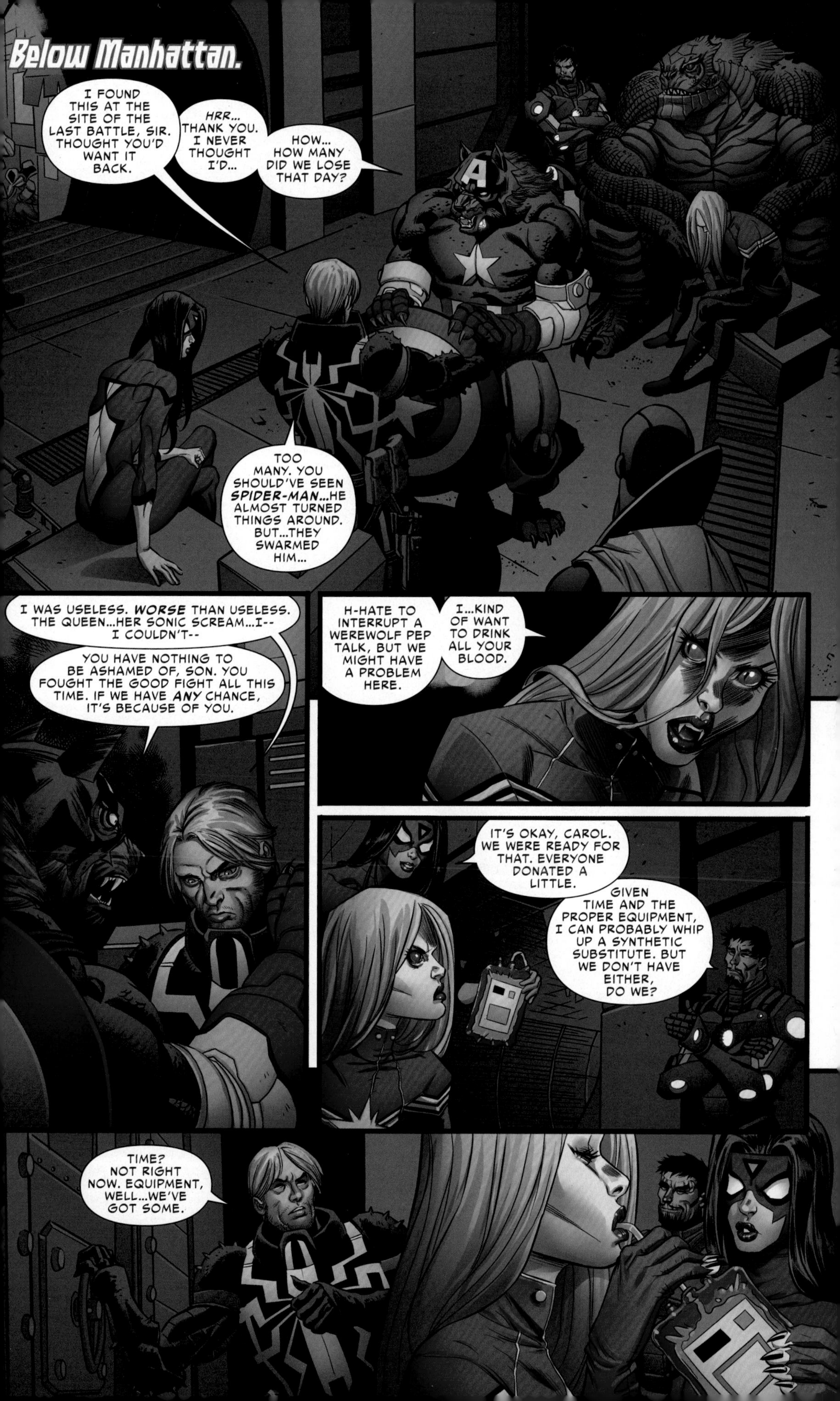
Below Manhattan.
I FOUND THIS AT THE SITE OF THE LAST BATTLE, SIR. THOUGHT YOU'D WANT IT BACK.
HRR... THANK YOU. I NEVER THOUGHT I'D...
HOW... HOW MANY DID WE LOSE THAT DAY?
TOO MANY. YOU SHOULD'VE SEEN SPIDER-MAN...HE ALMOST TURNED THINGS AROUND. BUT...THEY SWARMED HIM...
I WAS USELESS. WORSE THAN USELESS. THE QUEEN...HER SONIC SCREAM...I-- I COULDN'T--
YOU HAVE NOTHING TO BE ASHAMED OF, SON. YOU FOUGHT THE GOOD FIGHT ALL THIS TIME. IF WE HAVE ANY CHANCE, IT'S BECAUSE OF YOU.
H-HATE TO INTERRUPT A WEREWOLF PEP TALK, BUT WE MIGHT HAVE A PROBLEM HERE.
I...KIND OF WANT TO DRINK ALL YOUR BLOOD.
IT'S OKAY, CAROL. WE WERE READY FOR THAT. EVERYONE DONATED A LITTLE.
GIVEN TIME AND THE PROPER EQUIPMENT, I CAN PROBABLY WHIP UP A SYNTHETIC SUBSTITUTE. BUT WE DON'T HAVE EITHER, DO WE?
TIME? NOT RIGHT NOW. EQUIPMENT, WELL...WE'VE GOT SOME.

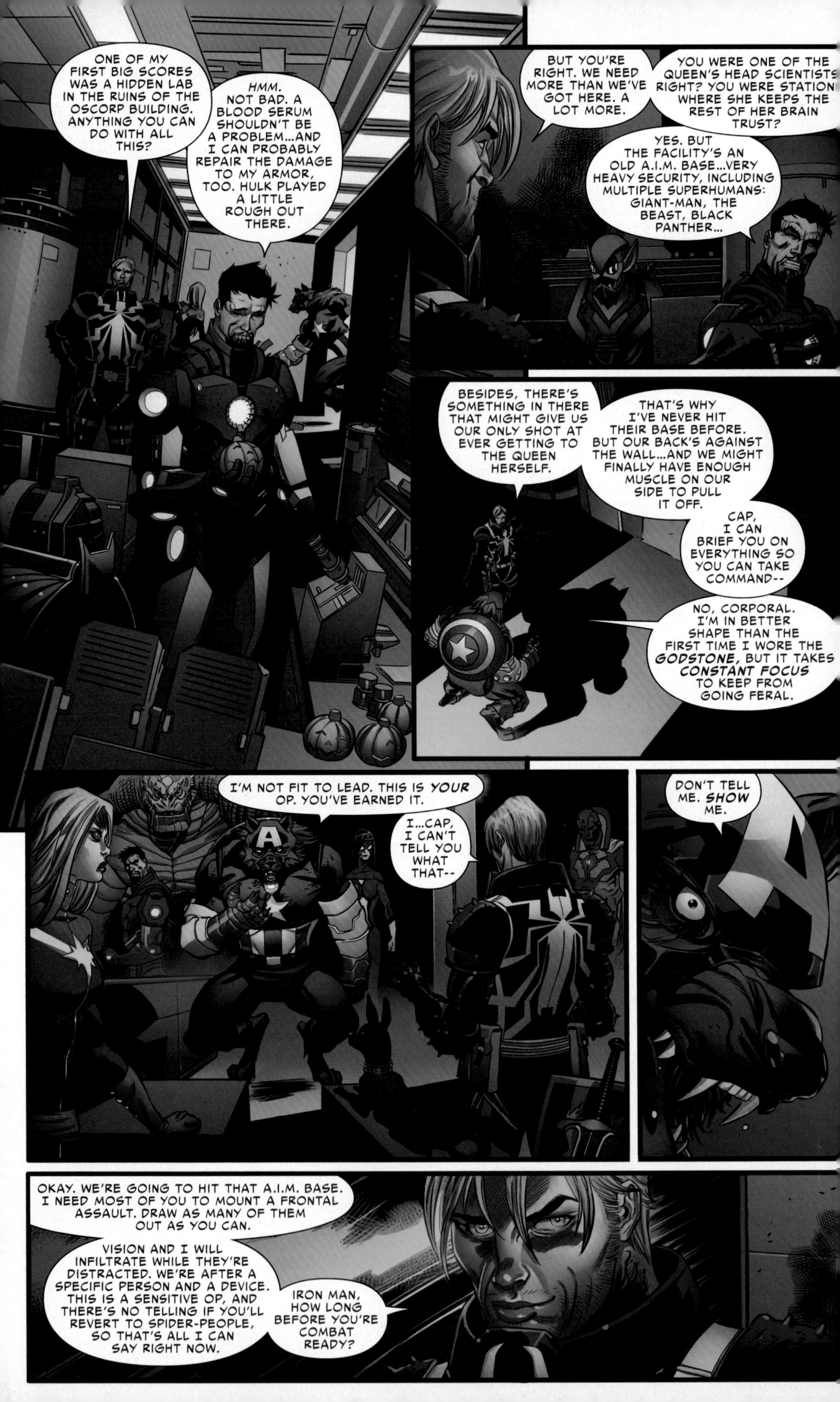
ONE OF MY FIRST BIG SCORES WAS A HIDDEN LAB IN THE RUINS OF THE OSCORP BUILDING. ANYTHING YOU CAN DO WITH ALL THIS?
HMM. NOT BAD. A BLOOD SERUM SHOULDN'T BE A PROBLEM...AND I CAN PROBABLY REPAIR THE DAMAGE TO MY ARMOR, TOO. HULK PLAYED A LITTLE ROUGH OUT THERE.
BUT YOU'RE RIGHT. WE NEED MORE THAN WE'VE GOT HERE. A LOT MORE.
YOU WERE ONE OF THE QUEEN'S HEAD SCIENTISTS RIGHT? YOU WERE STATION WHERE SHE KEEPS THE REST OF HER BRAIN TRUST?
YES. BUT THE FACILITY'S AN OLD A.I.M. BASE...VERY HEAVY SECURITY, INCLUDING MULTIPLE SUPERHUMANS: GIANT-MAN, THE BEAST, BLACK PANTHER...
BESIDES, THERE'S SOMETHING IN THERE THAT MIGHT GIVE US OUR ONLY SHOT AT EVER GETTING TO THE QUEEN HERSELF.
THAT'S WHY I'VE NEVER HIT THEIR BASE BEFORE. BUT OUR BACK'S AGAINST THE WALL...AND WE MIGHT FINALLY HAVE ENOUGH MUSCLE ON OUR SIDE TO PULL IT OFF.
CAP, I CAN BRIEF YOU ON EVERYTHING SO YOU CAN TAKE COMMAND--
NO, CORPORAL. I'M IN BETTER SHAPE THAN THE FIRST TIME I WORE THE GODSTONE, BUT IT TAKES CONSTANT FOCUS TO KEEP FROM GOING FERAL.
I'M NOT FIT TO LEAD. THIS IS YOUR OP. YOU'VE EARNED IT.
I...CAP, I CAN'T TELL YOU WHAT THAT--
DON'T TELL ME. SHOW ME.
OKAY. WE'RE GOING TO HIT THAT A.I.M. BASE. I NEED MOST OF YOU TO MOUNT A FRONTAL ASSAULT. DRAW AS MANY OF THEM OUT AS YOU CAN.
VISION AND I WILL INFILTRATE WHILE THEY'RE DISTRACTED. WE'RE AFTER A SPECIFIC PERSON AND A DEVICE. THIS IS A SENSITIVE OP, AND THERE'S NO TELLING IF YOU'LL REVERT TO SPIDER-PEOPLE, SO THAT'S ALL I CAN SAY RIGHT NOW.
IRON MAN, HOW LONG BEFORE YOU'RE COMBAT READY?

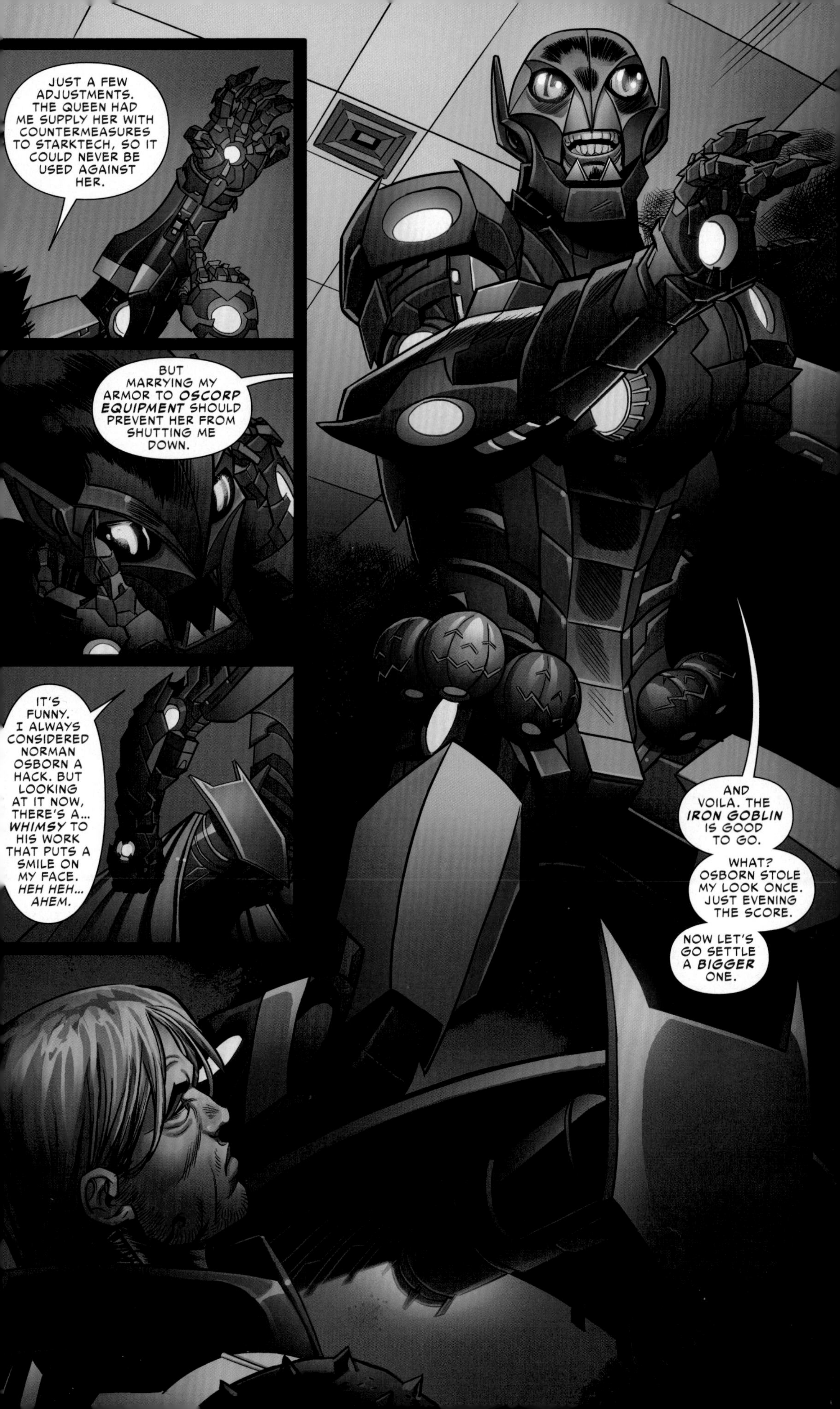

JUST A FEW ADJUSTMENTS. THE QUEEN HAD ME SUPPLY HER WITH COUNTERMEASURES TO STARKTECH, SO IT COULD NEVER BE USED AGAINST HER.
BUT MARRYING MY ARMOR TO *OSCORP EQUIPMENT* SHOULD PREVENT HER FROM SHUTTING ME DOWN.
IT'S FUNNY. I ALWAYS CONSIDERED NORMAN OSBORN A HACK. BUT LOOKING AT IT NOW, THERE'S A... *WHIMSY* TO HIS WORK THAT PUTS A SMILE ON MY FACE. *HEH HEH...* *AHEM.*
AND VOILA. THE *IRON GOBLIN* IS GOOD TO GO.
WHAT? OSBORN STOLE MY LOOK ONCE. JUST EVENING THE SCORE.
NOW LET'S GO SETTLE A *BIGGER* ONE.

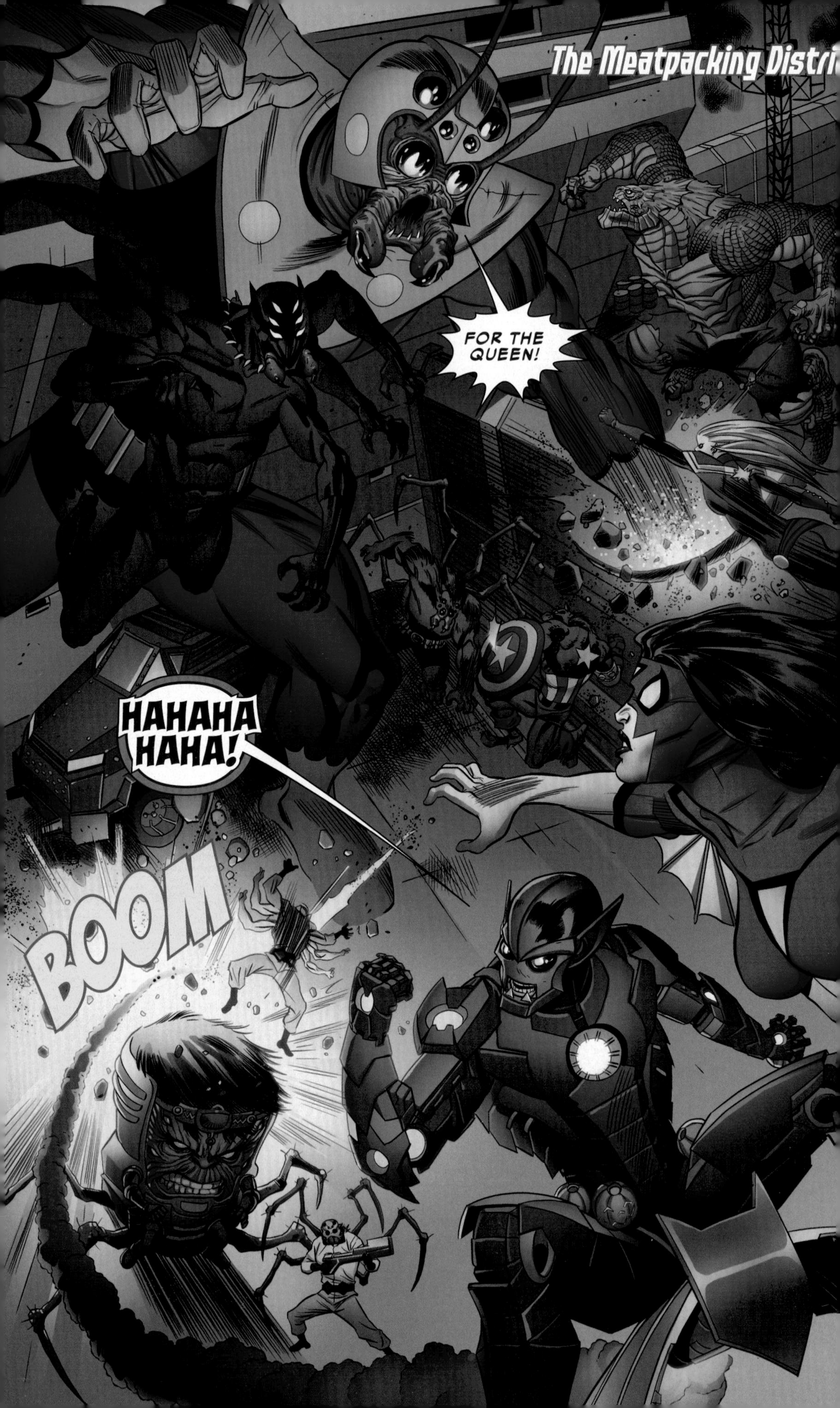
The Meatpacking Distri
FOR THE QUEEN!
HAHAHA HAHA!
BOOM

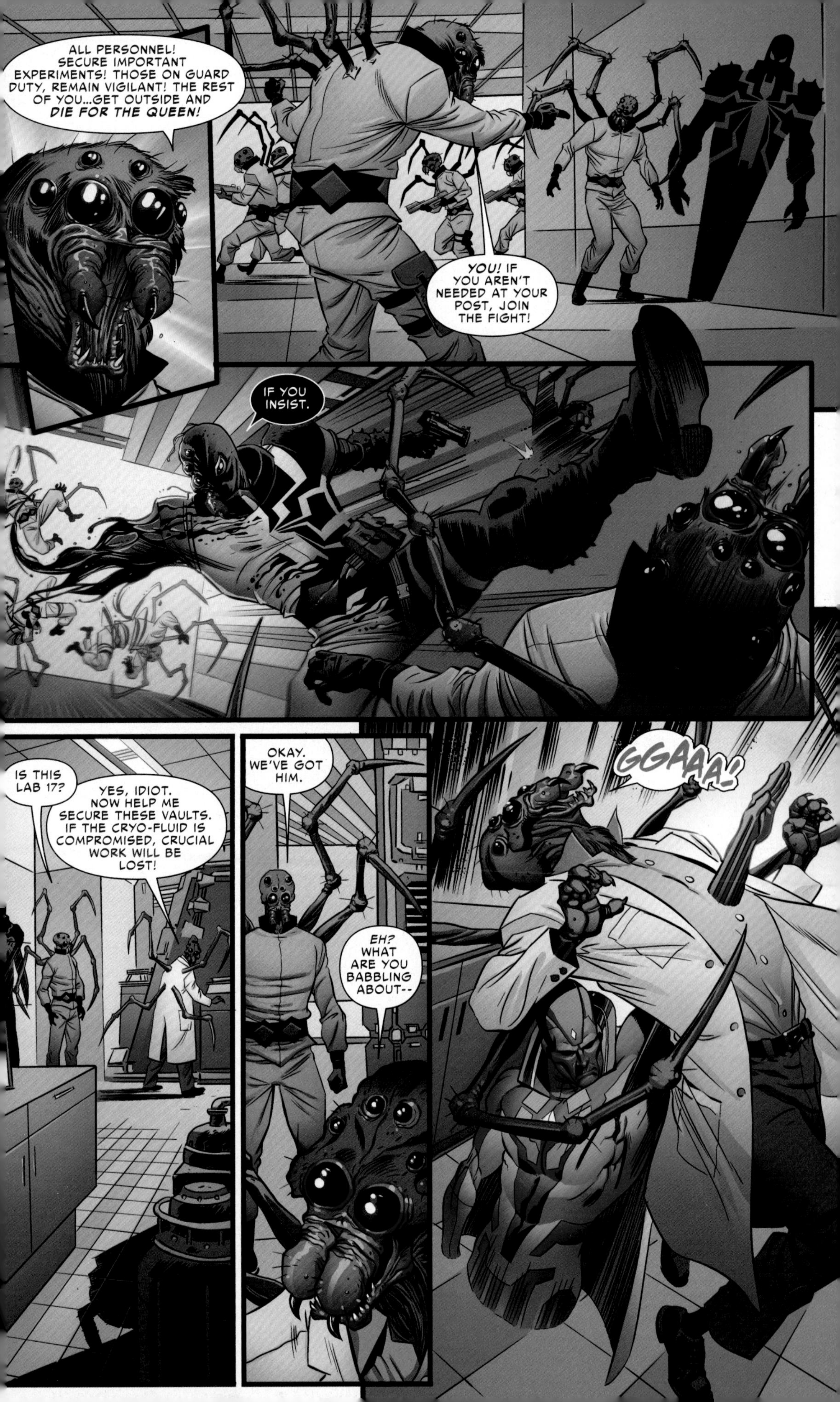
ALL PERSONNEL! SECURE IMPORTANT EXPERIMENTS! THOSE ON GUARD DUTY, REMAIN VIGILANT! THE REST OF YOU...GET OUTSIDE AND DIE FOR THE QUEEN!
YOU! IF YOU AREN'T NEEDED AT YOUR POST, JOIN THE FIGHT!
IF YOU INSIST.
IS THIS LAB 17?
YES, IDIOT. NOW HELP ME SECURE THESE VAULTS. IF THE CRYO-FLUID IS COMPROMISED, CRUCIAL WORK WILL BE LOST!
OKAY. WE'VE GOT HIM.
EH? WHAT ARE YOU BABBLING ABOUT--
GGAAA!

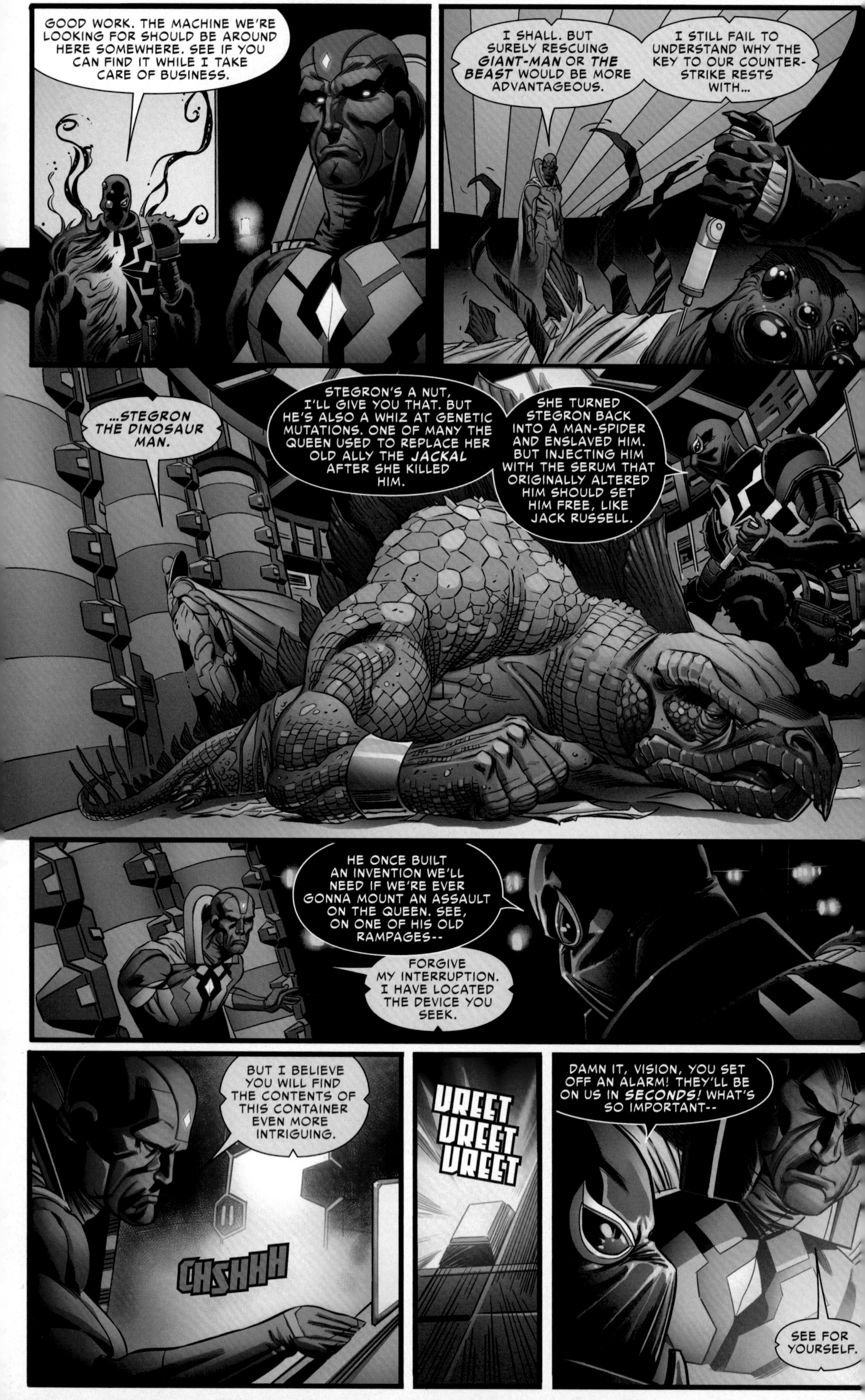
GOOD WORK. THE MACHINE WE'RE LOOKING FOR SHOULD BE AROUND HERE SOMEWHERE. SEE IF YOU CAN FIND IT WHILE I TAKE CARE OF BUSINESS.
I SHALL. BUT SURELY RESCUING GIANT-MAN OR THE BEAST WOULD BE MORE ADVANTAGEOUS.
I STILL FAIL TO UNDERSTAND WHY THE KEY TO OUR COUNTER-STRIKE RESTS WITH...
...STEGRON THE DINOSAUR MAN.
STEGRON'S A NUT, I'LL GIVE YOU THAT. BUT HE'S ALSO A WHIZ AT GENETIC MUTATIONS. ONE OF MANY THE QUEEN USED TO REPLACE HER OLD ALLY THE JACKAL AFTER SHE KILLED HIM.
SHE TURNED STEGRON BACK INTO A MAN-SPIDER AND ENSLAVED HIM. BUT INJECTING HIM WITH THE SERUM THAT ORIGINALLY ALTERED HIM SHOULD SET HIM FREE, LIKE JACK RUSSELL.
HE ONCE BUILT AN INVENTION WE'LL NEED IF WE'RE EVER GONNA MOUNT AN ASSAULT ON THE QUEEN. SEE, ON ONE OF HIS OLD RAMPAGES--
FORGIVE MY INTERRUPTION. I HAVE LOCATED THE DEVICE YOU SEEK.
BUT I BELIEVE YOU WILL FIND THE CONTENTS OF THIS CONTAINER EVEN MORE INTRIGUING.
CHSHHH
VREET VREET VREET
DAMN IT, VISION, YOU SET OFF AN ALARM! THEY'LL BE ON US IN SECONDS! WHAT'S SO IMPORTANT--
SEE FOR YOURSELF.

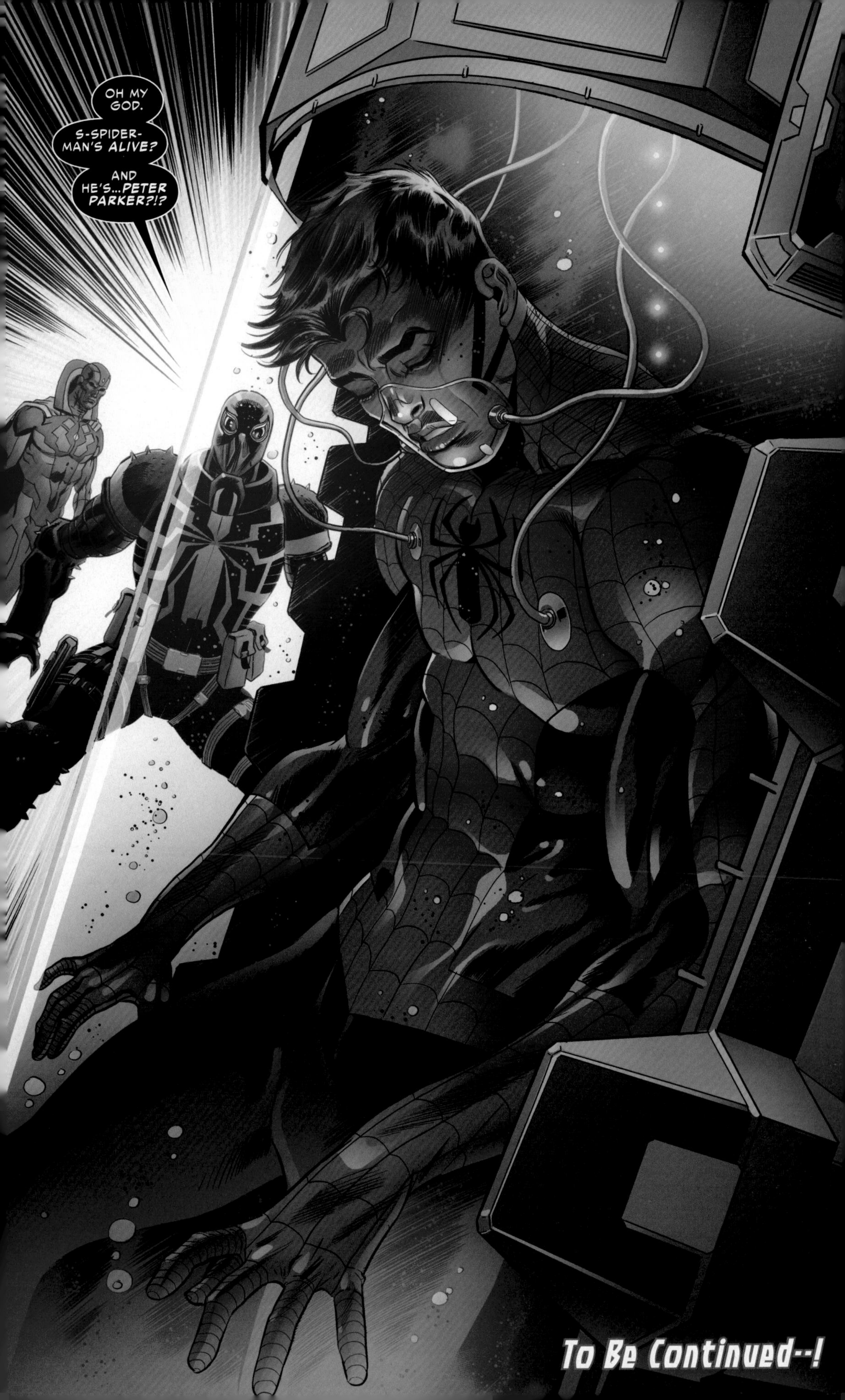
OH MY GOD.
S-SPIDER-MAN'S ALIVE?
AND HE'S...PETER PARKER?!?
To Be Continued--!

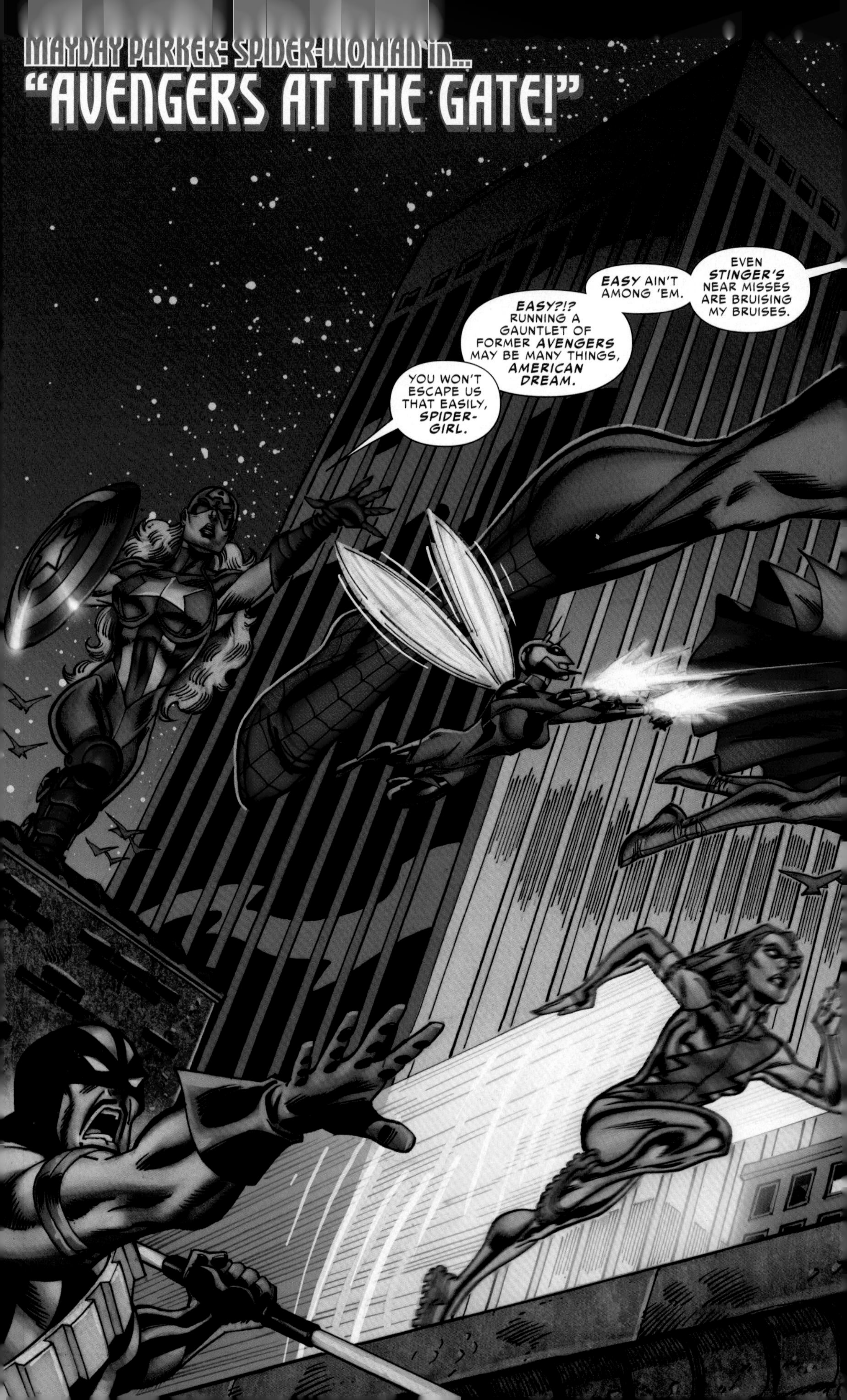
MAYDAY PARKER: SPIDER-WOMAN in...
"AVENGERS AT THE GATE!"
YOU WON'T ESCAPE US THAT EASILY, SPIDER-GIRL.
EASY?!? RUNNING A GAUNTLET OF FORMER AVENGERS MAY BE MANY THINGS, AMERICAN DREAM.
EASY AIN'T AMONG 'EM.
EVEN STINGER'S NEAR MISSES ARE BRUISING MY BRUISES.

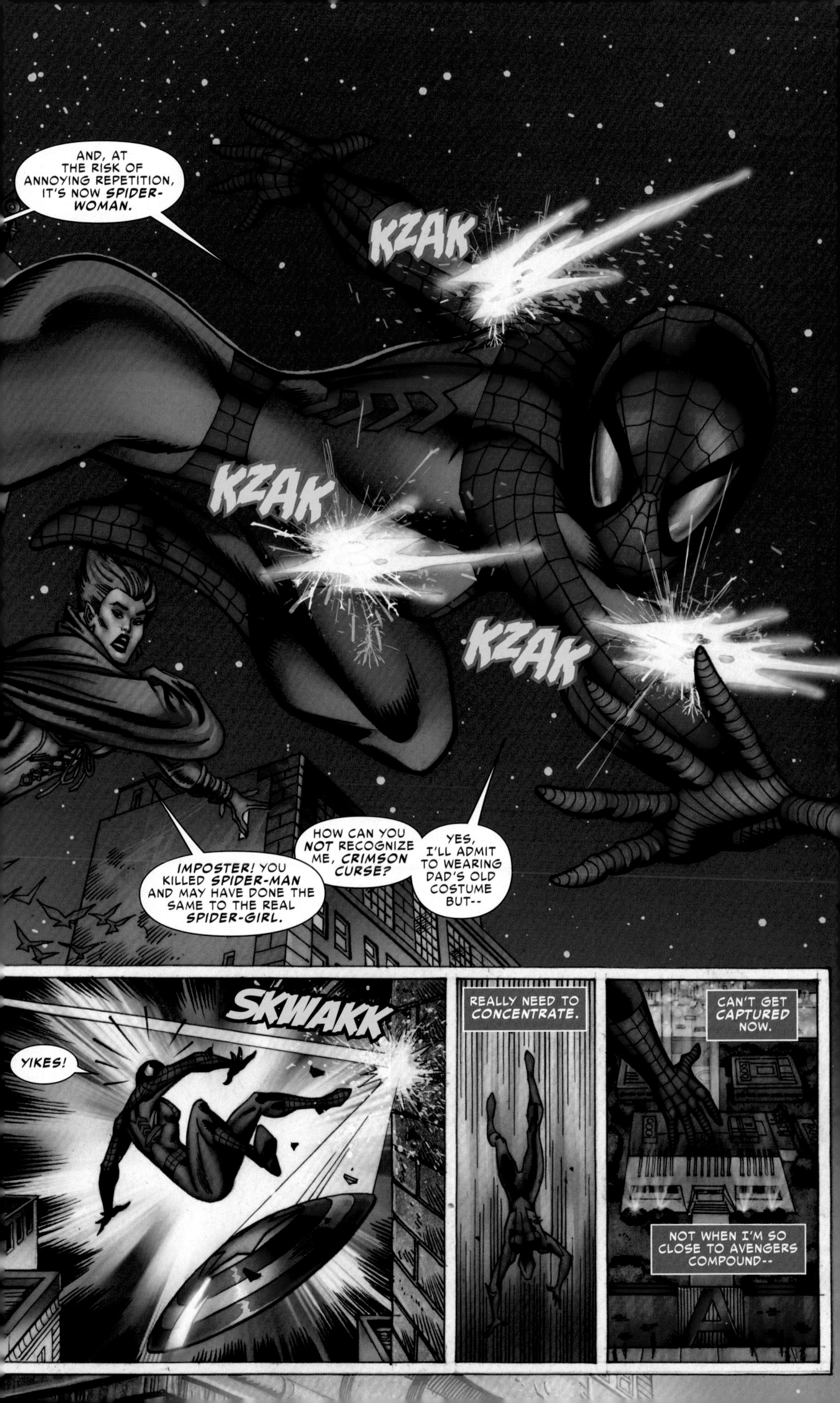

AND, AT THE RISK OF ANNOYING REPETITION, IT'S NOW SPIDER-WOMAN.
KZAK
KZAK
KZAK
IMPOSTER! YOU KILLED SPIDER-MAN AND MAY HAVE DONE THE SAME TO THE REAL SPIDER-GIRL.
HOW CAN YOU NOT RECOGNIZE ME, CRIMSON CURSE?
YES, I'LL ADMIT TO WEARING DAD'S OLD COSTUME BUT--
SKWAKK
YIKES!
REALLY NEED TO CONCENTRATE.
CAN'T GET CAPTURED NOW.
NOT WHEN I'M SO CLOSE TO AVENGERS COMPOUND--

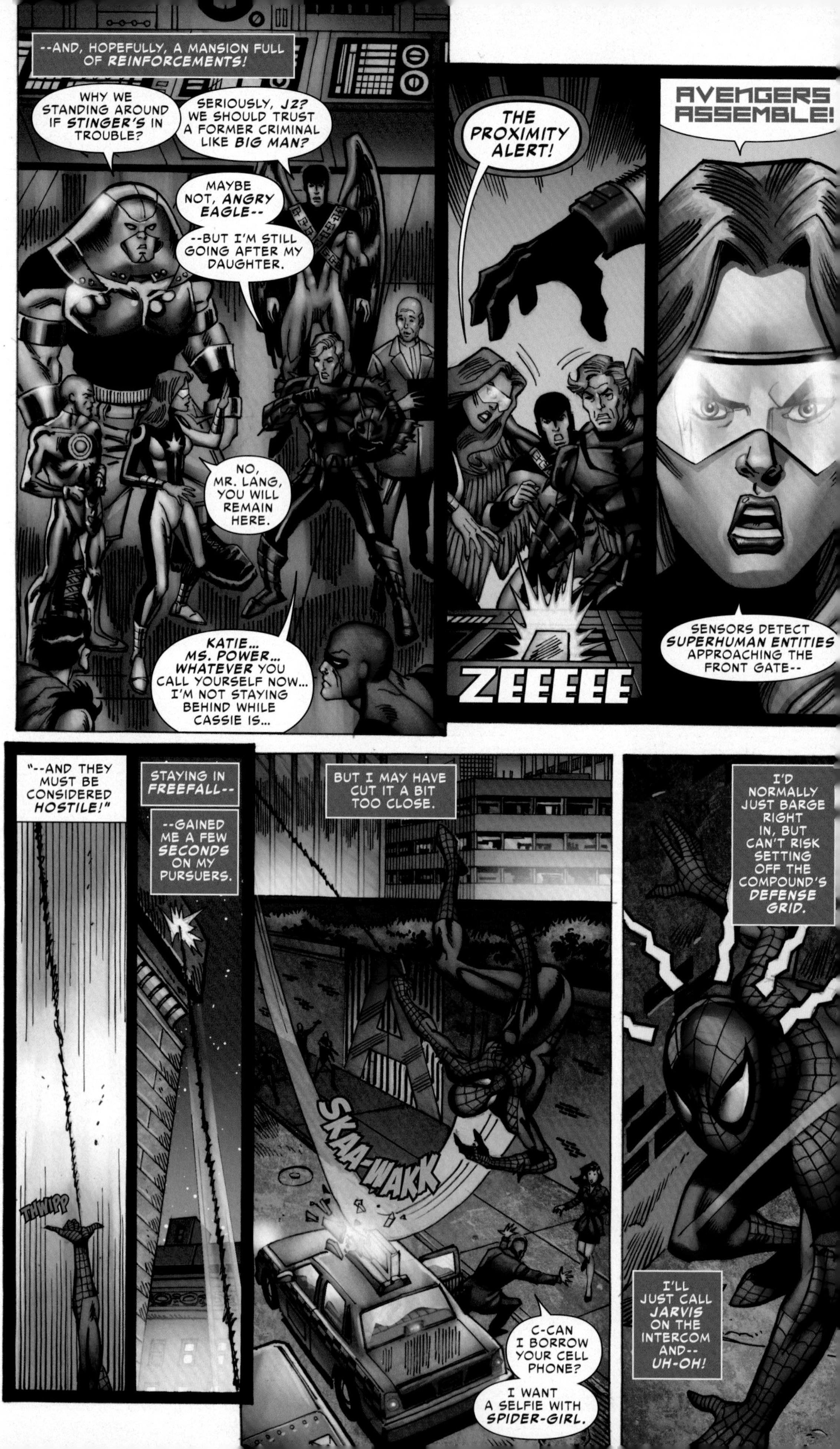
--AND, HOPEFULLY, A MANSION FULL OF REINFORCEMENTS!
WHY WE STANDING AROUND IF STINGER'S IN TROUBLE?
SERIOUSLY, J2? WE SHOULD TRUST A FORMER CRIMINAL LIKE BIG MAN?
MAYBE NOT, ANGRY EAGLE--
--BUT I'M STILL GOING AFTER MY DAUGHTER.
NO, MR. LANG, YOU WILL REMAIN HERE.
KATIE... MS. POWER... WHATEVER YOU CALL YOURSELF NOW... I'M NOT STAYING BEHIND WHILE CASSIE IS...
THE PROXIMITY ALERT!
ZEEEEE
AVENGERS ASSEMBLE!
SENSORS DETECT SUPERHUMAN ENTITIES APPROACHING THE FRONT GATE--
"--AND THEY MUST BE CONSIDERED HOSTILE!"
THWIPP
STAYING IN FREEFALL--
--GAINED ME A FEW SECONDS ON MY PURSUERS.
BUT I MAY HAVE CUT IT A BIT TOO CLOSE.
SKAA-WAKK
C-CAN I BORROW YOUR CELL PHONE?
I WANT A SELFIE WITH SPIDER-GIRL.
I'D NORMALLY JUST BARGE RIGHT IN, BUT CAN'T RISK SETTING OFF THE COMPOUND'S DEFENSE GRID.
I'LL JUST CALL JARVIS ON THE INTERCOM AND-- UH-OH!

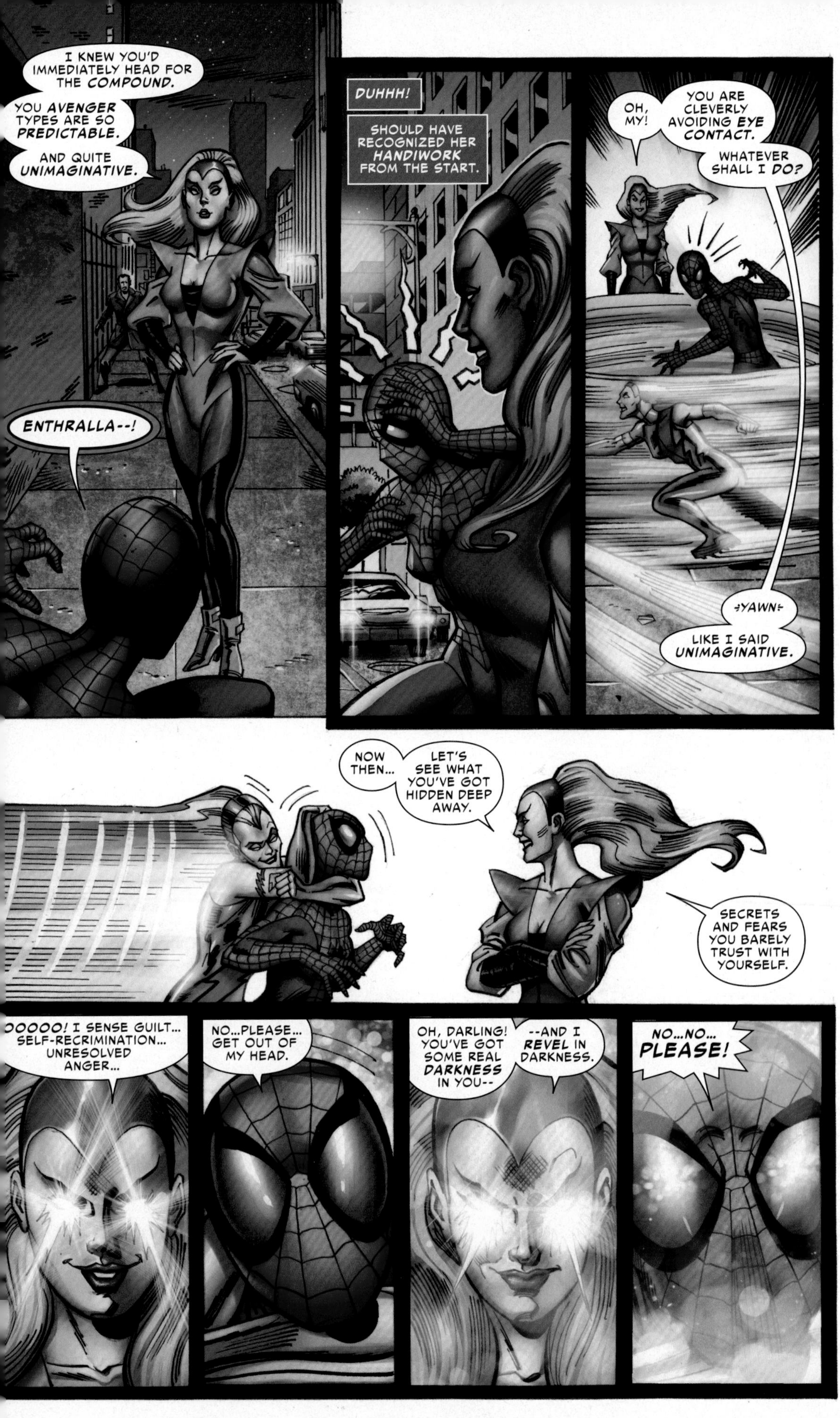
I KNEW YOU'D IMMEDIATELY HEAD FOR THE *COMPOUND*.
YOU *AVENGER* TYPES ARE SO *PREDICTABLE*.
AND QUITE *UNIMAGINATIVE*.
ENTHRALLA--!
DUHHH!
SHOULD HAVE RECOGNIZED HER *HANDIWORK* FROM THE START.
OH, MY!
YOU ARE CLEVERLY AVOIDING *EYE CONTACT*.
WHATEVER SHALL I *DO?*
YAWN
LIKE I SAID *UNIMAGINATIVE*.
NOW THEN...
LET'S SEE WHAT YOU'VE GOT HIDDEN DEEP AWAY.
SECRETS AND FEARS YOU BARELY TRUST WITH YOURSELF.
OOOOO! I SENSE GUILT... SELF-RECRIMINATION... UNRESOLVED ANGER...
NO...PLEASE... GET OUT OF MY HEAD.
OH, DARLING! YOU'VE GOT SOME REAL *DARKNESS* IN YOU--
--AND I *REVEL* IN DARKNESS.
NO...NO... *PLEASE!*

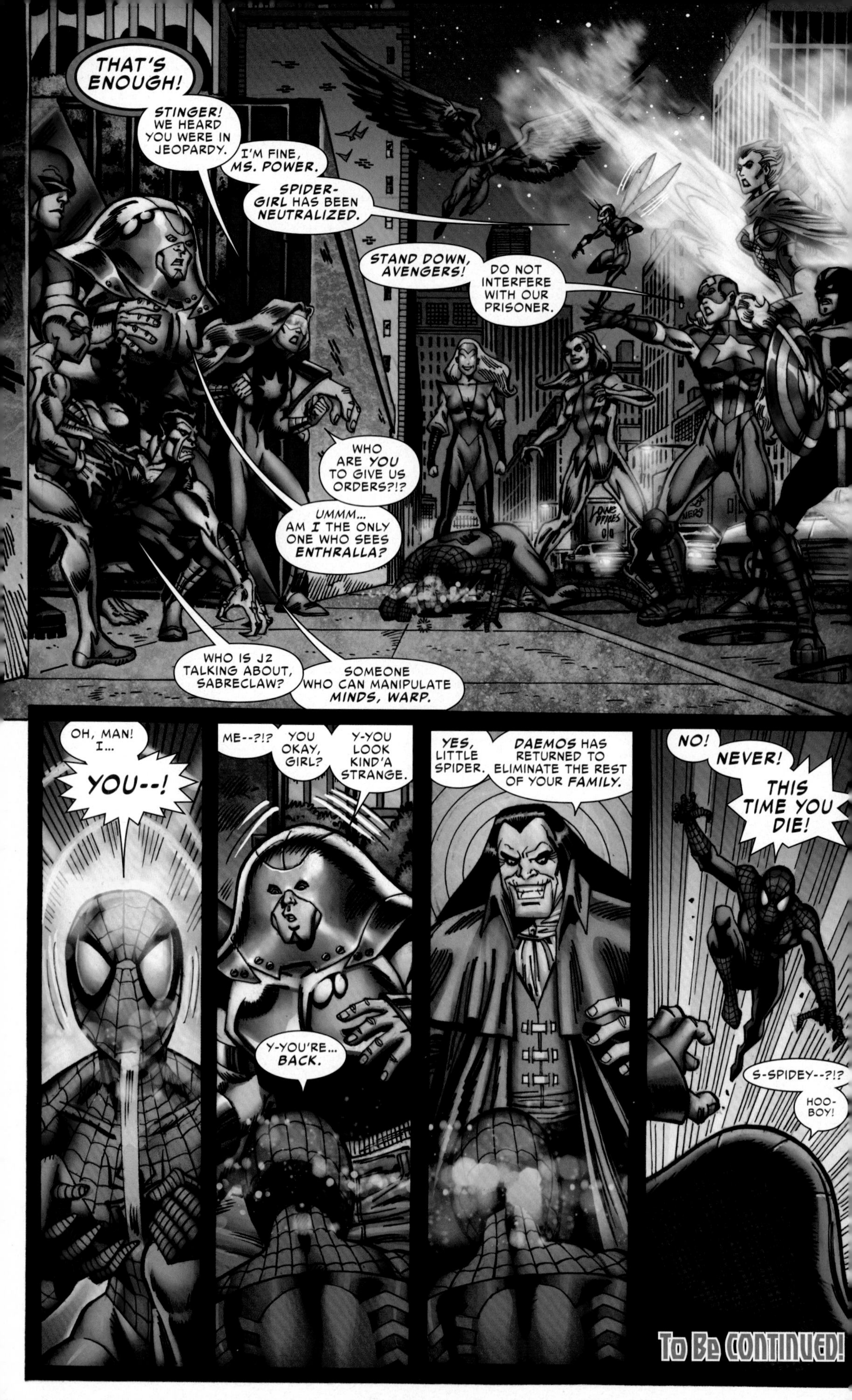
THAT'S ENOUGH!
STINGER! WE HEARD YOU WERE IN JEOPARDY.
I'M FINE, MS. POWER.
SPIDER-GIRL HAS BEEN NEUTRALIZED.
STAND DOWN, AVENGERS!
DO NOT INTERFERE WITH OUR PRISONER.
WHO ARE YOU TO GIVE US ORDERS?!?
UMMM... AM I THE ONLY ONE WHO SEES ENTHRALLA?
WHO IS J2 TALKING ABOUT, SABRECLAW?
SOMEONE WHO CAN MANIPULATE MINDS, WARP.
OH, MAN! I...
YOU--!
ME--?!?
YOU OKAY, GIRL?
Y-YOU LOOK KIND'A STRANGE.
Y-YOU'RE... BACK.
YES, LITTLE SPIDER.
DAEMOS HAS RETURNED TO ELIMINATE THE REST OF YOUR FAMILY.
NO!
NEVER!
THIS TIME YOU DIE!
S-SPIDEY--?!?
HOO-BOY!
To Be CONTINUED!

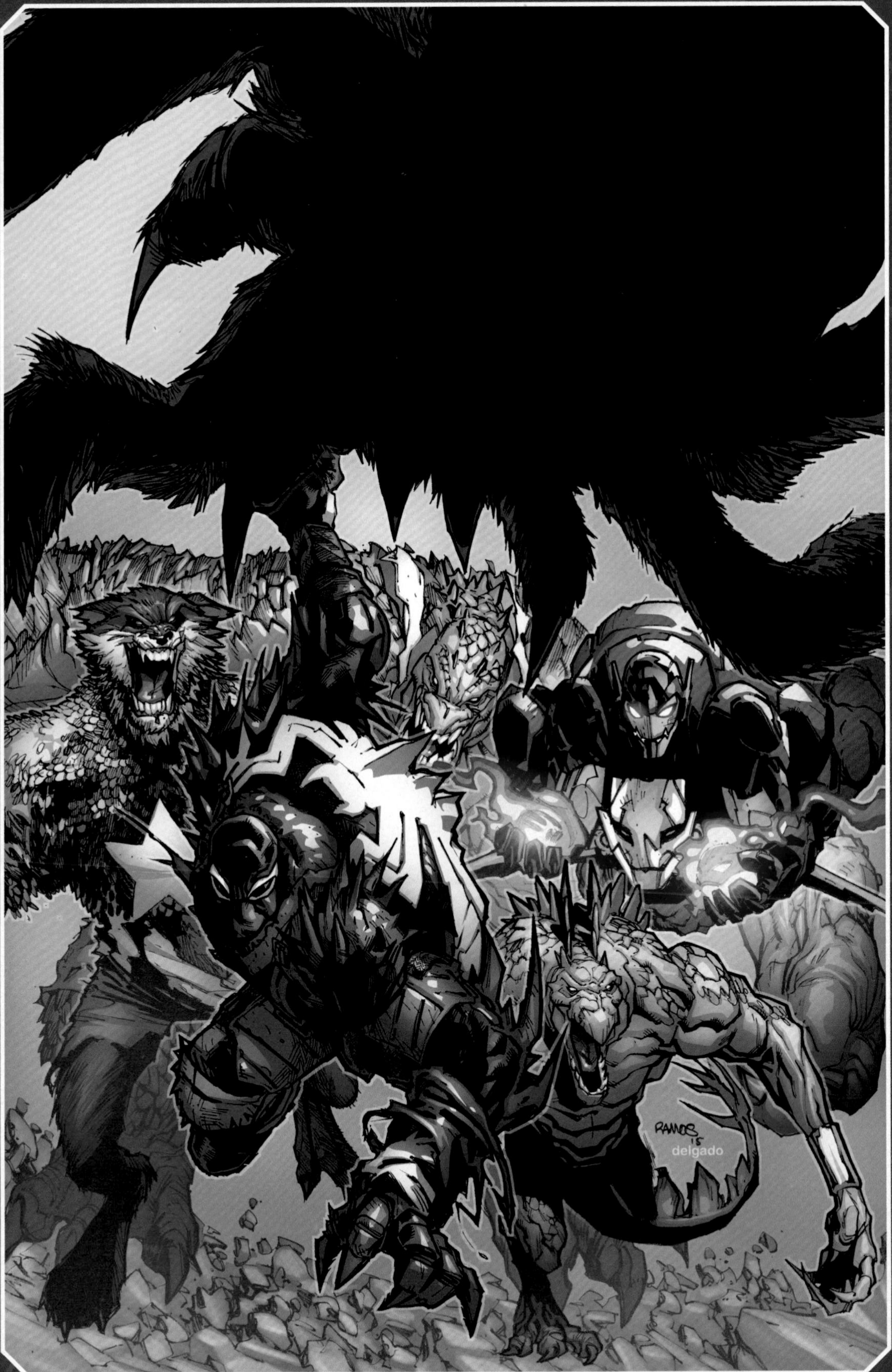
RAMOS '15
delgado

PART THREE: GOBLIN KNIGHT IN SHINING ARMOR

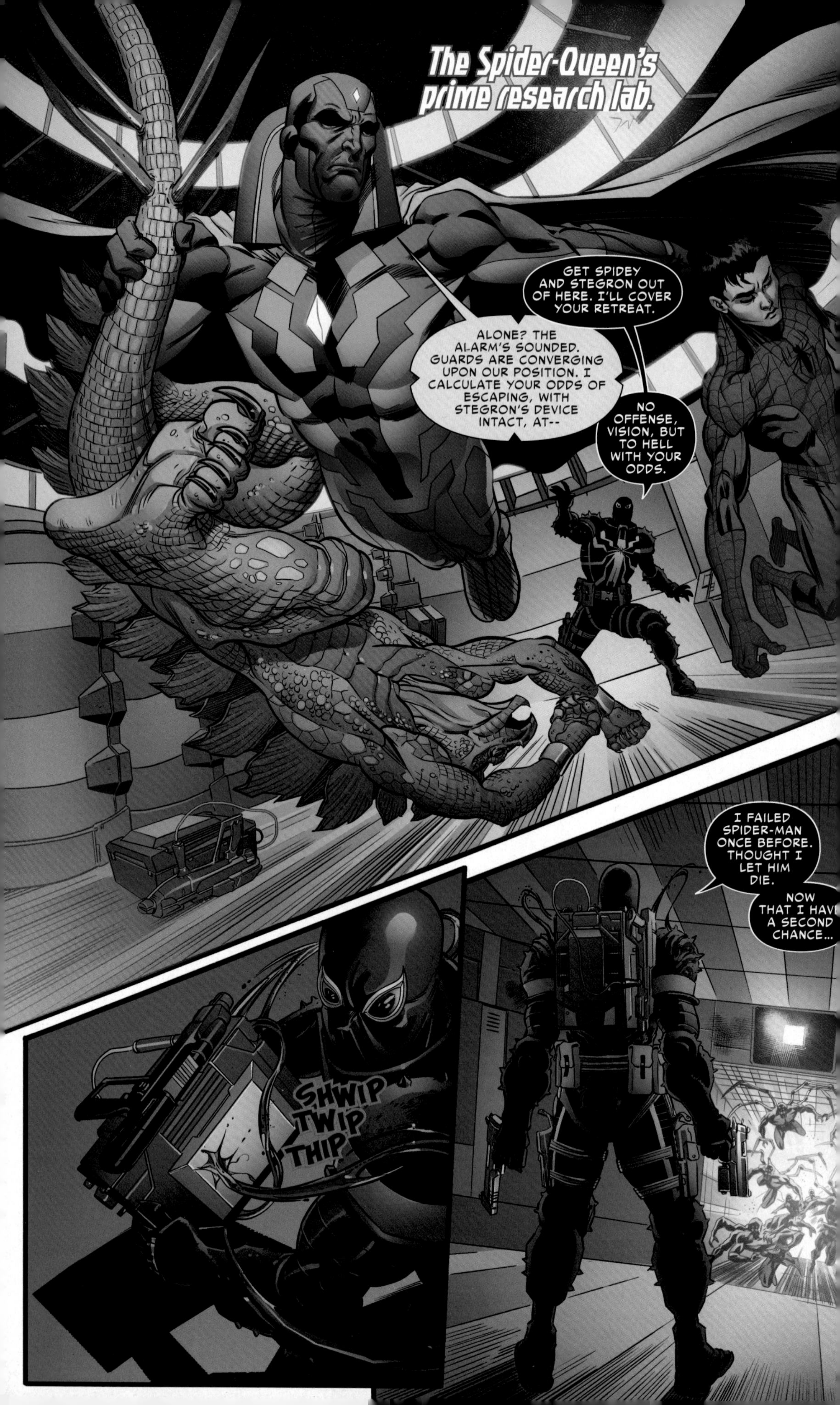
The Spider-Queen's prime research lab.
GET SPIDEY AND STEGRON OUT OF HERE. I'LL COVER YOUR RETREAT.
ALONE? THE ALARM'S SOUNDED. GUARDS ARE CONVERGING UPON OUR POSITION. I CALCULATE YOUR ODDS OF ESCAPING, WITH STEGRON'S DEVICE INTACT, AT--
NO OFFENSE, VISION, BUT TO HELL WITH YOUR ODDS.
I FAILED SPIDER-MAN ONCE BEFORE. THOUGHT I LET HIM DIE.
NOW THAT I HAVE A SECOND CHANCE...
SHWIP TWIP THIP

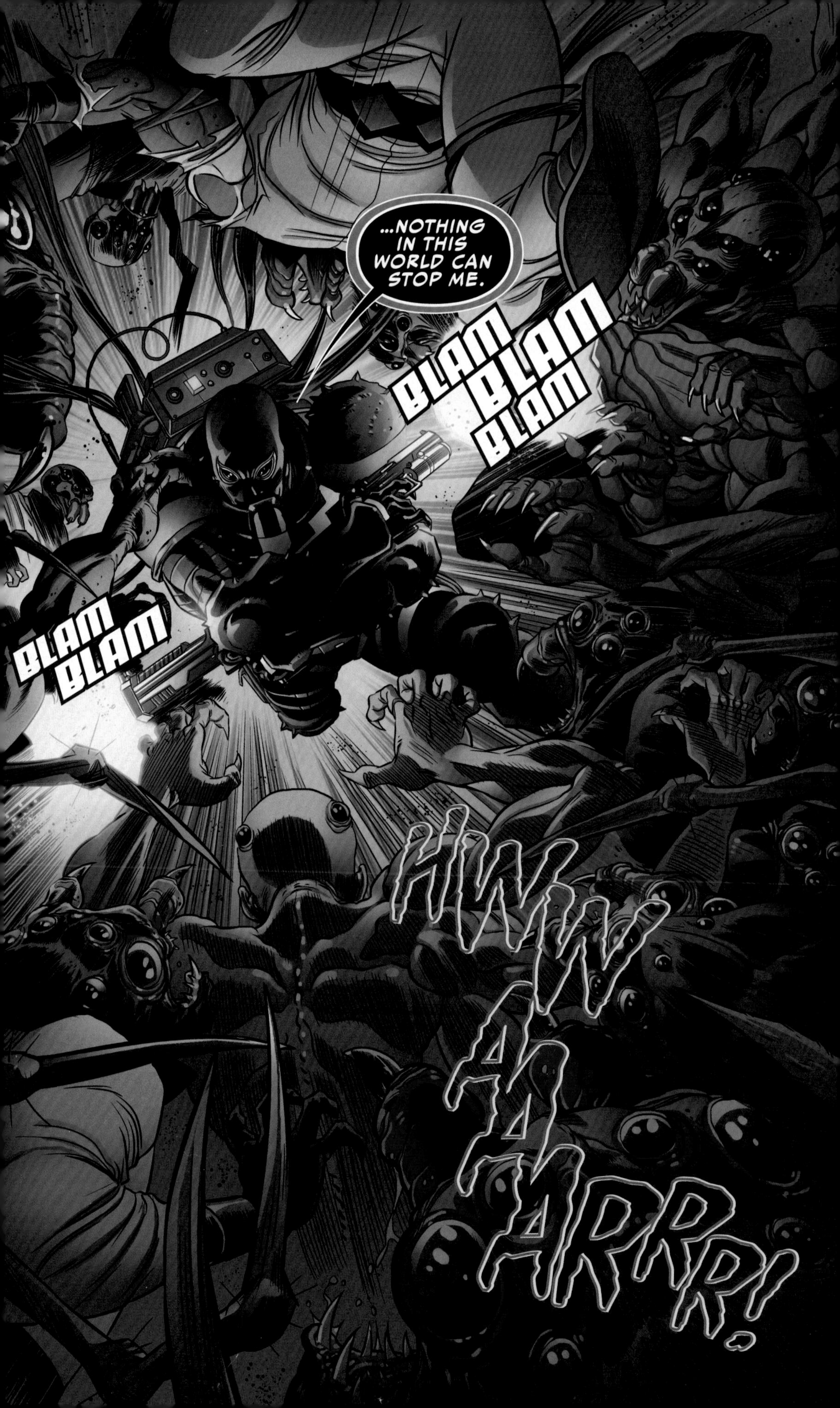

...NOTHING IN THIS WORLD CAN STOP ME.
BLAM BLAM BLAM
BLAM BLAM
HWWAARRR!

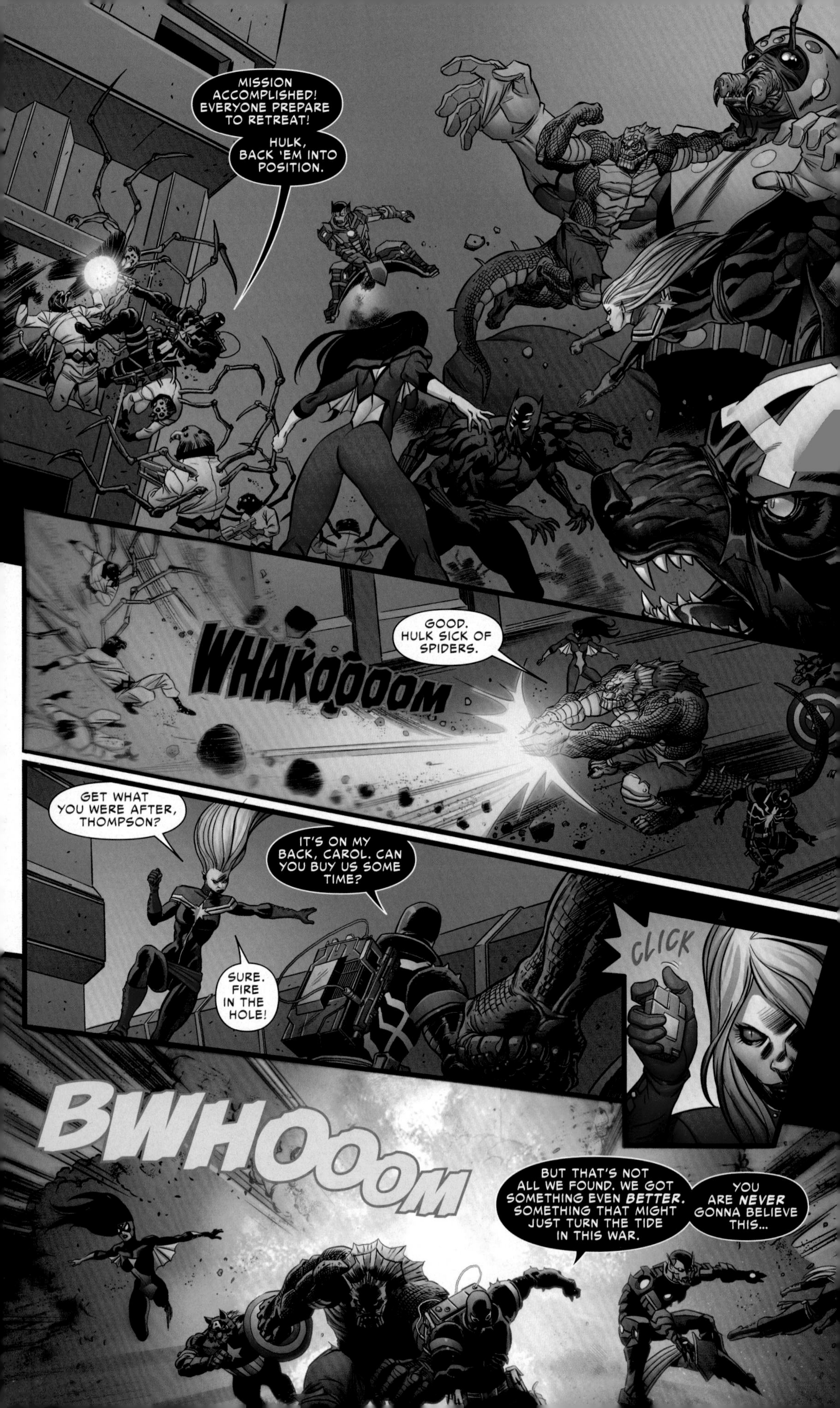

MISSION ACCOMPLISHED! EVERYONE PREPARE TO RETREAT!
HULK, BACK 'EM INTO POSITION.
GOOD. HULK SICK OF SPIDERS.
WHAKOOOOM
GET WHAT YOU WERE AFTER, THOMPSON?
IT'S ON MY BACK, CAROL. CAN YOU BUY US SOME TIME?
SURE. FIRE IN THE HOLE!
CLICK
BWHOOOOM
BUT THAT'S NOT ALL WE FOUND. WE GOT SOMETHING EVEN BETTER. SOMETHING THAT MIGHT JUST TURN THE TIDE IN THIS WAR.
YOU ARE NEVER GONNA BELIEVE THIS...

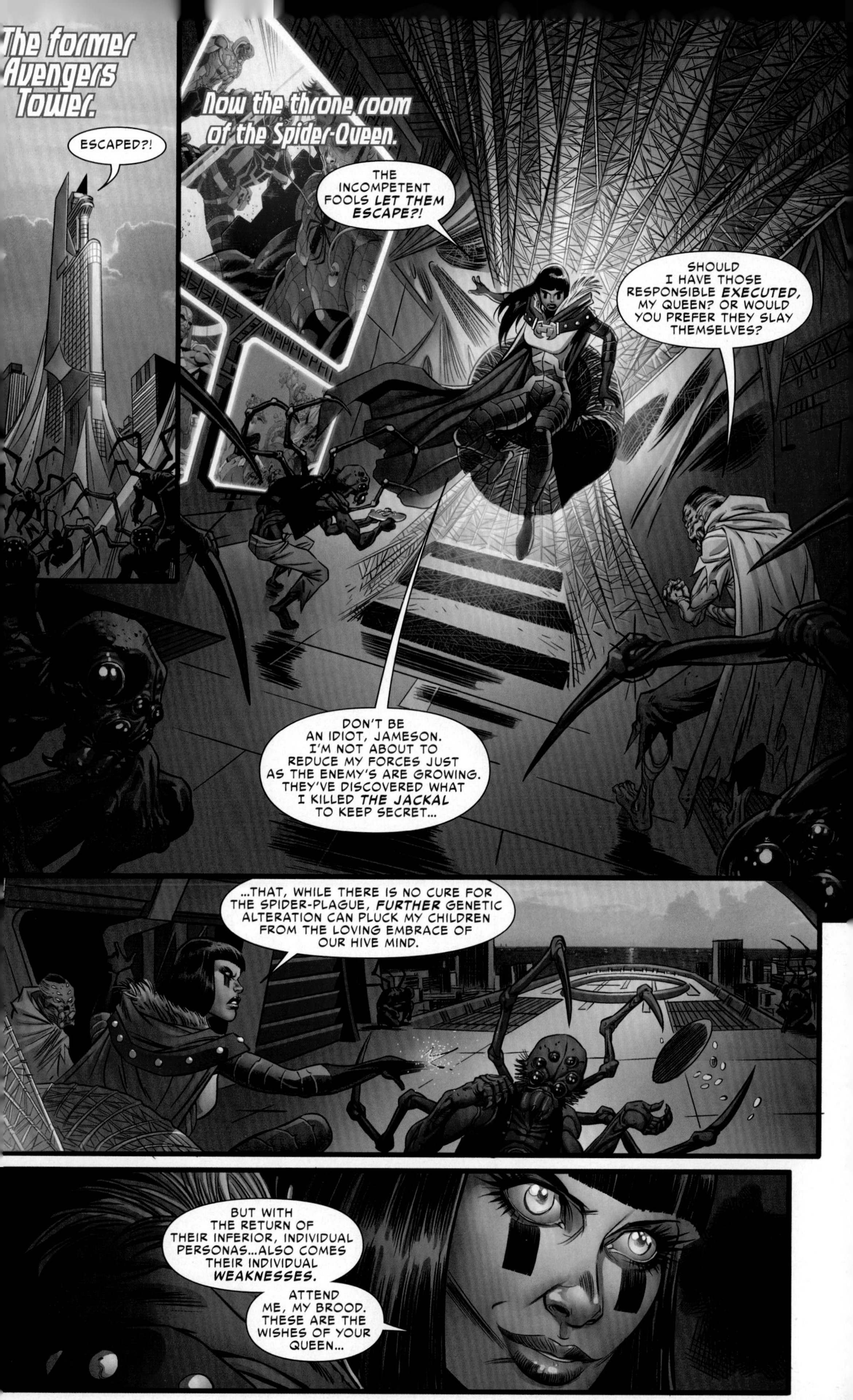
The former Avengers Tower.
ESCAPED?!
Now the throne room of the Spider-Queen.
THE INCOMPETENT FOOLS LET THEM ESCAPE?!
SHOULD I HAVE THOSE RESPONSIBLE EXECUTED, MY QUEEN? OR WOULD YOU PREFER THEY SLAY THEMSELVES?
DON'T BE AN IDIOT, JAMESON. I'M NOT ABOUT TO REDUCE MY FORCES JUST AS THE ENEMY'S ARE GROWING. THEY'VE DISCOVERED WHAT I KILLED THE JACKAL TO KEEP SECRET...
...THAT, WHILE THERE IS NO CURE FOR THE SPIDER-PLAGUE, FURTHER GENETIC ALTERATION CAN PLUCK MY CHILDREN FROM THE LOVING EMBRACE OF OUR HIVE MIND.
BUT WITH THE RETURN OF THEIR INFERIOR, INDIVIDUAL PERSONAS...ALSO COMES THEIR INDIVIDUAL WEAKNESSES.
ATTEND ME, MY BROOD. THESE ARE THE WISHES OF YOUR QUEEN...

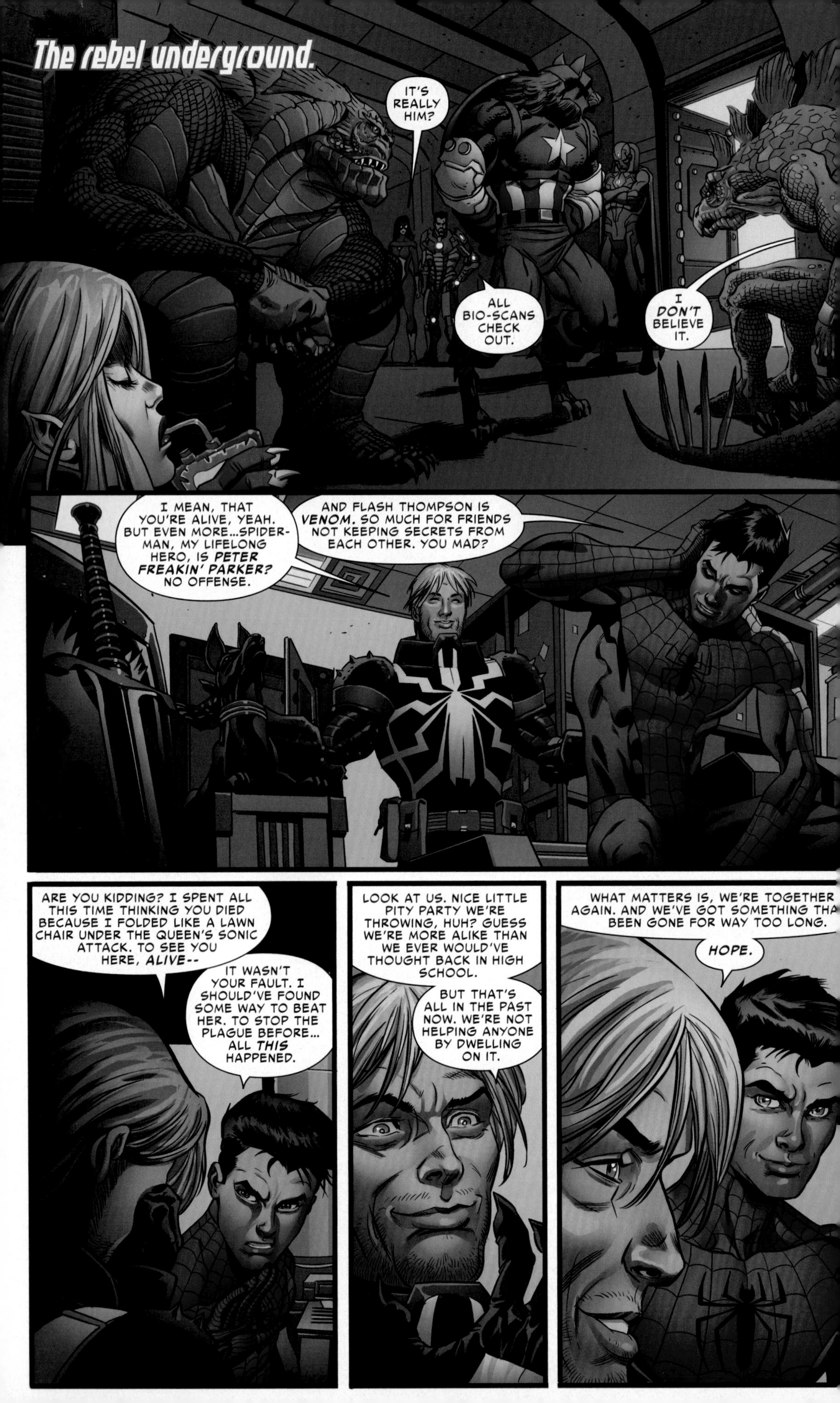

The rebel underground.
IT'S REALLY HIM?
ALL BIO-SCANS CHECK OUT.
I DON'T BELIEVE IT.
I MEAN, THAT YOU'RE ALIVE, YEAH. BUT EVEN MORE...SPIDER-MAN, MY LIFELONG HERO, IS PETER FREAKIN' PARKER? NO OFFENSE.
AND FLASH THOMPSON IS VENOM. SO MUCH FOR FRIENDS NOT KEEPING SECRETS FROM EACH OTHER. YOU MAD?
ARE YOU KIDDING? I SPENT ALL THIS TIME THINKING YOU DIED BECAUSE I FOLDED LIKE A LAWN CHAIR UNDER THE QUEEN'S SONIC ATTACK. TO SEE YOU HERE, ALIVE--
IT WASN'T YOUR FAULT. I SHOULD'VE FOUND SOME WAY TO BEAT HER. TO STOP THE PLAGUE BEFORE... ALL THIS HAPPENED.
LOOK AT US. NICE LITTLE PITY PARTY WE'RE THROWING, HUH? GUESS WE'RE MORE ALIKE THAN WE EVER WOULD'VE THOUGHT BACK IN HIGH SCHOOL.
BUT THAT'S ALL IN THE PAST NOW. WE'RE NOT HELPING ANYONE BY DWELLING ON IT.
WHAT MATTERS IS, WE'RE TOGETHER AGAIN. AND WE'VE GOT SOMETHING THA BEEN GONE FOR WAY TOO LONG.
HOPE.

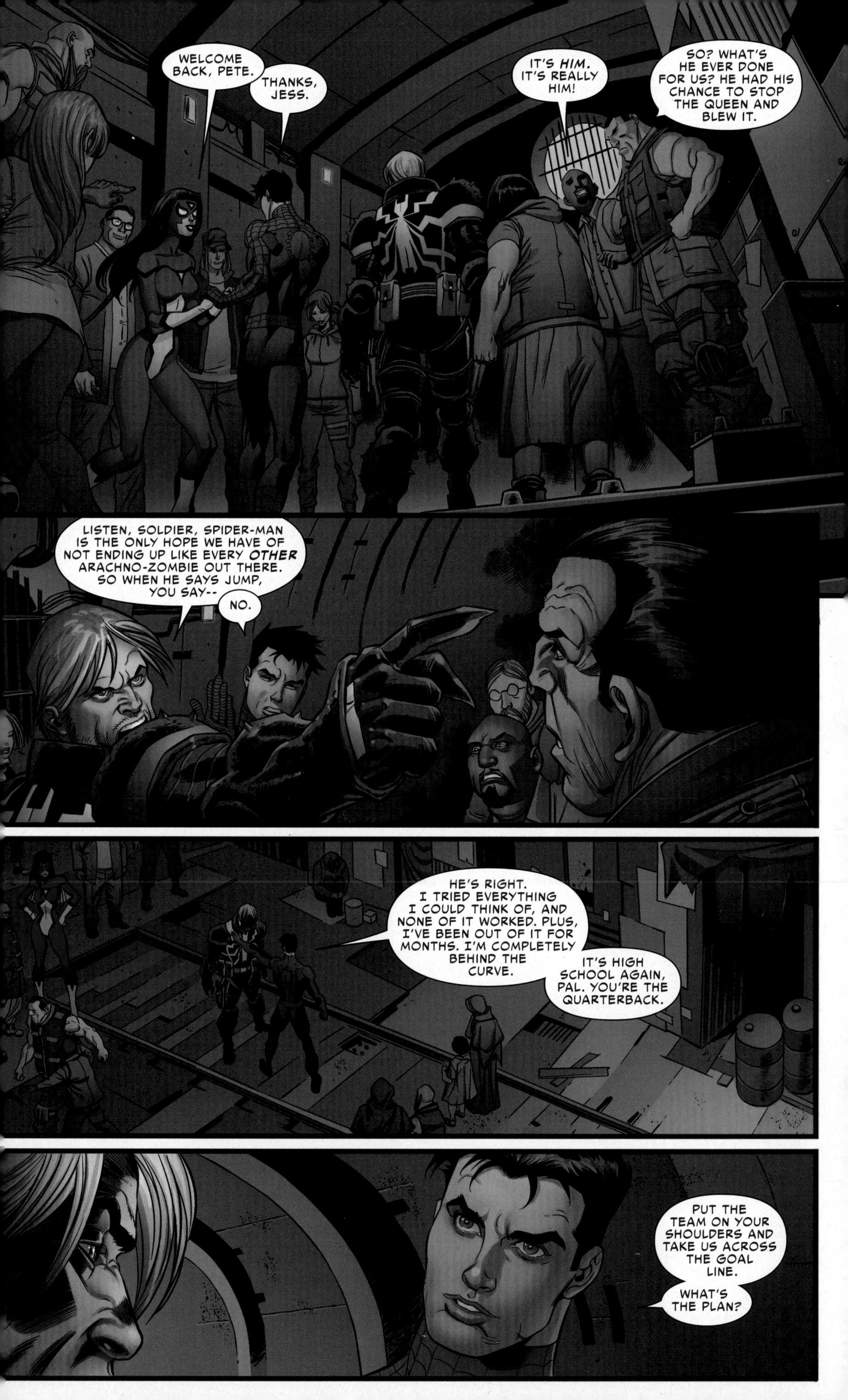
WELCOME BACK, PETE.
THANKS, JESS.
IT'S *HIM*. IT'S REALLY HIM!
SO? WHAT'S HE EVER DONE FOR US? HE HAD HIS CHANCE TO STOP THE QUEEN AND BLEW IT.
LISTEN, SOLDIER, SPIDER-MAN IS THE ONLY HOPE WE HAVE OF NOT ENDING UP LIKE EVERY *OTHER* ARACHNO-ZOMBIE OUT THERE. SO WHEN HE SAYS JUMP, YOU SAY--
NO.
HE'S RIGHT. I TRIED EVERYTHING I COULD THINK OF, AND NONE OF IT WORKED. PLUS, I'VE BEEN OUT OF IT FOR MONTHS. I'M COMPLETELY BEHIND THE CURVE.
IT'S HIGH SCHOOL AGAIN, PAL. YOU'RE THE QUARTERBACK.
PUT THE TEAM ON YOUR SHOULDERS AND TAKE US ACROSS THE GOAL LINE.
WHAT'S THE PLAN?

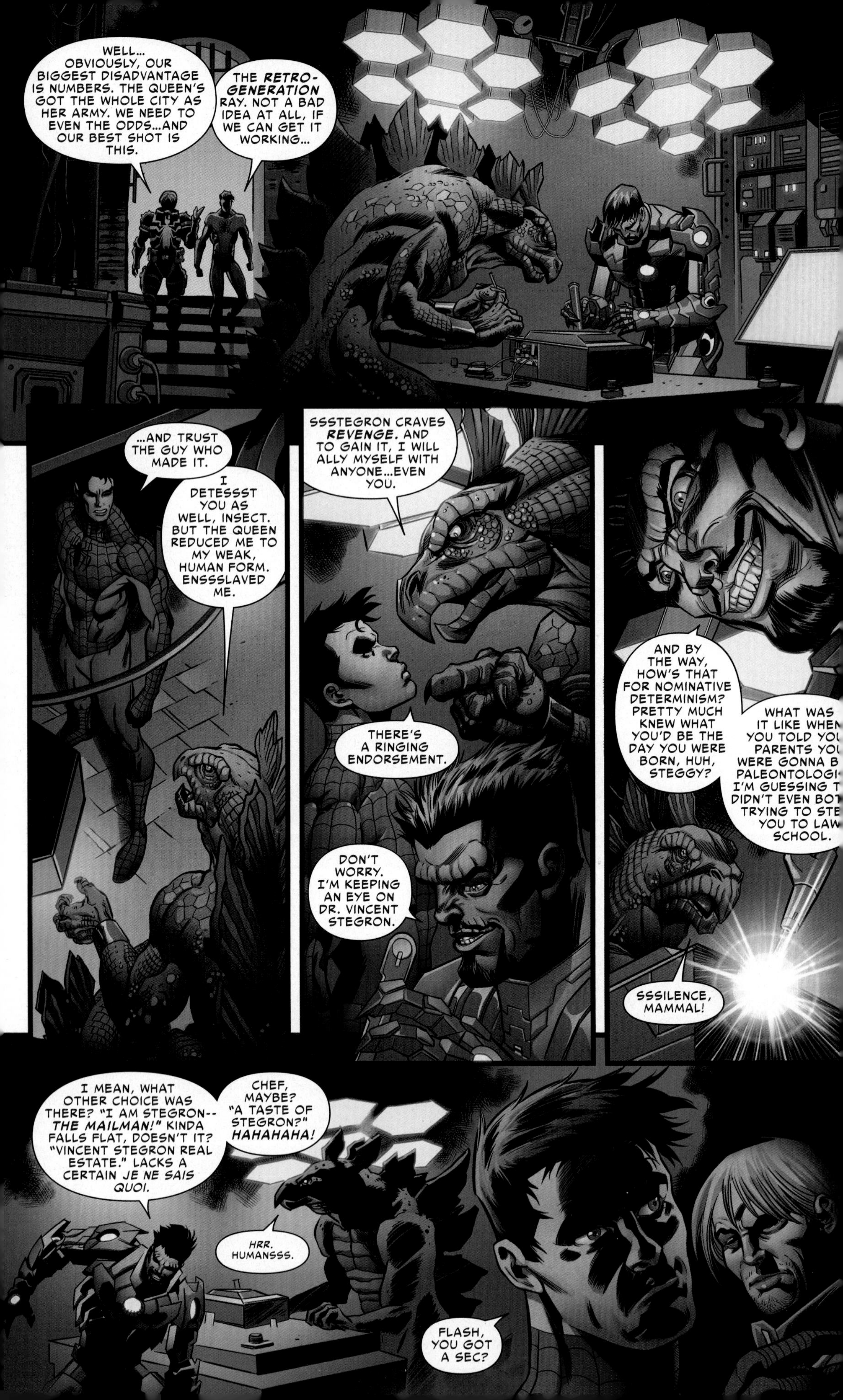
WELL... OBVIOUSLY, OUR BIGGEST DISADVANTAGE IS NUMBERS. THE QUEEN'S GOT THE WHOLE CITY AS HER ARMY. WE NEED TO EVEN THE ODDS...AND OUR BEST SHOT IS THIS.
THE *RETRO-GENERATION* RAY. NOT A BAD IDEA AT ALL, IF WE CAN GET IT WORKING...
...AND TRUST THE GUY WHO MADE IT.
I DETESSST YOU AS WELL, INSECT. BUT THE QUEEN REDUCED ME TO MY WEAK, HUMAN FORM. ENSSSLAVED ME.
SSSTEGRON CRAVES *REVENGE.* AND TO GAIN IT, I WILL ALLY MYSELF WITH ANYONE...EVEN YOU.
THERE'S A RINGING ENDORSEMENT.
DON'T WORRY. I'M KEEPING AN EYE ON DR. VINCENT STEGRON.
AND BY THE WAY, HOW'S THAT FOR NOMINATIVE DETERMINISM? PRETTY MUCH KNEW WHAT YOU'D BE THE DAY YOU WERE BORN, HUH, STEGGY?
SSSILENCE, MAMMAL!
I MEAN, WHAT OTHER CHOICE WAS THERE? "I AM STEGRON--*THE MAILMAN!*" KINDA FALLS FLAT, DOESN'T IT? "VINCENT STEGRON REAL ESTATE." LACKS A CERTAIN *JE NE SAIS QUOI.*
CHEF, MAYBE? "A TASTE OF STEGRON?" *HAHAHAHA!*
HRR. HUMANSSS.
FLASH, YOU GOT A SEC?

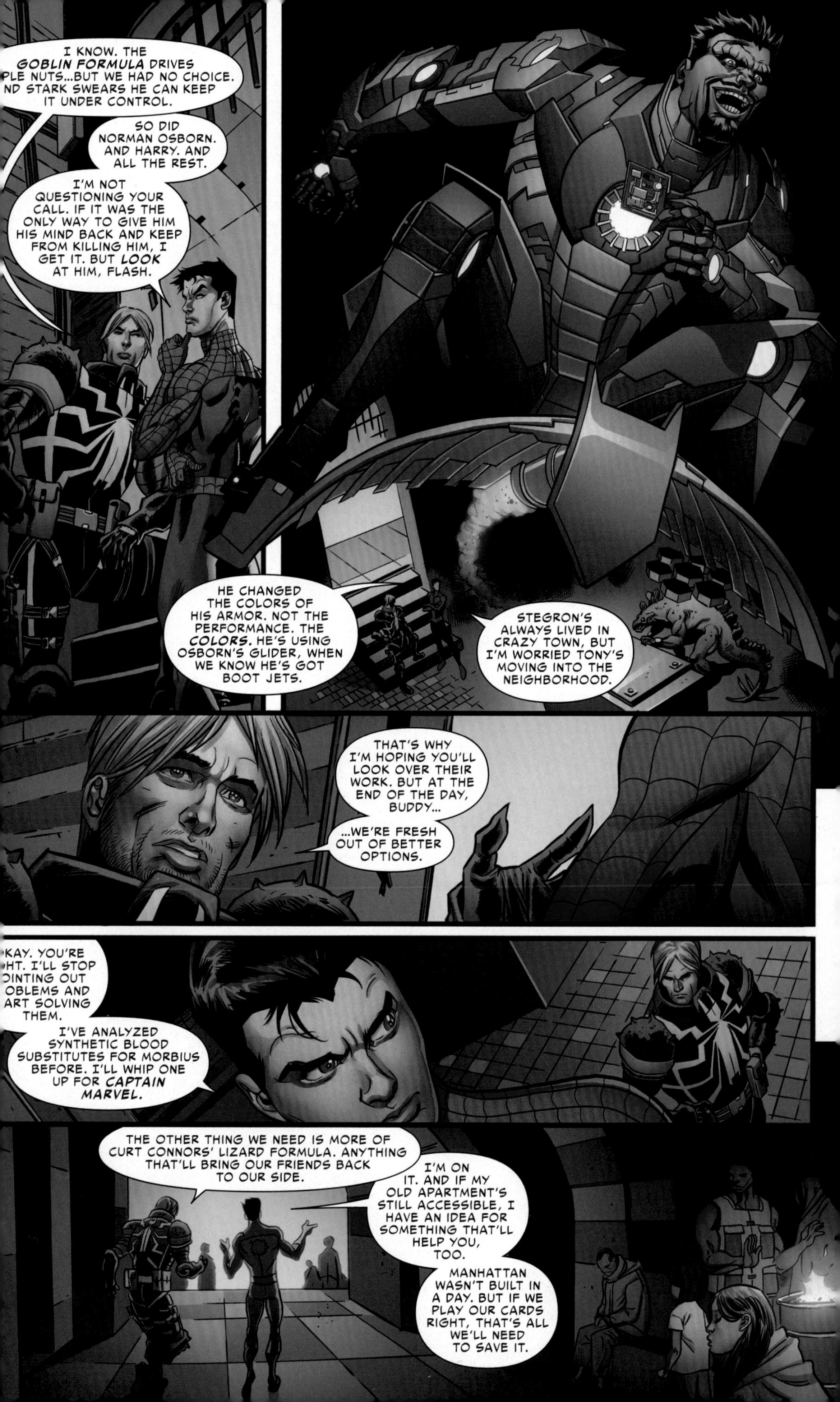
I KNOW. THE GOBLIN FORMULA DRIVES PLE NUTS...BUT WE HAD NO CHOICE. ND STARK SWEARS HE CAN KEEP IT UNDER CONTROL.
SO DID NORMAN OSBORN. AND HARRY. AND ALL THE REST.
I'M NOT QUESTIONING YOUR CALL. IF IT WAS THE ONLY WAY TO GIVE HIM HIS MIND BACK AND KEEP FROM KILLING HIM, I GET IT. BUT LOOK AT HIM, FLASH.
HE CHANGED THE COLORS OF HIS ARMOR. NOT THE PERFORMANCE. THE COLORS. HE'S USING OSBORN'S GLIDER, WHEN WE KNOW HE'S GOT BOOT JETS.
STEGRON'S ALWAYS LIVED IN CRAZY TOWN, BUT I'M WORRIED TONY'S MOVING INTO THE NEIGHBORHOOD.
THAT'S WHY I'M HOPING YOU'LL LOOK OVER THEIR WORK. BUT AT THE END OF THE DAY, BUDDY...
...WE'RE FRESH OUT OF BETTER OPTIONS.
KAY. YOU'RE HT. I'LL STOP OINTING OUT OBLEMS AND ART SOLVING THEM.
I'VE ANALYZED SYNTHETIC BLOOD SUBSTITUTES FOR MORBIUS BEFORE. I'LL WHIP ONE UP FOR CAPTAIN MARVEL.
THE OTHER THING WE NEED IS MORE OF CURT CONNORS' LIZARD FORMULA. ANYTHING THAT'LL BRING OUR FRIENDS BACK TO OUR SIDE.
I'M ON IT. AND IF MY OLD APARTMENT'S STILL ACCESSIBLE, I HAVE AN IDEA FOR SOMETHING THAT'LL HELP YOU, TOO.
MANHATTAN WASN'T BUILT IN A DAY. BUT IF WE PLAY OUR CARDS RIGHT, THAT'S ALL WE'LL NEED TO SAVE IT.

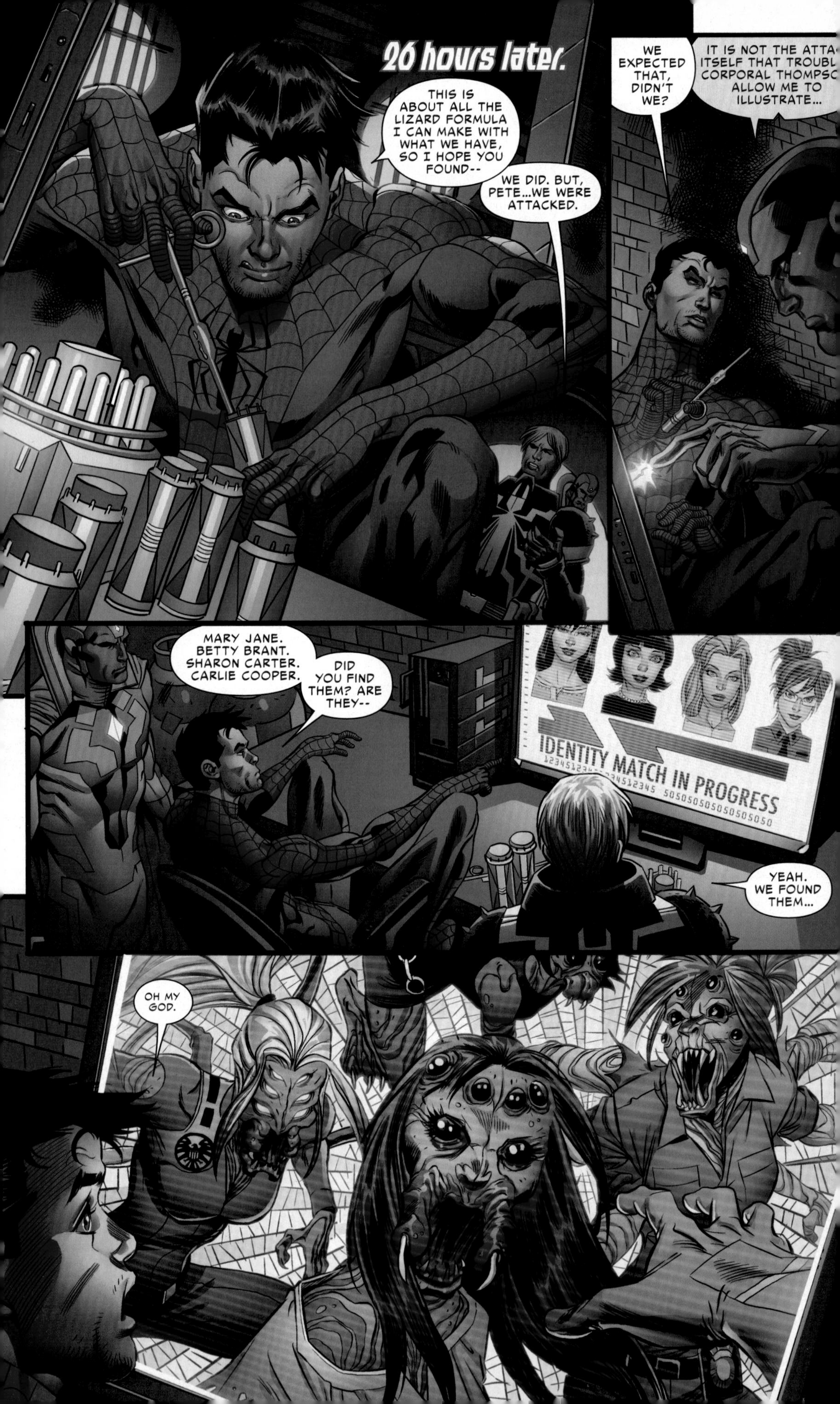
26 hours later.
THIS IS ABOUT ALL THE LIZARD FORMULA I CAN MAKE WITH WHAT WE HAVE, SO I HOPE YOU FOUND--
WE DID. BUT, PETE...WE WERE ATTACKED.
WE EXPECTED THAT, DIDN'T WE?
IT IS NOT THE ATTA ITSELF THAT TROUBL CORPORAL THOMPSC ALLOW ME TO ILLUSTRATE...
MARY JANE. BETTY BRANT. SHARON CARTER. CARLIE COOPER.
DID YOU FIND THEM? ARE THEY--
IDENTITY MATCH IN PROGRESS
YEAH. WE FOUND THEM...
OH MY GOD.

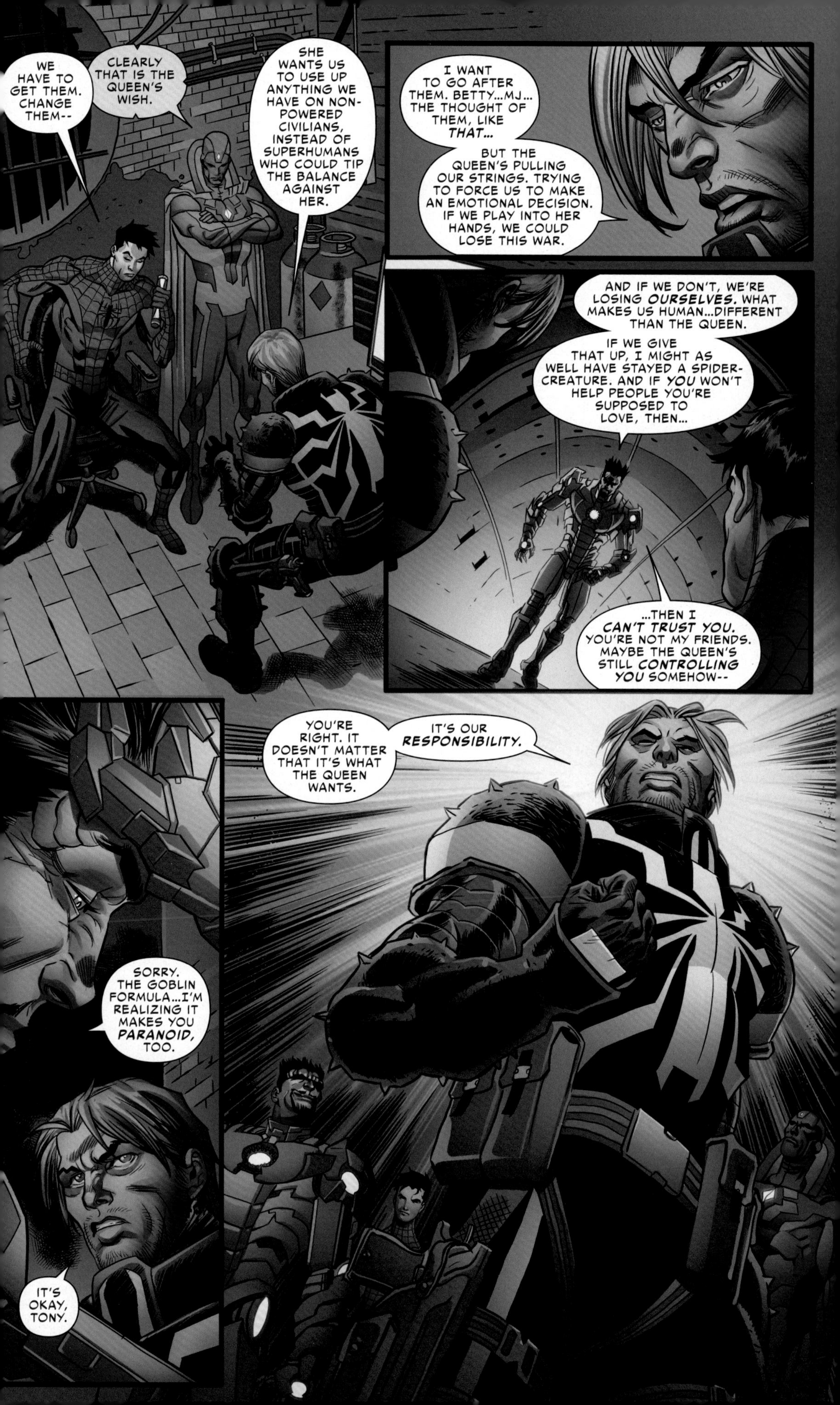

WE HAVE TO GET THEM. CHANGE THEM--
CLEARLY THAT IS THE QUEEN'S WISH.
SHE WANTS US TO USE UP ANYTHING WE HAVE ON NON-POWERED CIVILIANS, INSTEAD OF SUPERHUMANS WHO COULD TIP THE BALANCE AGAINST HER.
I WANT TO GO AFTER THEM. BETTY...MJ... THE THOUGHT OF THEM, LIKE THAT...
BUT THE QUEEN'S PULLING OUR STRINGS. TRYING TO FORCE US TO MAKE AN EMOTIONAL DECISION. IF WE PLAY INTO HER HANDS, WE COULD LOSE THIS WAR.
AND IF WE DON'T, WE'RE LOSING OURSELVES. WHAT MAKES US HUMAN...DIFFERENT THAN THE QUEEN.
IF WE GIVE THAT UP, I MIGHT AS WELL HAVE STAYED A SPIDER-CREATURE. AND IF YOU WON'T HELP PEOPLE YOU'RE SUPPOSED TO LOVE, THEN...
...THEN I CAN'T TRUST YOU. YOU'RE NOT MY FRIENDS. MAYBE THE QUEEN'S STILL CONTROLLING YOU SOMEHOW--
SORRY. THE GOBLIN FORMULA...I'M REALIZING IT MAKES YOU PARANOID, TOO.
IT'S OKAY, TONY.
YOU'RE RIGHT. IT DOESN'T MATTER THAT IT'S WHAT THE QUEEN WANTS.
IT'S OUR RESPONSIBILITY.

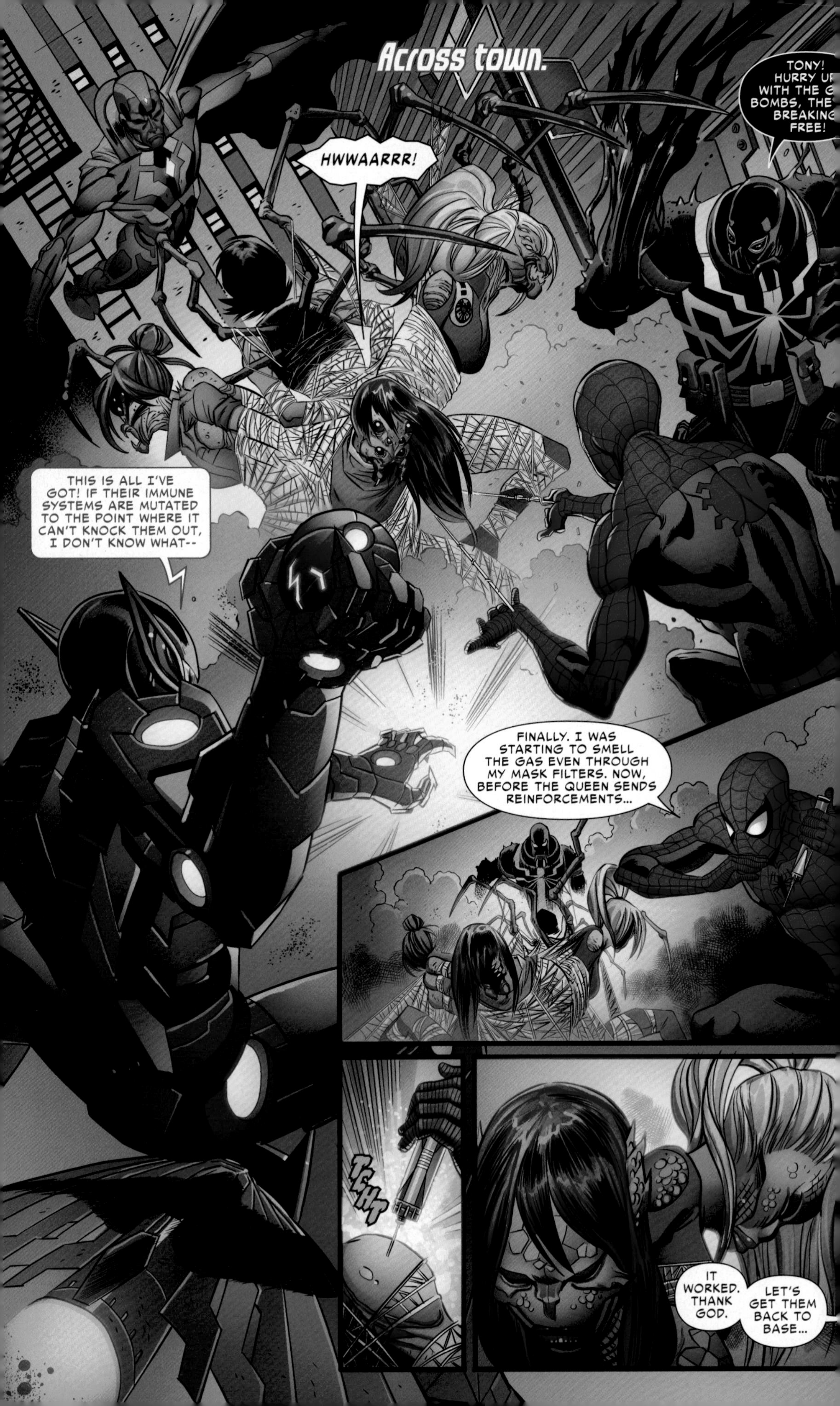
Across town.
TONY! HURRY UP WITH THE G BOMBS, THE BREAKING FREE!
HWWAARRR!
THIS IS ALL I'VE GOT! IF THEIR IMMUNE SYSTEMS ARE MUTATED TO THE POINT WHERE IT CAN'T KNOCK THEM OUT, I DON'T KNOW WHAT--
FINALLY. I WAS STARTING TO SMELL THE GAS EVEN THROUGH MY MASK FILTERS. NOW, BEFORE THE QUEEN SENDS REINFORCEMENTS...
TCHT
IT WORKED. THANK GOD.
LET'S GET THEM BACK TO BASE...

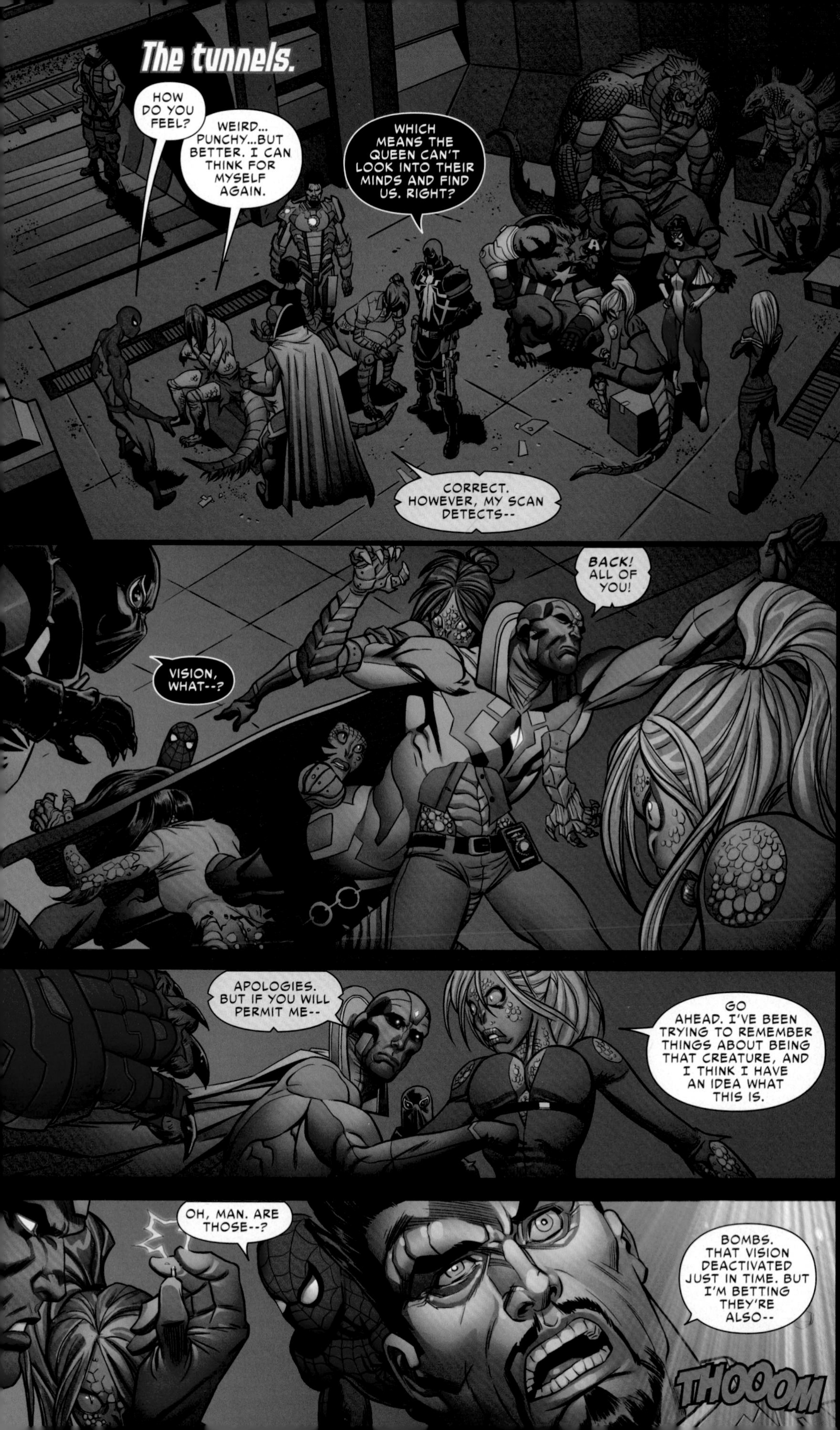
The tunnels.
HOW DO YOU FEEL?
WEIRD... PUNCHY...BUT BETTER. I CAN THINK FOR MYSELF AGAIN.
WHICH MEANS THE QUEEN CAN'T LOOK INTO THEIR MINDS AND FIND US. RIGHT?
CORRECT. HOWEVER, MY SCAN DETECTS--
BACK! ALL OF YOU!
VISION, WHAT--?
APOLOGIES. BUT IF YOU WILL PERMIT ME--
GO AHEAD. I'VE BEEN TRYING TO REMEMBER THINGS ABOUT BEING THAT CREATURE, AND I THINK I HAVE AN IDEA WHAT THIS IS.
OH, MAN. ARE THOSE--?
BOMBS. THAT VISION DEACTIVATED JUST IN TIME. BUT I'M BETTING THEY'RE ALSO--
THOOOM

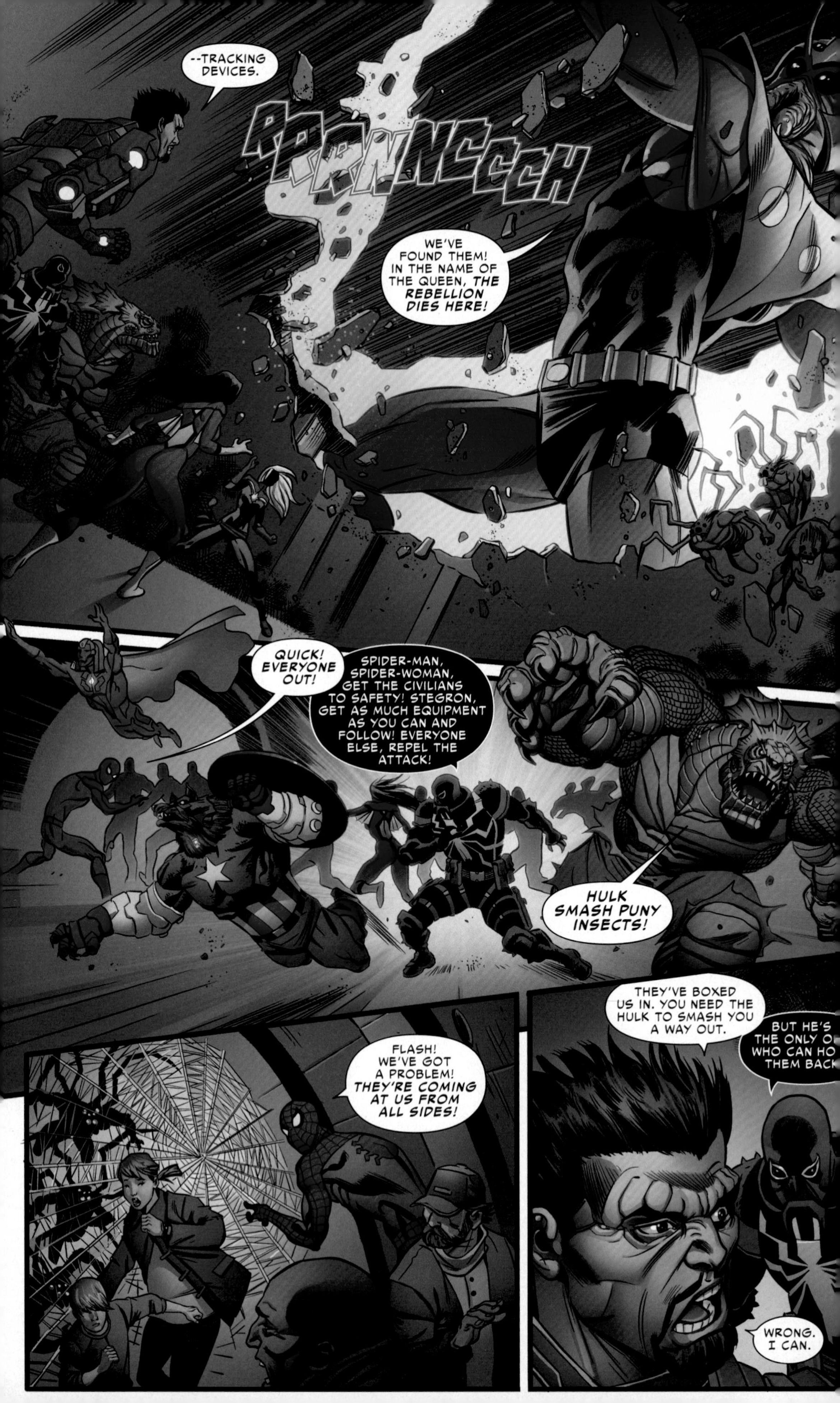
--TRACKING DEVICES.
RRRNNCCCH
WE'VE FOUND THEM! IN THE NAME OF THE QUEEN, THE REBELLION DIES HERE!
QUICK! EVERYONE OUT!
SPIDER-MAN, SPIDER-WOMAN, GET THE CIVILIANS TO SAFETY! STEGRON, GET AS MUCH EQUIPMENT AS YOU CAN AND FOLLOW! EVERYONE ELSE, REPEL THE ATTACK!
HULK SMASH PUNY INSECTS!
FLASH! WE'VE GOT A PROBLEM! THEY'RE COMING AT US FROM ALL SIDES!
THEY'VE BOXED US IN. YOU NEED THE HULK TO SMASH YOU A WAY OUT.
WRONG. I CAN.

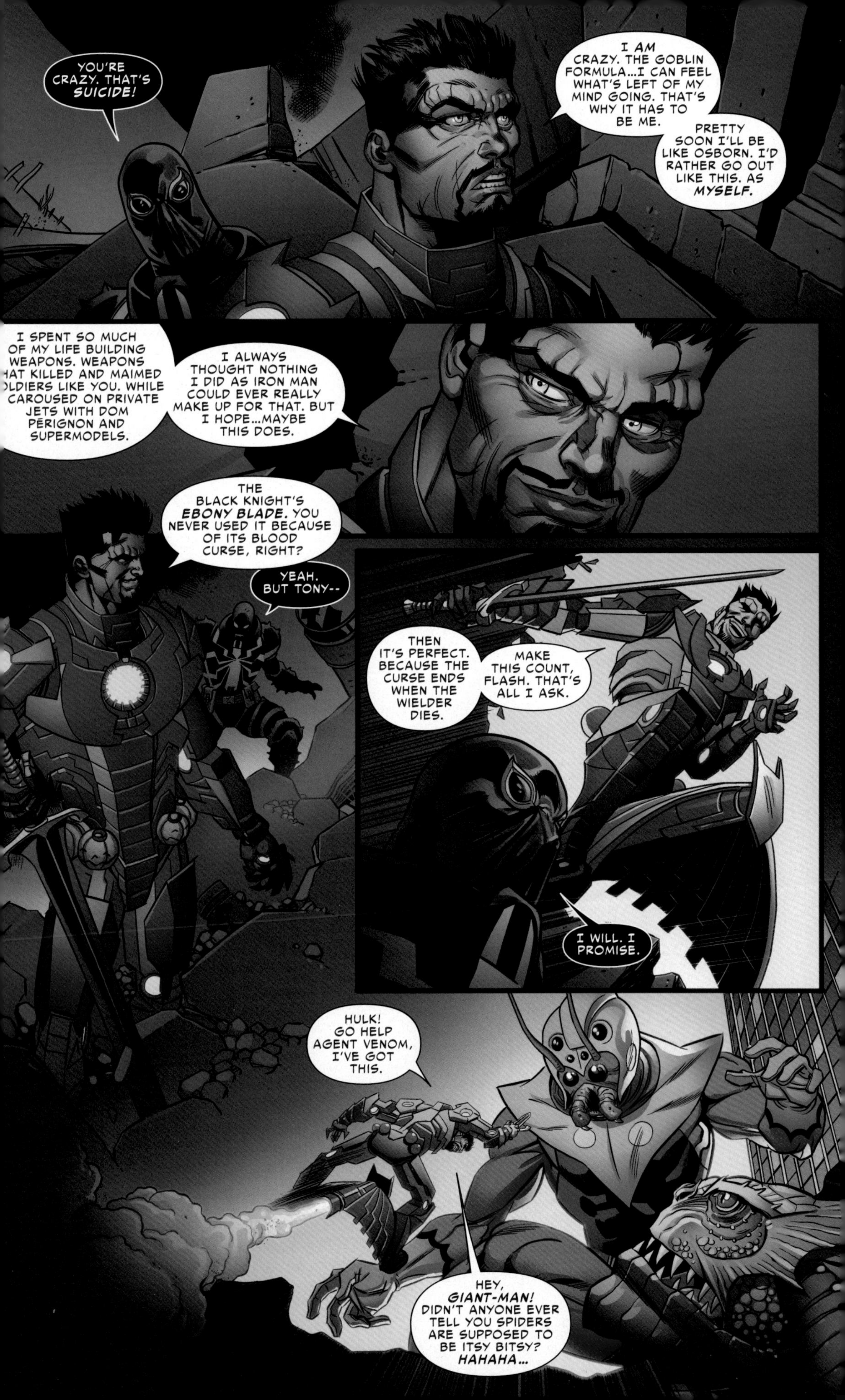
YOU'RE CRAZY. THAT'S SUICIDE!
I AM CRAZY. THE GOBLIN FORMULA...I CAN FEEL WHAT'S LEFT OF MY MIND GOING. THAT'S WHY IT HAS TO BE ME.
PRETTY SOON I'LL BE LIKE OSBORN. I'D RATHER GO OUT LIKE THIS. AS MYSELF.
I SPENT SO MUCH OF MY LIFE BUILDING WEAPONS. WEAPONS HAT KILLED AND MAIMED OLDIERS LIKE YOU. WHILE CAROUSED ON PRIVATE JETS WITH DOM PÉRIGNON AND SUPERMODELS.
I ALWAYS THOUGHT NOTHING I DID AS IRON MAN COULD EVER REALLY MAKE UP FOR THAT. BUT I HOPE...MAYBE THIS DOES.
THE BLACK KNIGHT'S EBONY BLADE. YOU NEVER USED IT BECAUSE OF ITS BLOOD CURSE, RIGHT?
YEAH. BUT TONY--
THEN IT'S PERFECT. BECAUSE THE CURSE ENDS WHEN THE WIELDER DIES.
MAKE THIS COUNT, FLASH. THAT'S ALL I ASK.
I WILL. I PROMISE.
HULK! GO HELP AGENT VENOM, I'VE GOT THIS.
HEY, GIANT-MAN! DIDN'T ANYONE EVER TELL YOU SPIDERS ARE SUPPOSED TO BE ITSY BITSY? HAHAHA...

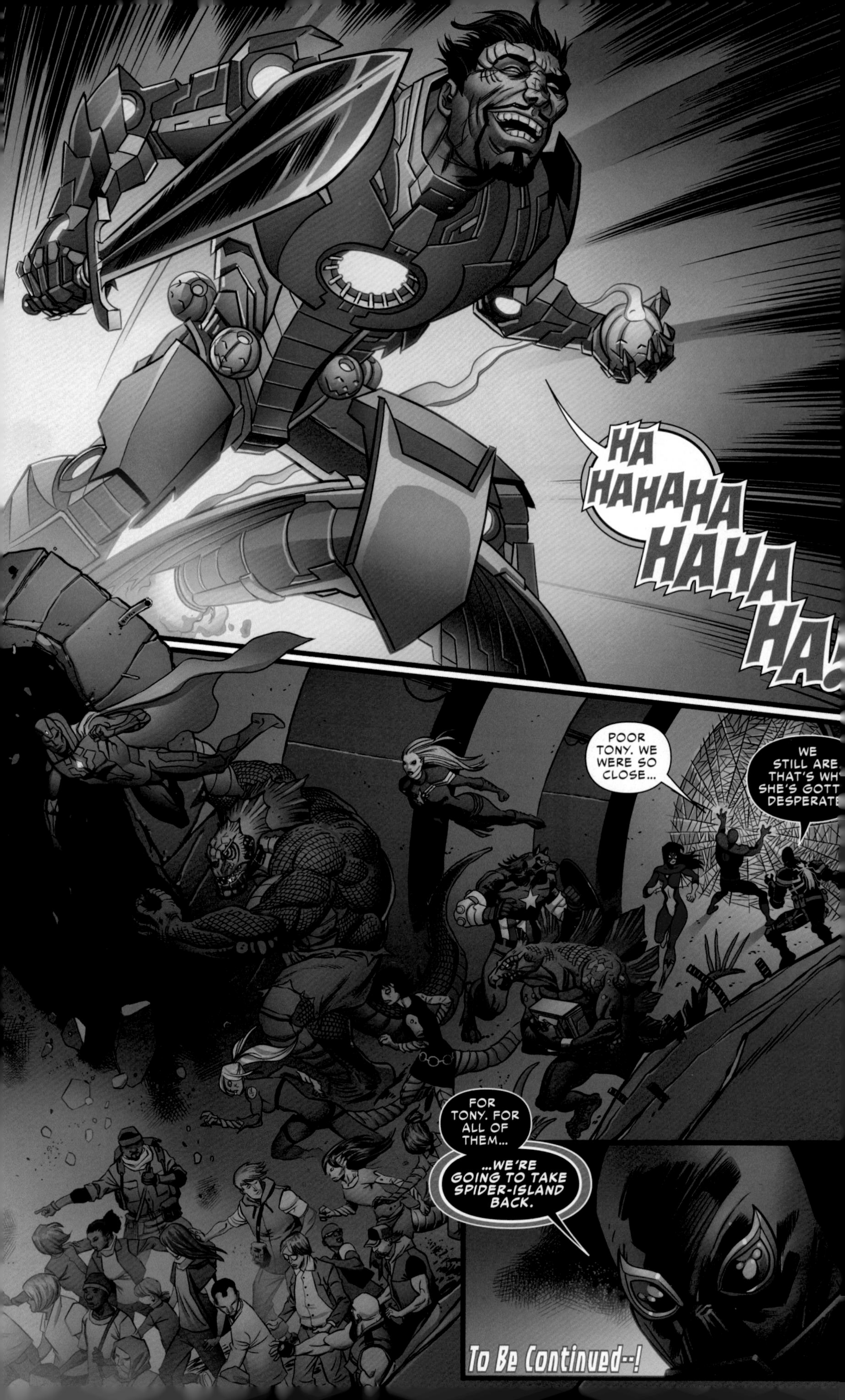
HA HAHAHA HAHAHA HA!
POOR TONY. WE WERE SO CLOSE...
WE STILL ARE. THAT'S WH SHE'S GOTT DESPERATE
FOR TONY. FOR ALL OF THEM...
...WE'RE GOING TO TAKE SPIDER-ISLAND BACK.
To Be Continued--!

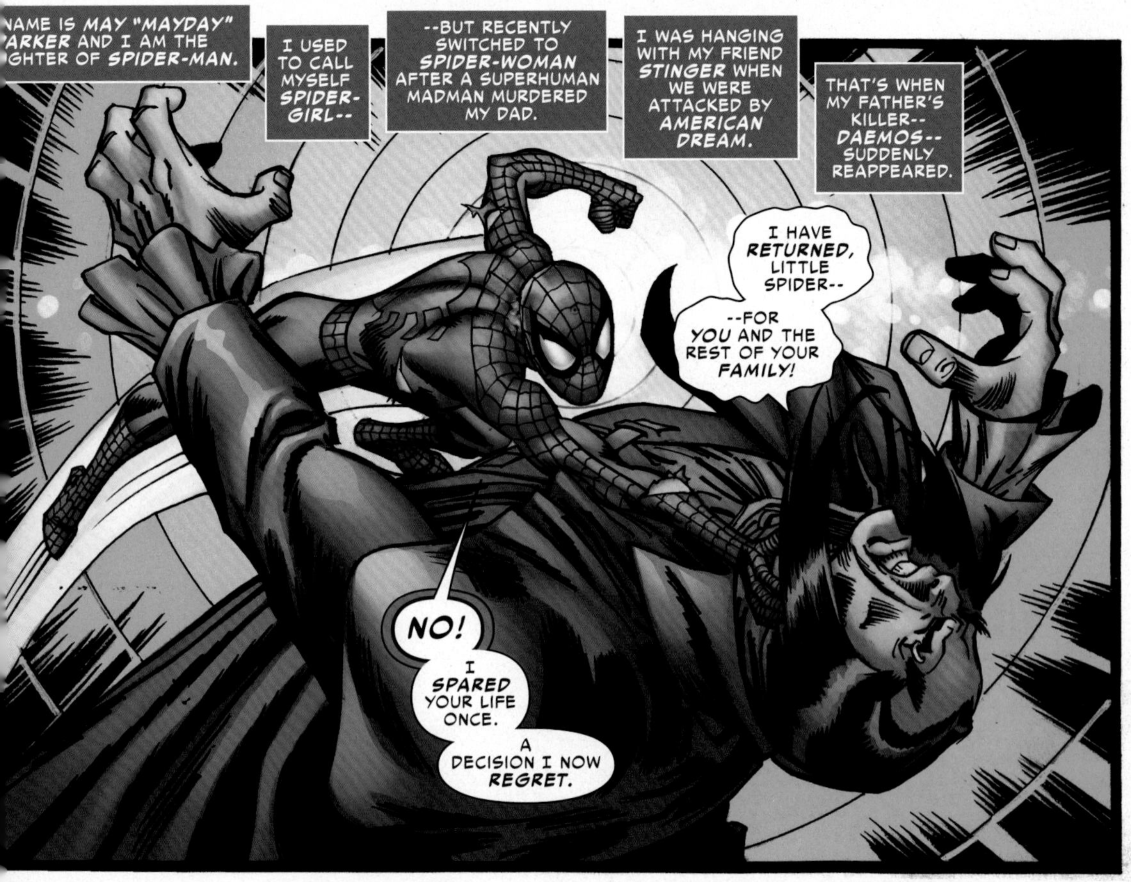
NAME IS MAY "MAYDAY" PARKER AND I AM THE GHTER OF SPIDER-MAN.
I USED TO CALL MYSELF SPIDER-GIRL--
--BUT RECENTLY SWITCHED TO SPIDER-WOMAN AFTER A SUPERHUMAN MADMAN MURDERED MY DAD.
I WAS HANGING WITH MY FRIEND STINGER WHEN WE WERE ATTACKED BY AMERICAN DREAM.
THAT'S WHEN MY FATHER'S KILLER-- DAEMOS-- SUDDENLY REAPPEARED.
I HAVE RETURNED, LITTLE SPIDER--
--FOR YOU AND THE REST OF YOUR FAMILY!
NO!
I SPARED YOUR LIFE ONCE.
A DECISION I NOW REGRET.

MAYDAY PARKER: SPIDER-WOMAN in...
"THE ENEMY WITHIN!"

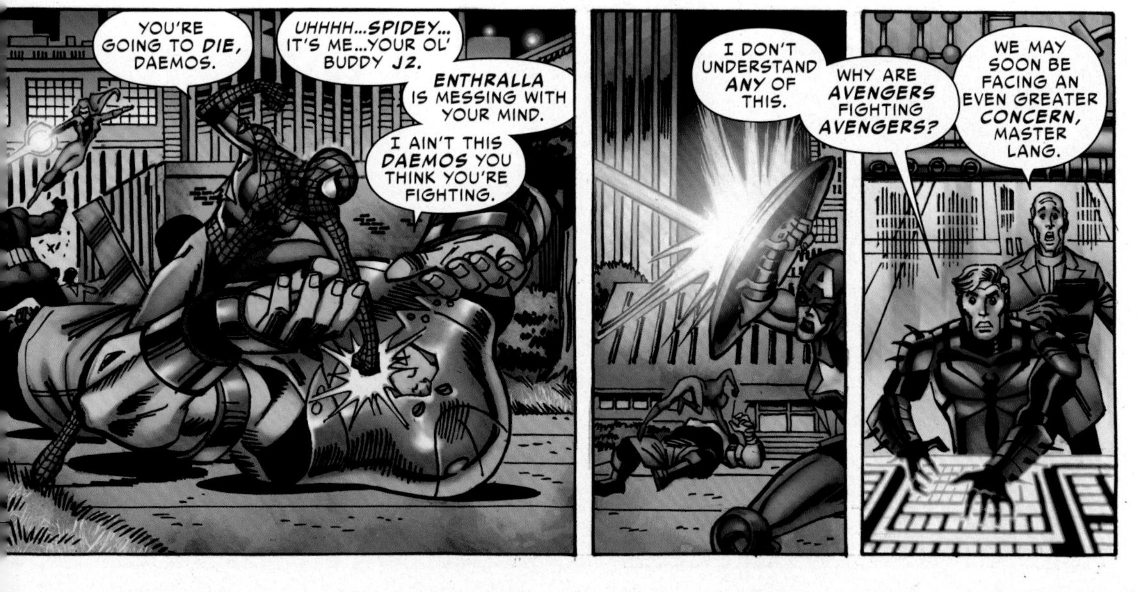
YOU'RE GOING TO DIE, DAEMOS.
UHHHH...SPIDEY... IT'S ME...YOUR OL' BUDDY J2.
ENTHRALLA IS MESSING WITH YOUR MIND.
I AIN'T THIS DAEMOS YOU THINK YOU'RE FIGHTING.
I DON'T UNDERSTAND ANY OF THIS.
WHY ARE AVENGERS FIGHTING AVENGERS?
WE MAY SOON BE FACING AN EVEN GREATER CONCERN, MASTER LANG.

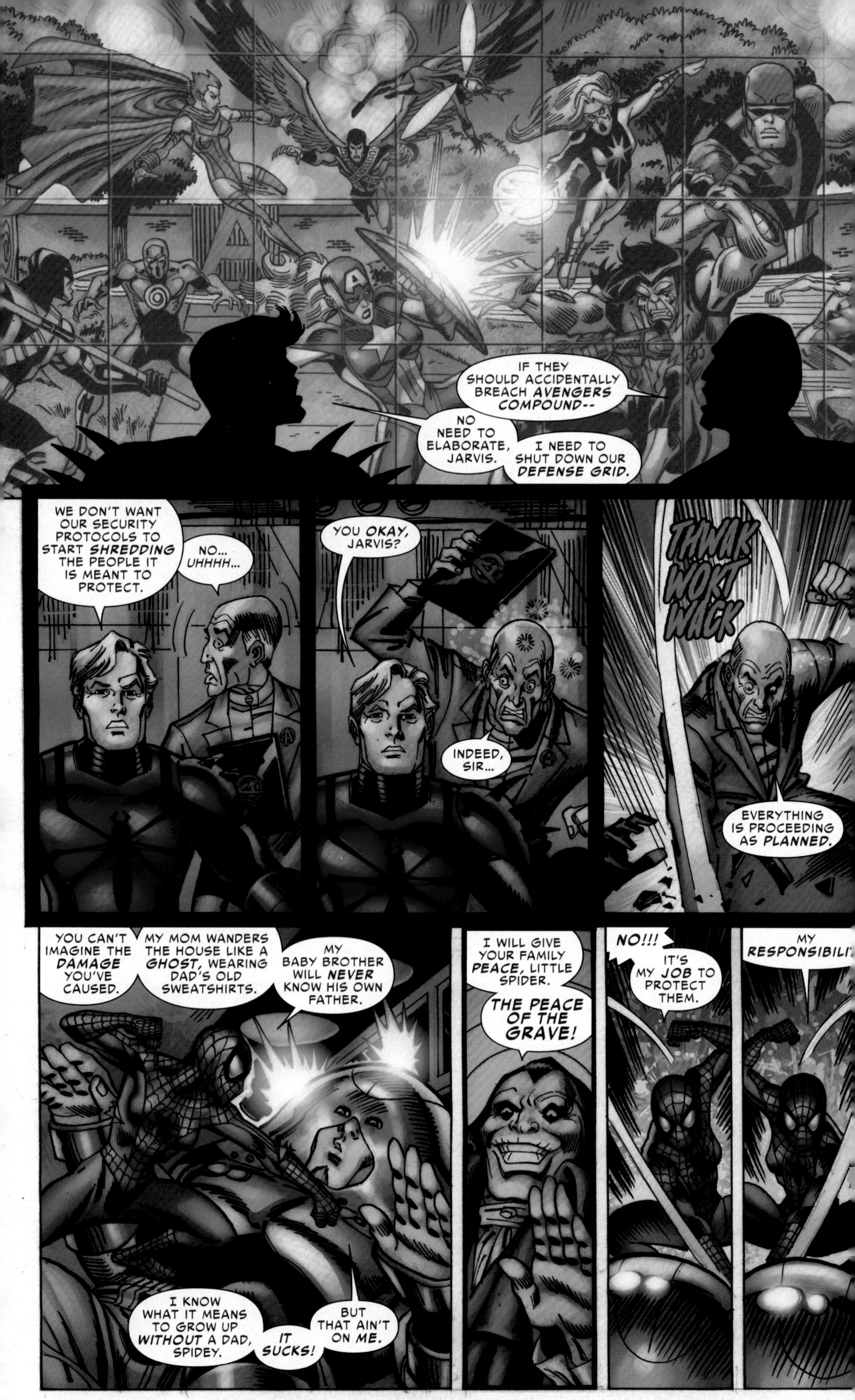

IF THEY SHOULD ACCIDENTALLY BREACH AVENGERS COMPOUND--
NO NEED TO ELABORATE, JARVIS.
I NEED TO SHUT DOWN OUR DEFENSE GRID.
WE DON'T WANT OUR SECURITY PROTOCOLS TO START SHREDDING THE PEOPLE IT IS MEANT TO PROTECT.
NO... UHHHH...
YOU OKAY, JARVIS?
INDEED, SIR...
THWAK
WOK
WACK
EVERYTHING IS PROCEEDING AS PLANNED.
YOU CAN'T IMAGINE THE DAMAGE YOU'VE CAUSED.
MY MOM WANDERS THE HOUSE LIKE A GHOST, WEARING DAD'S OLD SWEATSHIRTS.
MY BABY BROTHER WILL NEVER KNOW HIS OWN FATHER.
I KNOW WHAT IT MEANS TO GROW UP WITHOUT A DAD, SPIDEY.
IT SUCKS!
BUT THAT AIN'T ON ME.
I WILL GIVE YOUR FAMILY PEACE, LITTLE SPIDER.
THE PEACE OF THE GRAVE!
NO!!!
IT'S MY JOB TO PROTECT THEM.
MY RESPONSIBILI

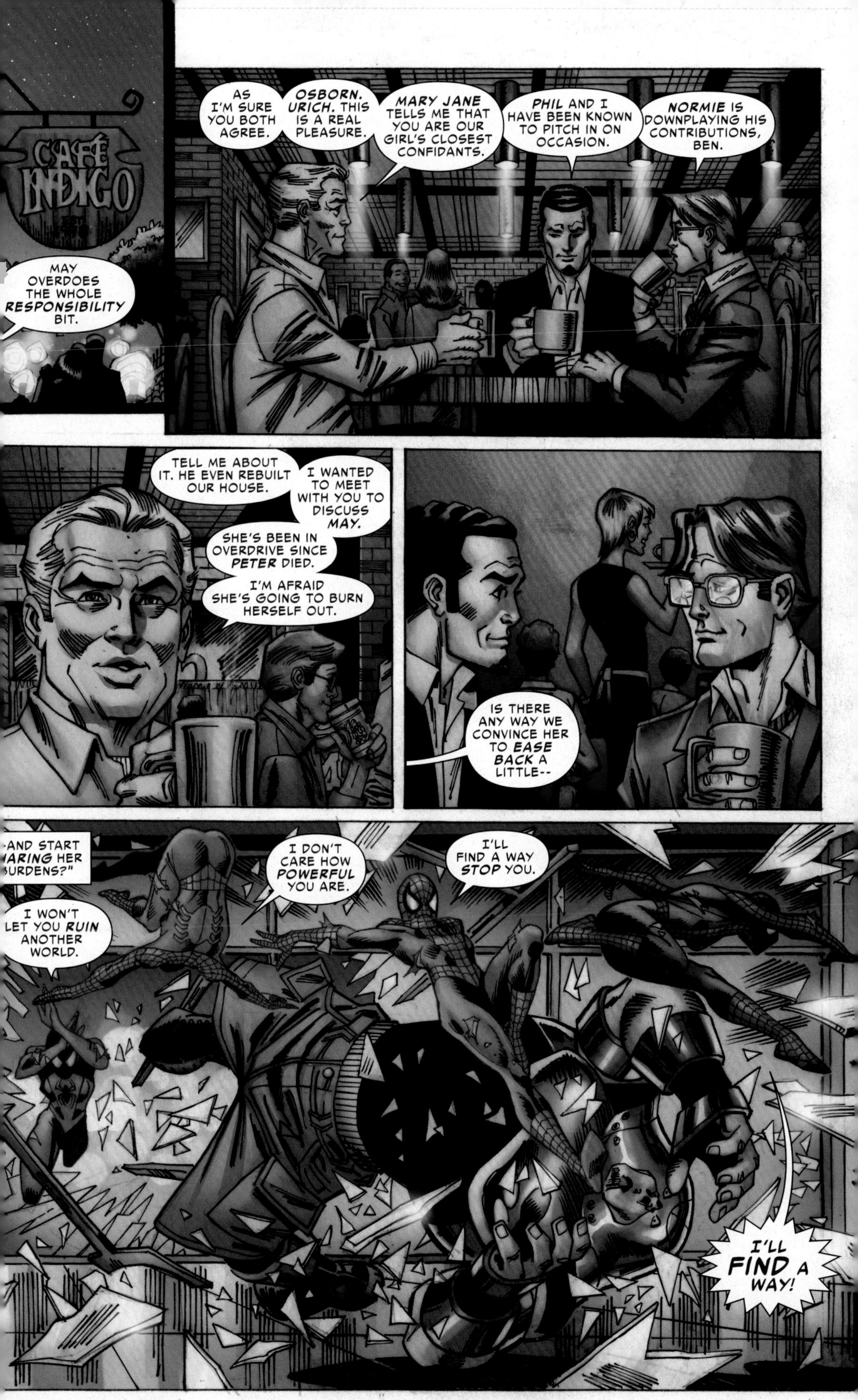

CAFÉ INDIGO
MAY OVERDOES THE WHOLE RESPONSIBILITY BIT.
AS I'M SURE YOU BOTH AGREE.
OSBORN. URICH. THIS IS A REAL PLEASURE.
MARY JANE TELLS ME THAT YOU ARE OUR GIRL'S CLOSEST CONFIDANTS.
PHIL AND I HAVE BEEN KNOWN TO PITCH IN ON OCCASION.
NORMIE IS DOWNPLAYING HIS CONTRIBUTIONS, BEN.
TELL ME ABOUT IT. HE EVEN REBUILT OUR HOUSE.
I WANTED TO MEET WITH YOU TO DISCUSS MAY.
SHE'S BEEN IN OVERDRIVE SINCE PETER DIED.
I'M AFRAID SHE'S GOING TO BURN HERSELF OUT.
IS THERE ANY WAY WE CONVINCE HER TO EASE BACK A LITTLE--
-AND START ARING HER URDENS?"
I WON'T LET YOU RUIN ANOTHER WORLD.
I DON'T CARE HOW POWERFUL YOU ARE.
I'LL FIND A WAY STOP YOU.
I'LL FIND A WAY!

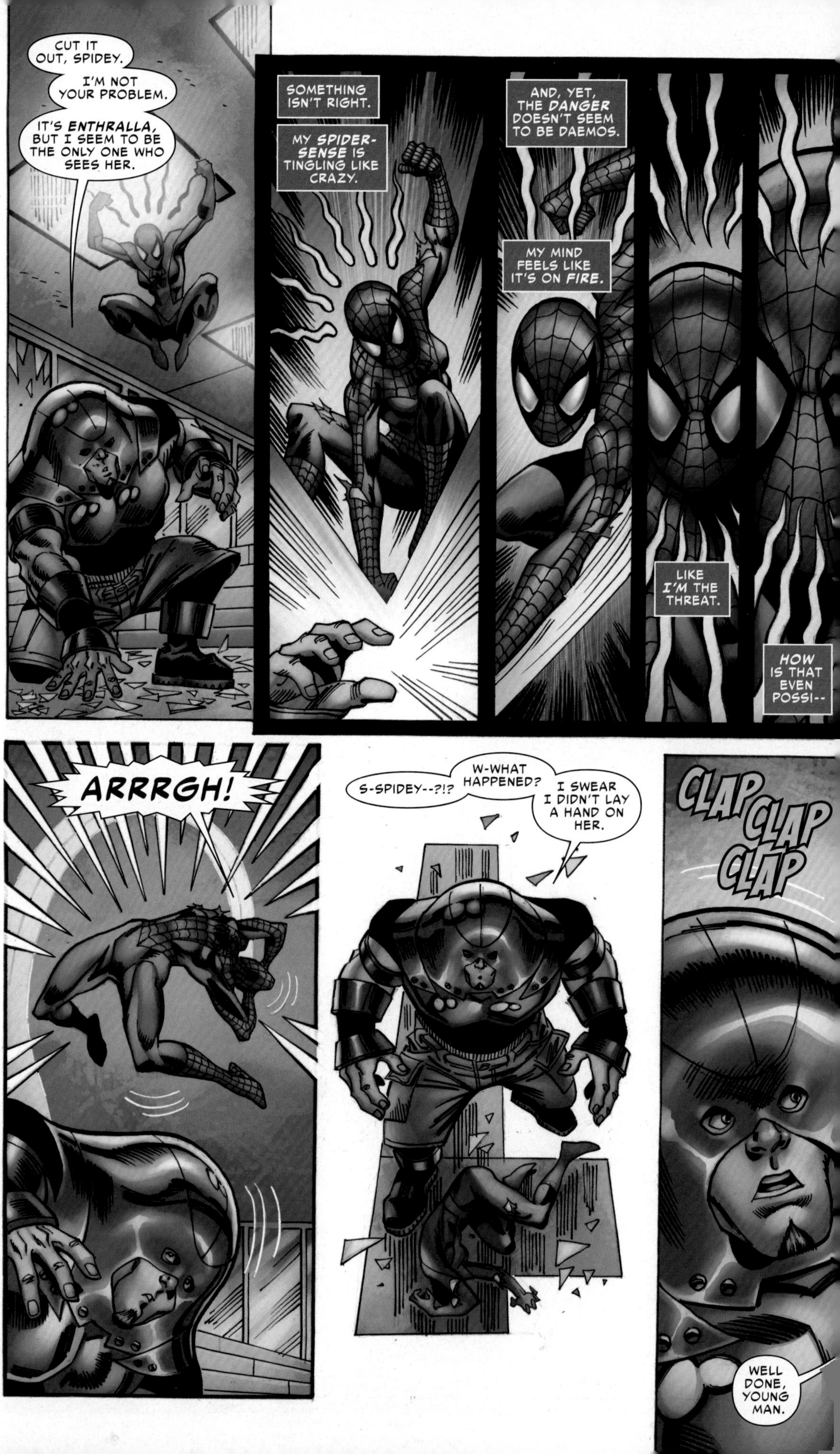

CUT IT OUT, SPIDEY.
I'M NOT YOUR PROBLEM.
IT'S ENTHRALLA, BUT I SEEM TO BE THE ONLY ONE WHO SEES HER.
SOMETHING ISN'T RIGHT.
MY SPIDER-SENSE IS TINGLING LIKE CRAZY.
AND, YET, THE DANGER DOESN'T SEEM TO BE DAEMOS.
MY MIND FEELS LIKE IT'S ON FIRE.
LIKE I'M THE THREAT.
HOW IS THAT EVEN POSSI--
ARRRGH!
S-SPIDEY--?!?
W-WHAT HAPPENED?
I SWEAR I DIDN'T LAY A HAND ON HER.
CLAP CLAP CLAP
WELL DONE, YOUNG MAN.

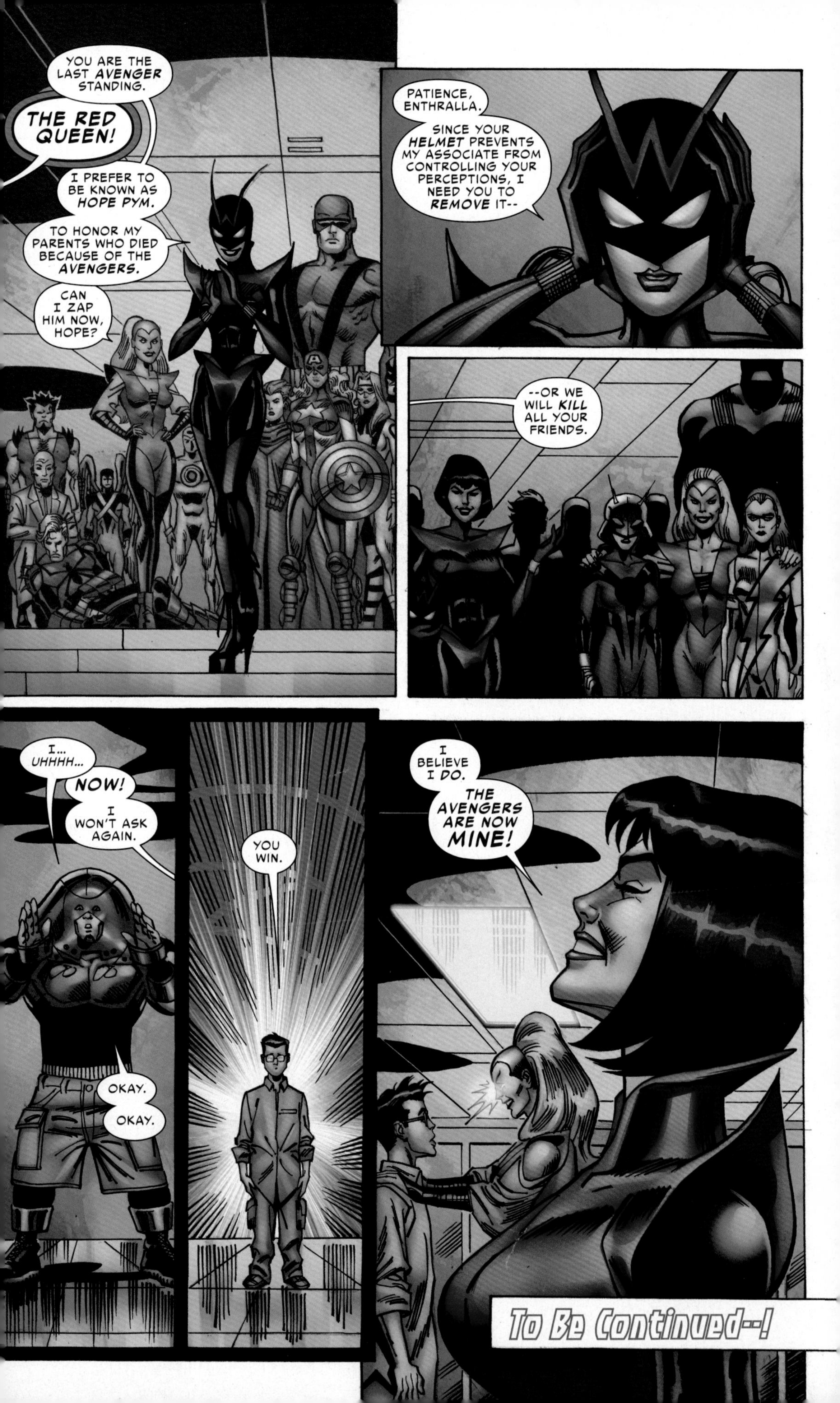

YOU ARE THE LAST AVENGER STANDING.
THE RED QUEEN!
I PREFER TO BE KNOWN AS HOPE PYM.
TO HONOR MY PARENTS WHO DIED BECAUSE OF THE AVENGERS.
CAN I ZAP HIM NOW, HOPE?
PATIENCE, ENTHRALLA.
SINCE YOUR HELMET PREVENTS MY ASSOCIATE FROM CONTROLLING YOUR PERCEPTIONS, I NEED YOU TO REMOVE IT--
--OR WE WILL KILL ALL YOUR FRIENDS.
I... UHHHH...
NOW!
I WON'T ASK AGAIN.
OKAY.
OKAY.
YOU WIN.
I BELIEVE I DO.
THE AVENGERS ARE NOW MINE!
To Be Continued--!

SPIDER-ISLAND #1 50 YEARS OF INHUMANS variant
by John Cassaday

SPIDER-ISLAND #1 variant by Ron Frenz

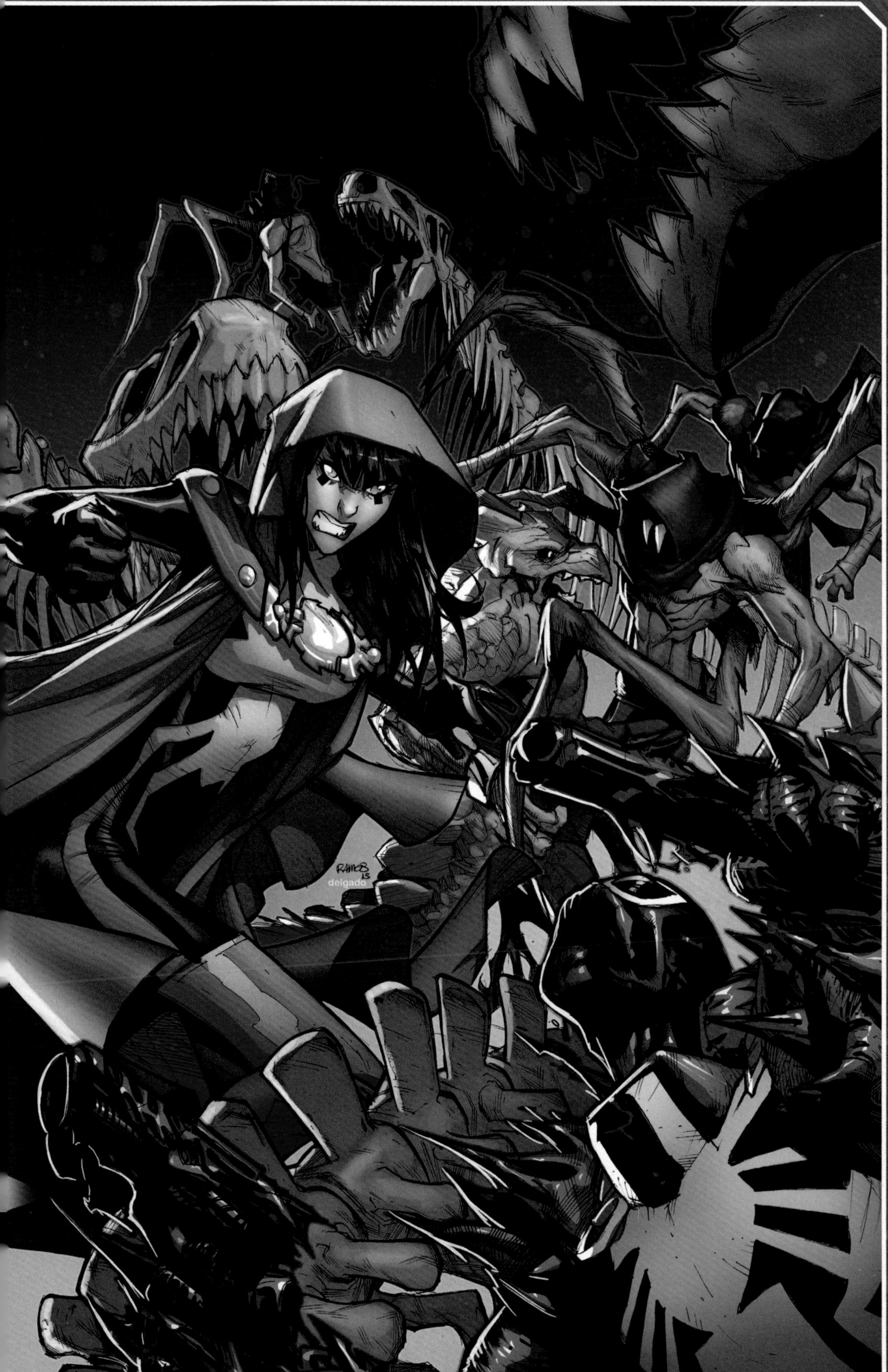
RAMOS 15
delgado

PART FOUR: **INTELLIGENT DESIGN**

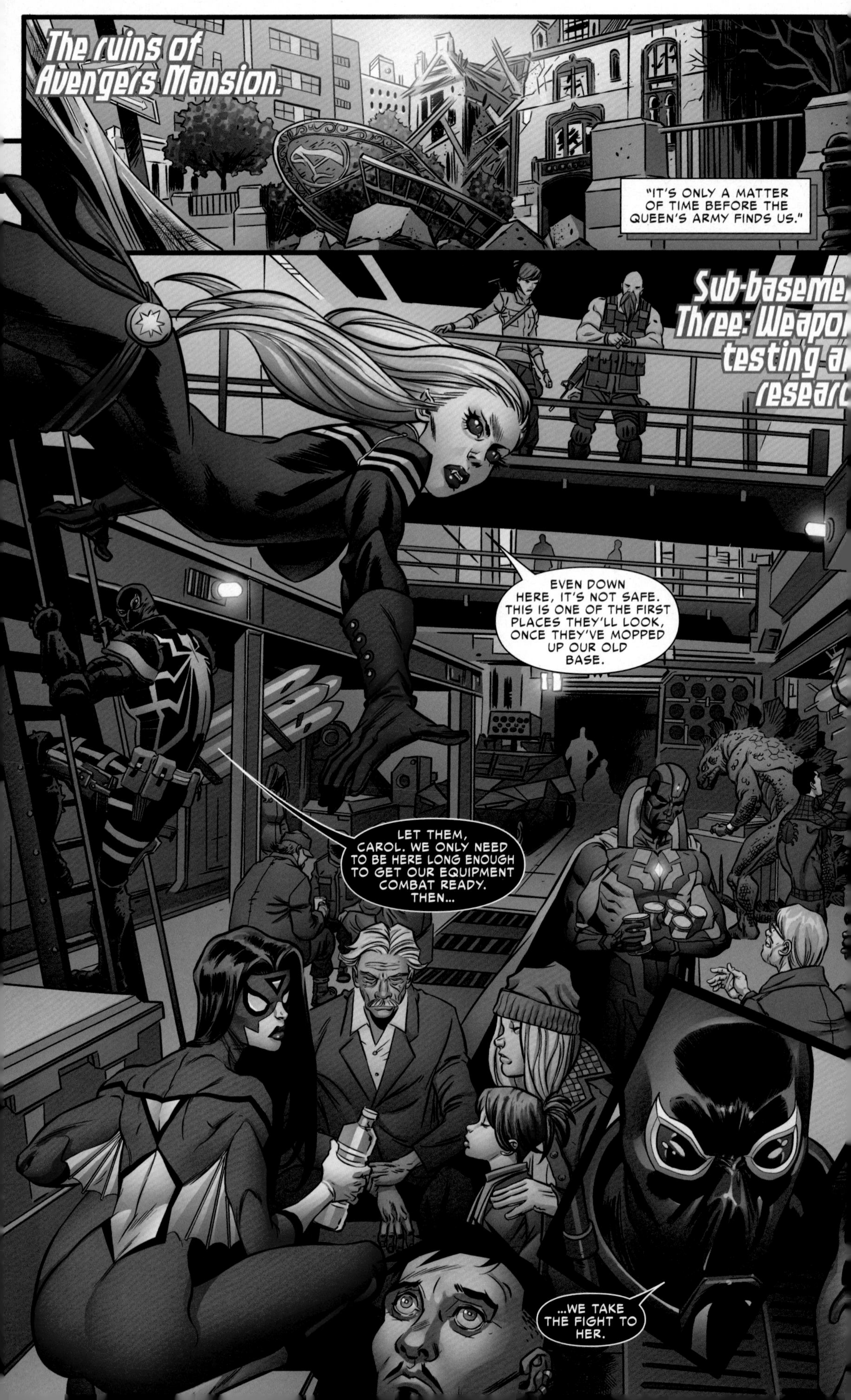
The ruins of Avengers Mansion.
"IT'S ONLY A MATTER OF TIME BEFORE THE QUEEN'S ARMY FINDS US."
Sub-baseme Three: Weapo testing a researc
EVEN DOWN HERE, IT'S NOT SAFE. THIS IS ONE OF THE FIRST PLACES THEY'LL LOOK, ONCE THEY'VE MOPPED UP OUR OLD BASE.
LET THEM, CAROL. WE ONLY NEED TO BE HERE LONG ENOUGH TO GET OUR EQUIPMENT COMBAT READY. THEN...
...WE TAKE THE FIGHT TO HER.

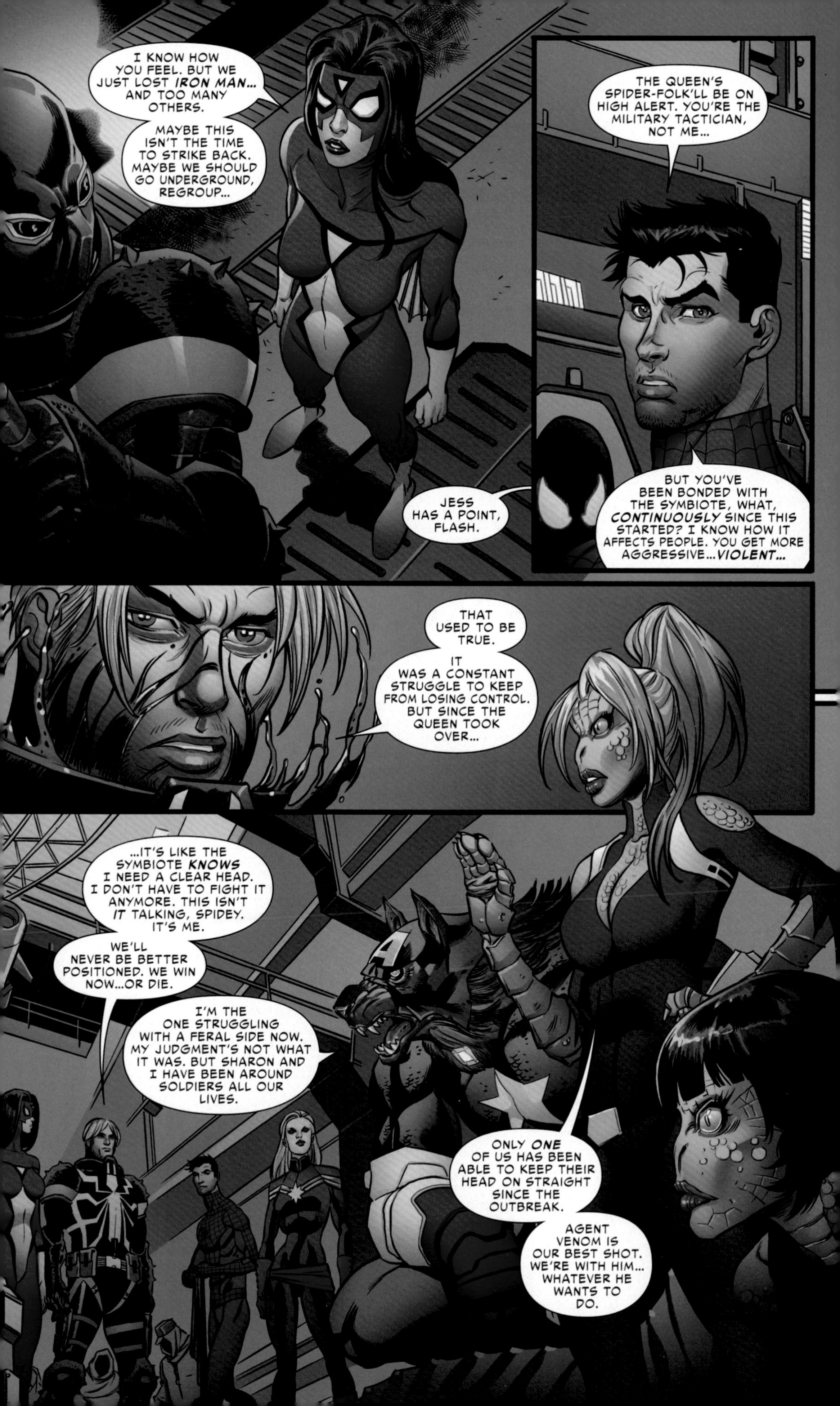

I KNOW HOW YOU FEEL. BUT WE JUST LOST *IRON MAN*... AND TOO MANY OTHERS.
MAYBE THIS ISN'T THE TIME TO STRIKE BACK. MAYBE WE SHOULD GO UNDERGROUND, REGROUP...
JESS HAS A POINT, FLASH.
THE QUEEN'S SPIDER-FOLK'LL BE ON HIGH ALERT. YOU'RE THE MILITARY TACTICIAN, NOT ME...
BUT YOU'VE BEEN BONDED WITH THE SYMBIOTE, WHAT, *CONTINUOUSLY* SINCE THIS STARTED? I KNOW HOW IT AFFECTS PEOPLE. YOU GET MORE AGGRESSIVE...*VIOLENT*...
THAT USED TO BE TRUE.
IT WAS A CONSTANT STRUGGLE TO KEEP FROM LOSING CONTROL. BUT SINCE THE QUEEN TOOK OVER...
...IT'S LIKE THE SYMBIOTE *KNOWS* I NEED A CLEAR HEAD. I DON'T HAVE TO FIGHT IT ANYMORE. THIS ISN'T *IT* TALKING, SPIDEY. IT'S ME.
WE'LL NEVER BE BETTER POSITIONED. WE WIN NOW...OR DIE.
I'M THE ONE STRUGGLING WITH A FERAL SIDE NOW. MY JUDGMENT'S NOT WHAT IT WAS. BUT SHARON AND I HAVE BEEN AROUND SOLDIERS ALL OUR LIVES.
ONLY *ONE* OF US HAS BEEN ABLE TO KEEP THEIR HEAD ON STRAIGHT SINCE THE OUTBREAK.
AGENT VENOM IS OUR BEST SHOT. WE'RE WITH HIM... WHATEVER HE WANTS TO DO.

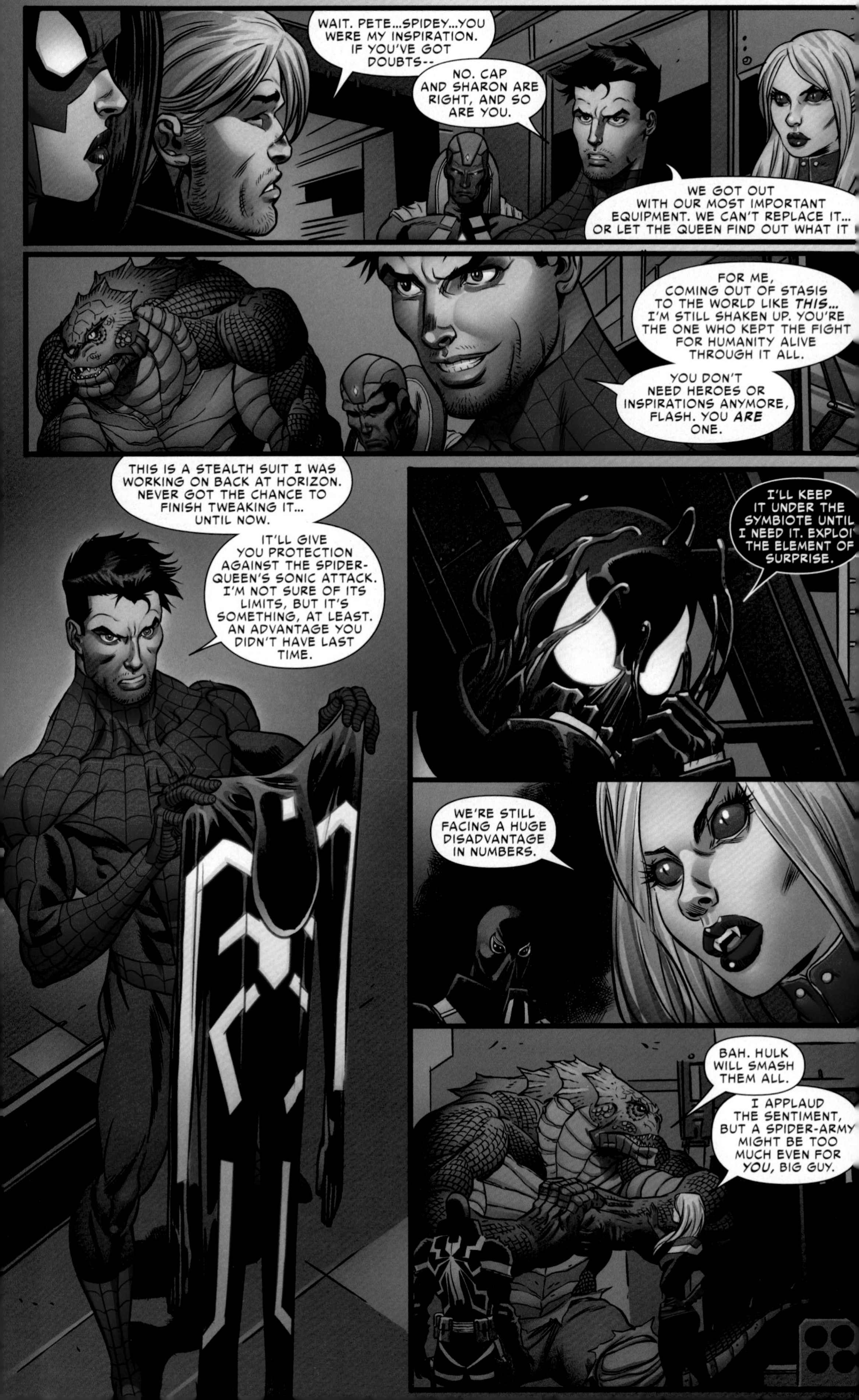

WAIT. PETE...SPIDEY...YOU WERE MY INSPIRATION. IF YOU'VE GOT DOUBTS--
NO. CAP AND SHARON ARE RIGHT, AND SO ARE YOU.
WE GOT OUT WITH OUR MOST IMPORTANT EQUIPMENT. WE CAN'T REPLACE IT... OR LET THE QUEEN FIND OUT WHAT IT
FOR ME, COMING OUT OF STASIS TO THE WORLD LIKE *THIS*... I'M STILL SHAKEN UP. YOU'RE THE ONE WHO KEPT THE FIGHT FOR HUMANITY ALIVE THROUGH IT ALL.
YOU DON'T NEED HEROES OR INSPIRATIONS ANYMORE, FLASH. YOU *ARE* ONE.
THIS IS A STEALTH SUIT I WAS WORKING ON BACK AT HORIZON. NEVER GOT THE CHANCE TO FINISH TWEAKING IT... UNTIL NOW.
IT'LL GIVE YOU PROTECTION AGAINST THE SPIDER-QUEEN'S SONIC ATTACK. I'M NOT SURE OF ITS LIMITS, BUT IT'S SOMETHING, AT LEAST. AN ADVANTAGE YOU DIDN'T HAVE LAST TIME.
I'LL KEEP IT UNDER THE SYMBIOTE UNTIL I NEED IT. EXPLOI THE ELEMENT OF SURPRISE.
WE'RE STILL FACING A HUGE DISADVANTAGE IN NUMBERS.
BAH. HULK WILL SMASH THEM ALL.
I APPLAUD THE SENTIMENT, BUT A SPIDER-ARMY MIGHT BE TOO MUCH EVEN FOR *YOU*, BIG GUY.

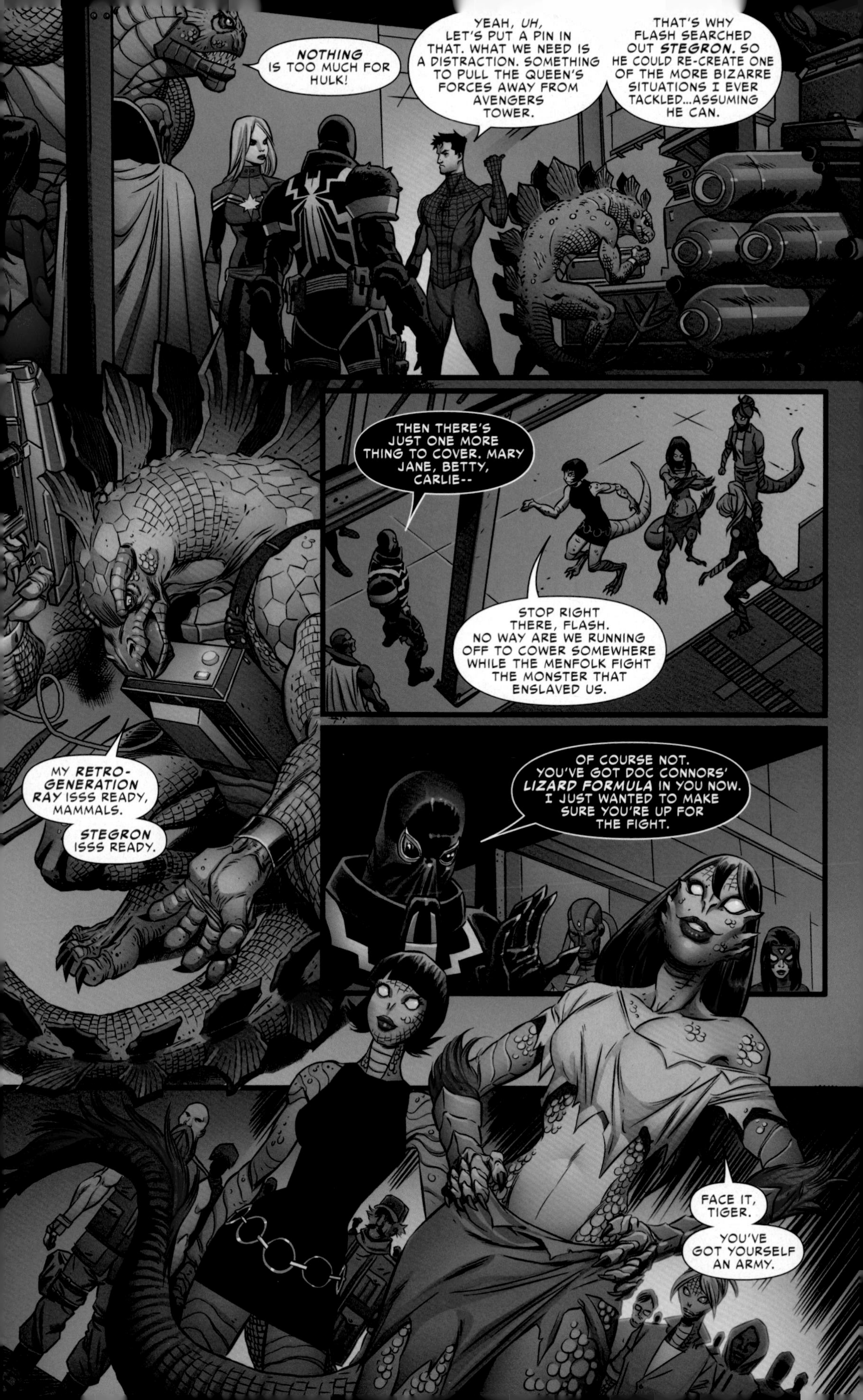
NOTHING IS TOO MUCH FOR HULK!
YEAH, UH, LET'S PUT A PIN IN THAT. WHAT WE NEED IS A DISTRACTION. SOMETHING TO PULL THE QUEEN'S FORCES AWAY FROM AVENGERS TOWER.
THAT'S WHY FLASH SEARCHED OUT STEGRON. SO HE COULD RE-CREATE ONE OF THE MORE BIZARRE SITUATIONS I EVER TACKLED...ASSUMING HE CAN.
THEN THERE'S JUST ONE MORE THING TO COVER. MARY JANE, BETTY, CARLIE--
STOP RIGHT THERE, FLASH. NO WAY ARE WE RUNNING OFF TO COWER SOMEWHERE WHILE THE MENFOLK FIGHT THE MONSTER THAT ENSLAVED US.
MY RETRO-GENERATION RAY ISSS READY, MAMMALS.
STEGRON ISSS READY.
OF COURSE NOT. YOU'VE GOT DOC CONNORS' LIZARD FORMULA IN YOU NOW. I JUST WANTED TO MAKE SURE YOU'RE UP FOR THE FIGHT.
FACE IT, TIGER.
YOU'VE GOT YOURSELF AN ARMY.

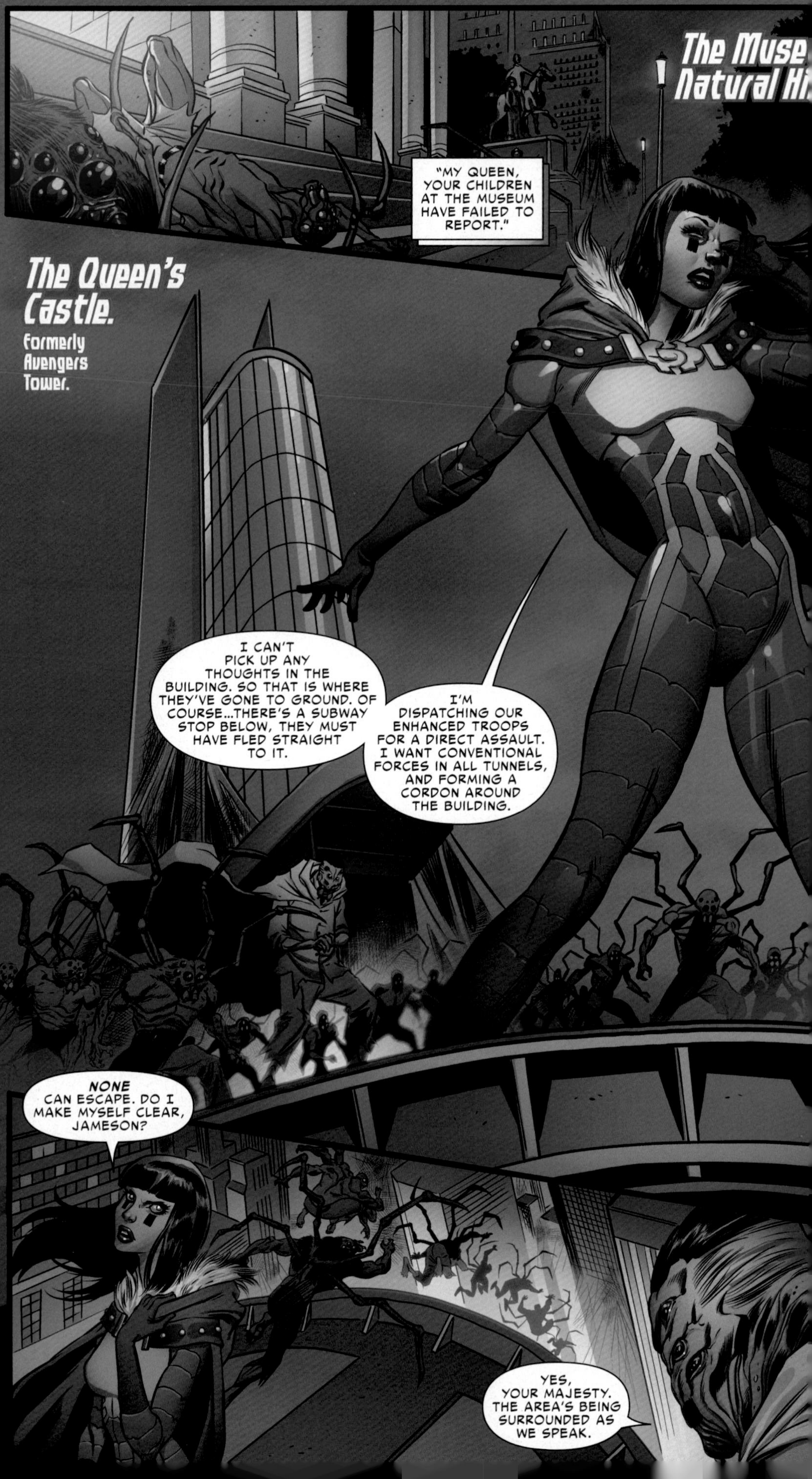

The Muse
Natural Hi
"MY QUEEN, YOUR CHILDREN AT THE MUSEUM HAVE FAILED TO REPORT."
The Queen's Castle.
Formerly Avengers Tower.
I CAN'T PICK UP ANY THOUGHTS IN THE BUILDING. SO THAT IS WHERE THEY'VE GONE TO GROUND. OF COURSE...THERE'S A SUBWAY STOP BELOW, THEY MUST HAVE FLED STRAIGHT TO IT.
I'M DISPATCHING OUR ENHANCED TROOPS FOR A DIRECT ASSAULT. I WANT CONVENTIONAL FORCES IN ALL TUNNELS, AND FORMING A CORDON AROUND THE BUILDING.
NONE CAN ESCAPE. DO I MAKE MYSELF CLEAR, JAMESON?
YES, YOUR MAJESTY. THE AREA'S BEING SURROUNDED AS WE SPEAK.

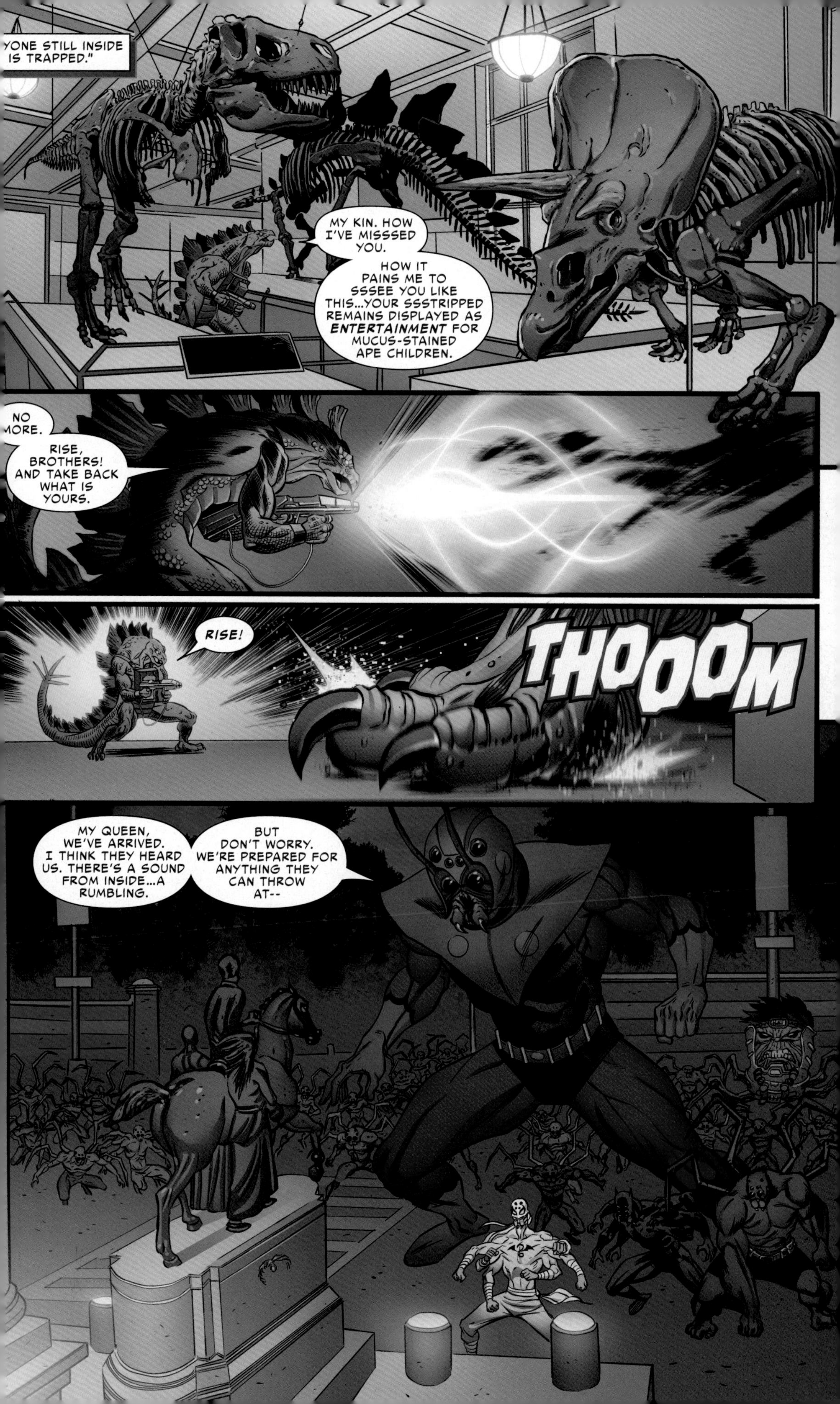
YONE STILL INSIDE IS TRAPPED."
MY KIN. HOW I'VE MISSSED YOU.
HOW IT PAINS ME TO SSSEE YOU LIKE THIS...YOUR SSSTRIPPED REMAINS DISPLAYED AS ENTERTAINMENT FOR MUCUS-STAINED APE CHILDREN.
NO MORE.
RISE, BROTHERS! AND TAKE BACK WHAT IS YOURS.
RISE!
THOOOM
MY QUEEN, WE'VE ARRIVED. I THINK THEY HEARD US. THERE'S A SOUND FROM INSIDE...A RUMBLING.
BUT DON'T WORRY. WE'RE PREPARED FOR ANYTHING THEY CAN THROW AT--

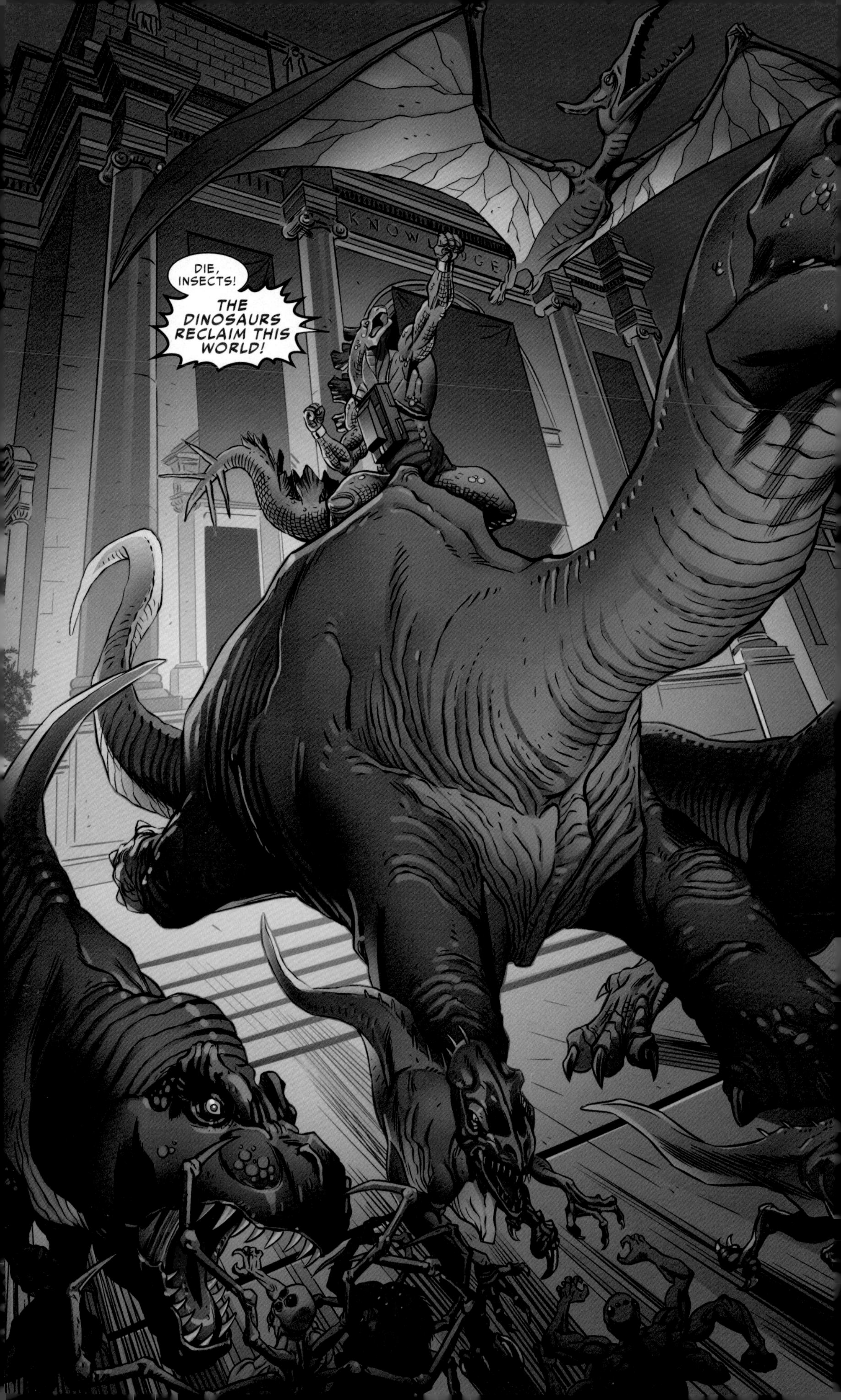
DIE, INSECTS!
THE DINOSAURS RECLAIM THIS WORLD!

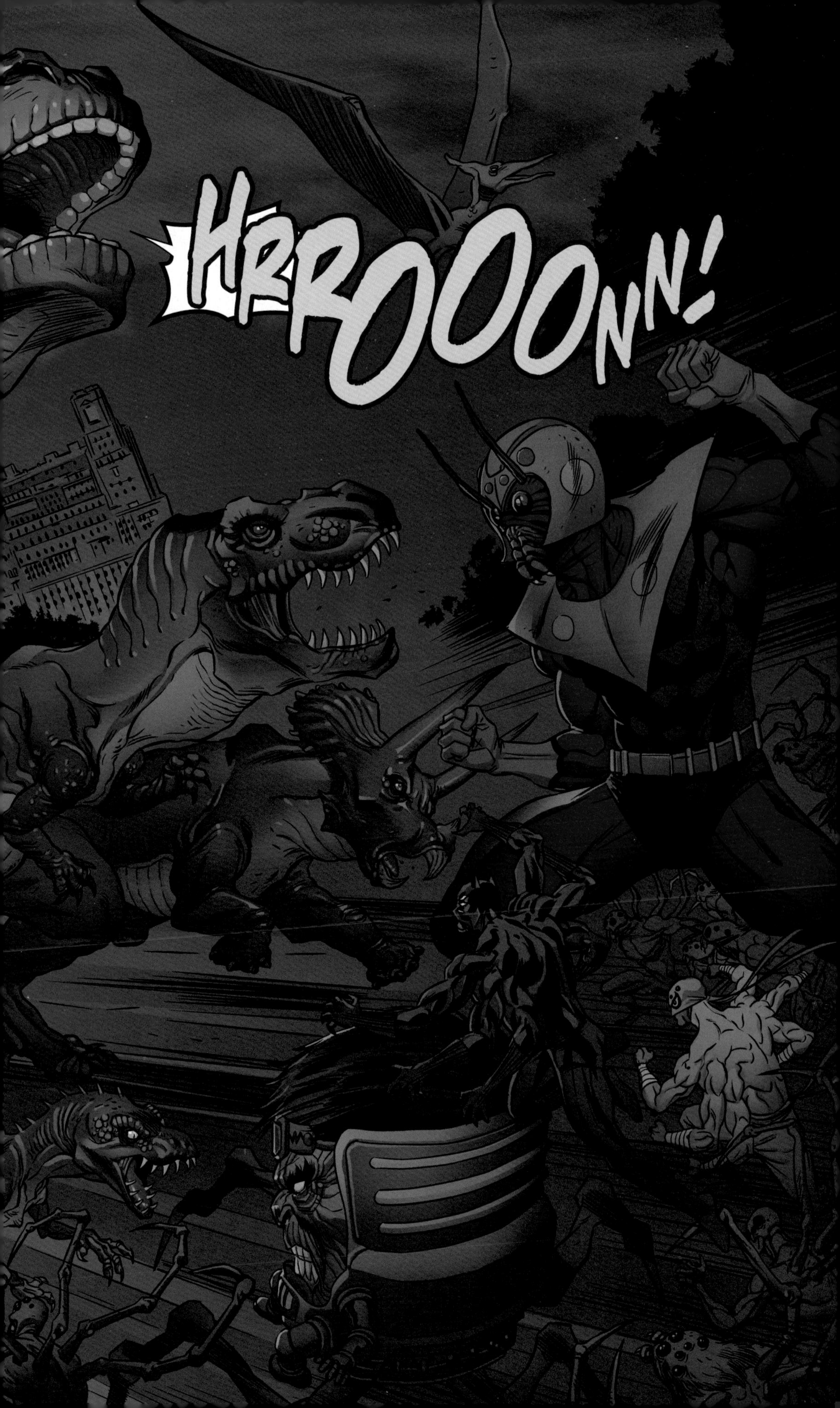
HRROOOONN!

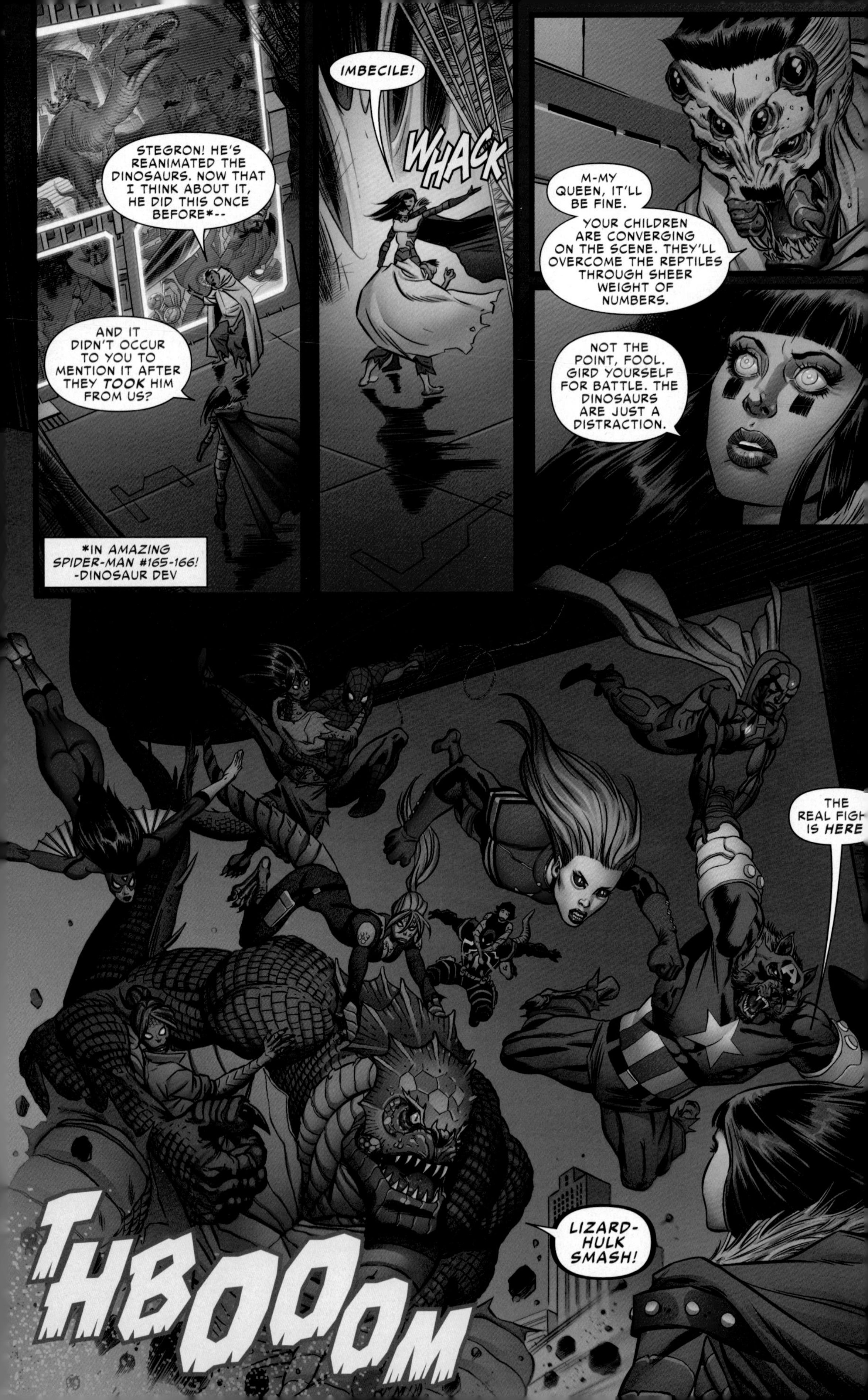
STEGRON! HE'S REANIMATED THE DINOSAURS. NOW THAT I THINK ABOUT IT, HE DID THIS ONCE BEFORE*--
AND IT DIDN'T OCCUR TO YOU TO MENTION IT AFTER THEY TOOK HIM FROM US?
*IN AMAZING SPIDER-MAN #165-166! -DINOSAUR DEV
IMBECILE!
WHACK
M-MY QUEEN, IT'LL BE FINE.
YOUR CHILDREN ARE CONVERGING ON THE SCENE. THEY'LL OVERCOME THE REPTILES THROUGH SHEER WEIGHT OF NUMBERS.
NOT THE POINT, FOOL. GIRD YOURSELF FOR BATTLE. THE DINOSAURS ARE JUST A DISTRACTION.
THE REAL FIGH IS HERE
LIZARD-HULK SMASH!
THBOOOM

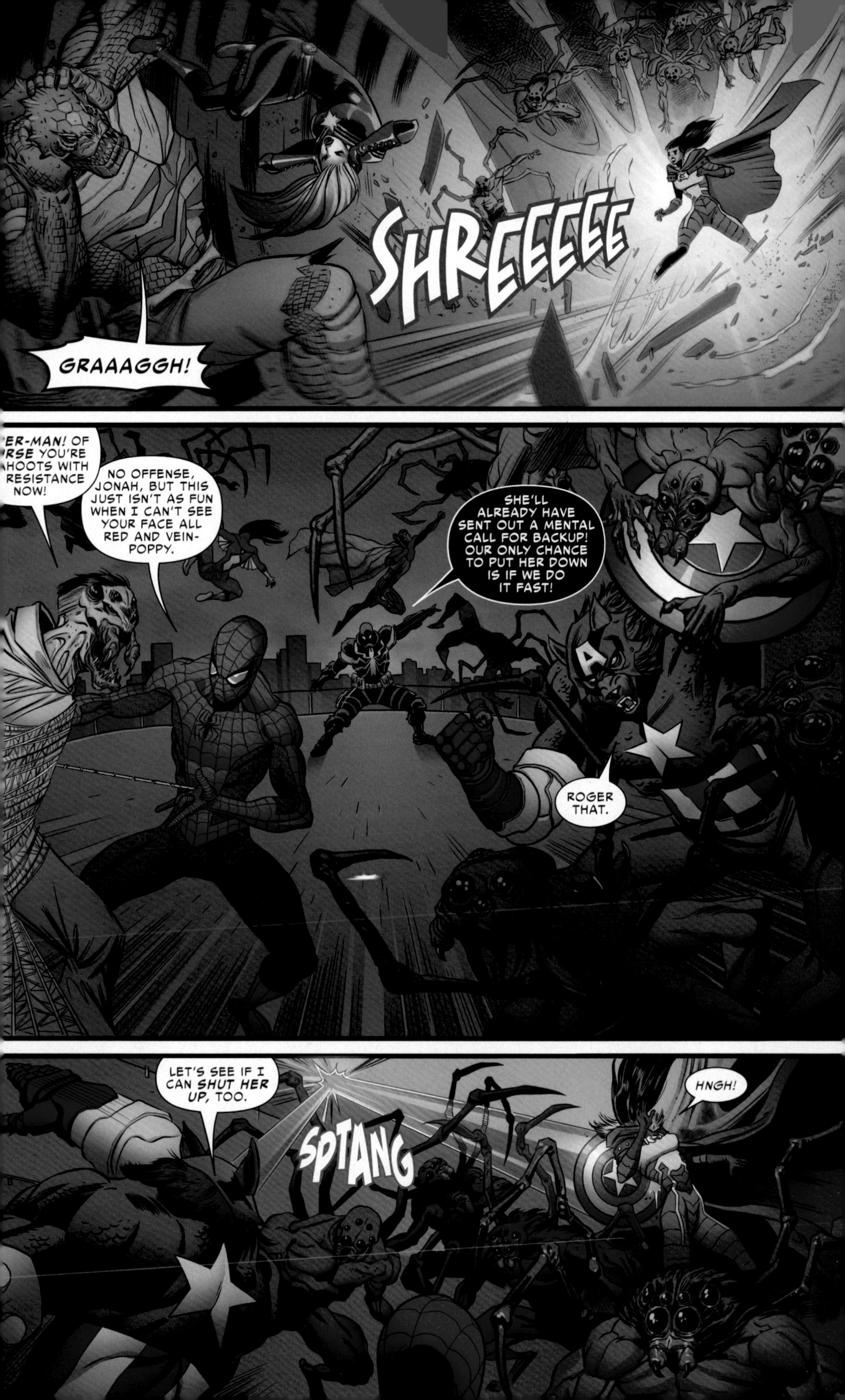
SHREEEEE
GRAAAGGH!
ER-MAN! OF RSE YOU'RE HOOTS WITH RESISTANCE NOW!
NO OFFENSE, JONAH, BUT THIS JUST ISN'T AS FUN WHEN I CAN'T SEE YOUR FACE ALL RED AND VEIN-POPPY.
SHE'LL ALREADY HAVE SENT OUT A MENTAL CALL FOR BACKUP! OUR ONLY CHANCE TO PUT HER DOWN IS IF WE DO IT FAST!
ROGER THAT.
LET'S SEE IF I CAN SHUT HER UP, TOO.
SPTANG
HNGH!

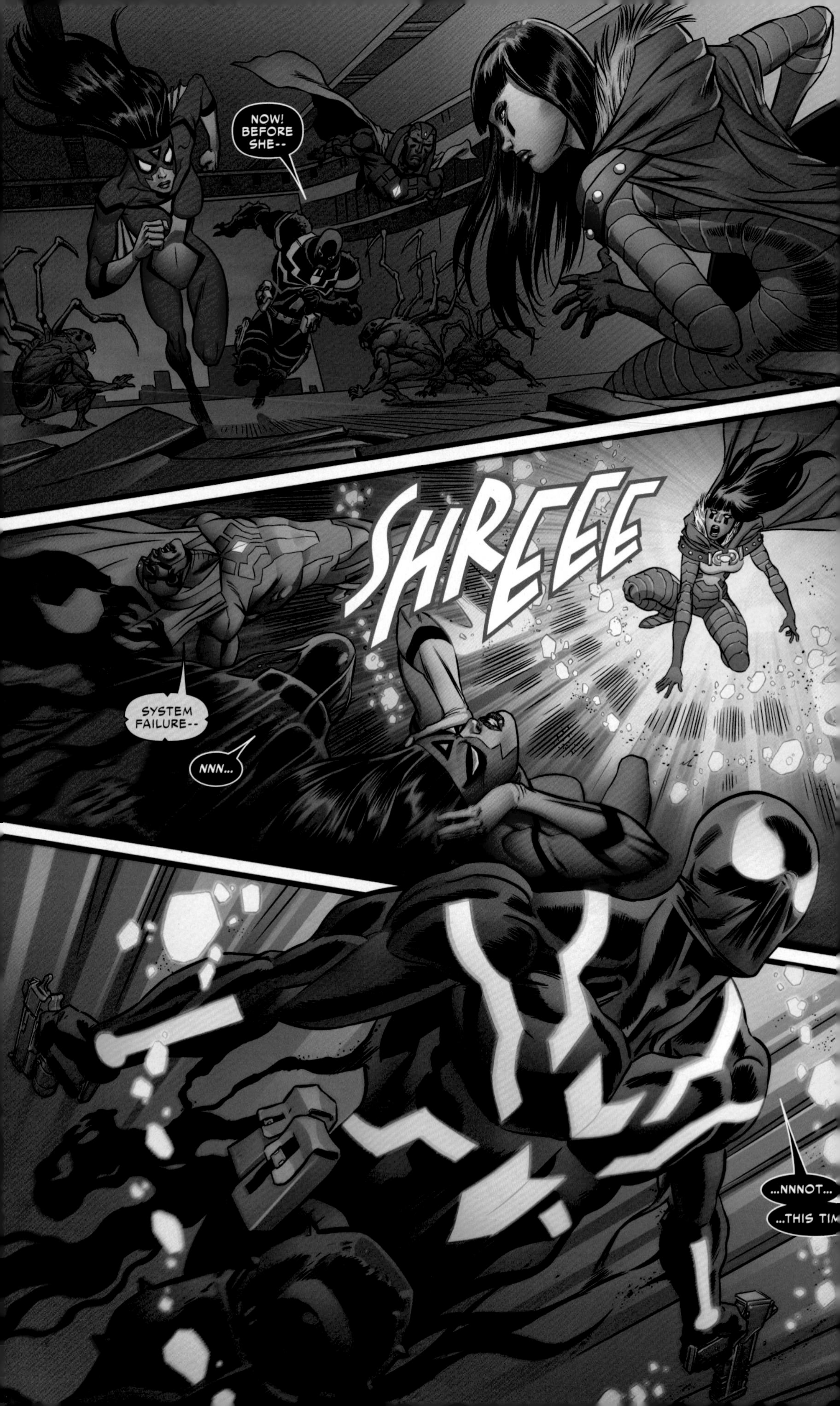

NOW! BEFORE SHE--
SHREEE
SYSTEM FAILURE--
NNN...
...NNNOT...
...THIS TIM

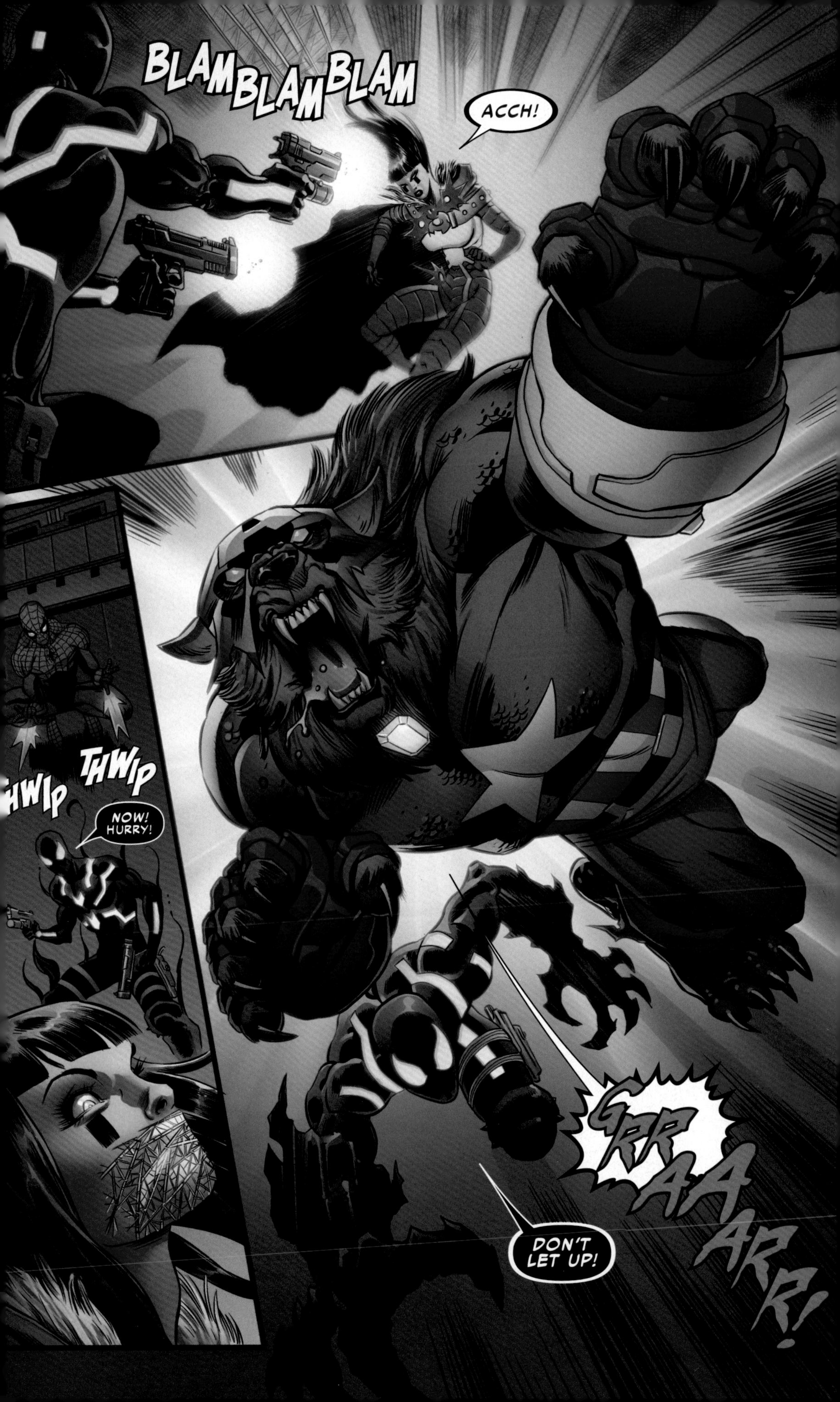
BLAMBLAMBLAM
ACCH!
THWIP
THWIP
NOW! HURRY!
GRRAAARR!
DON'T LET UP!

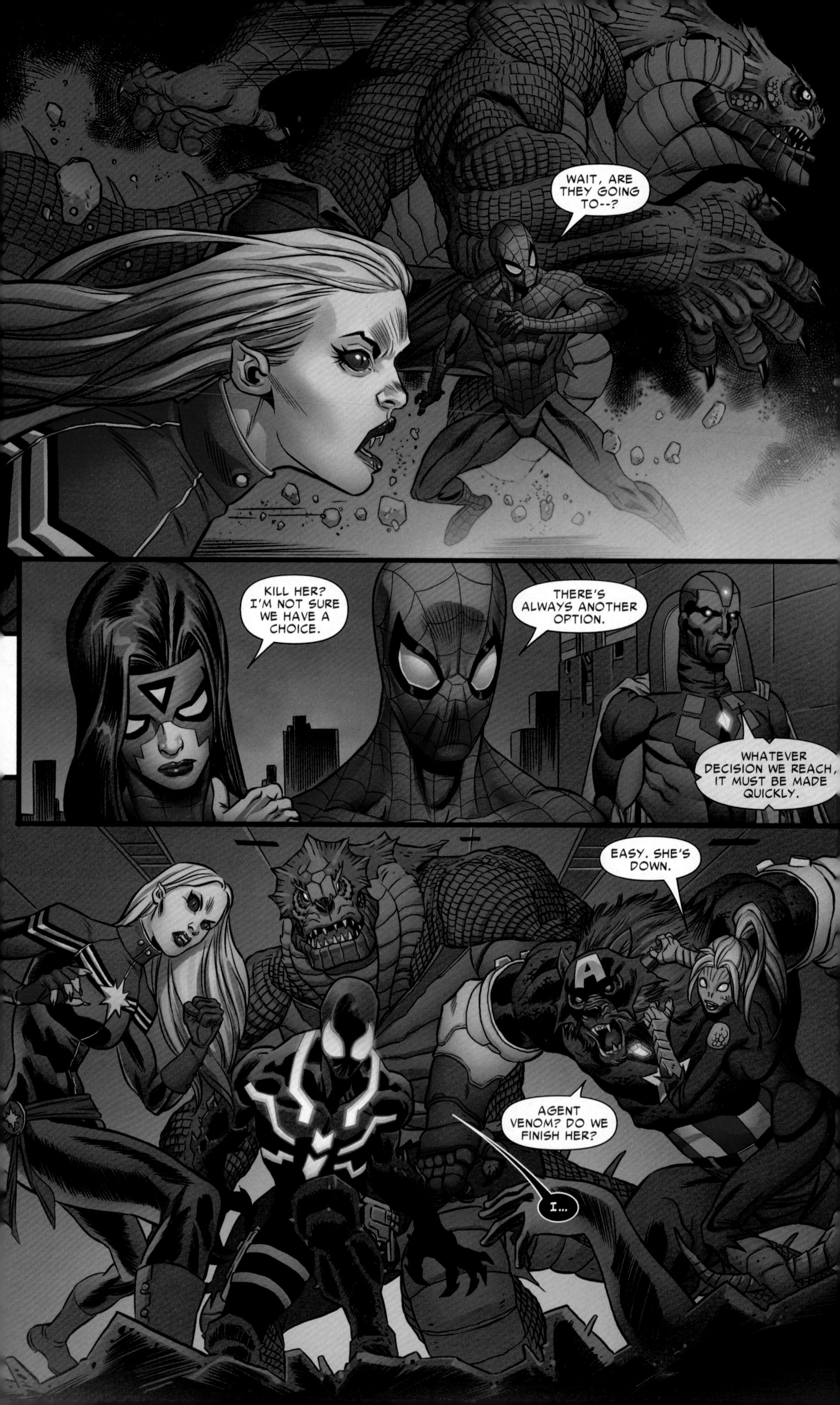

WAIT, ARE THEY GOING TO--?
KILL HER? I'M NOT SURE WE HAVE A CHOICE.
THERE'S ALWAYS ANOTHER OPTION.
WHATEVER DECISION WE REACH, IT MUST BE MADE QUICKLY.
EASY. SHE'S DOWN.
AGENT VENOM? DO WE FINISH HER?
I...

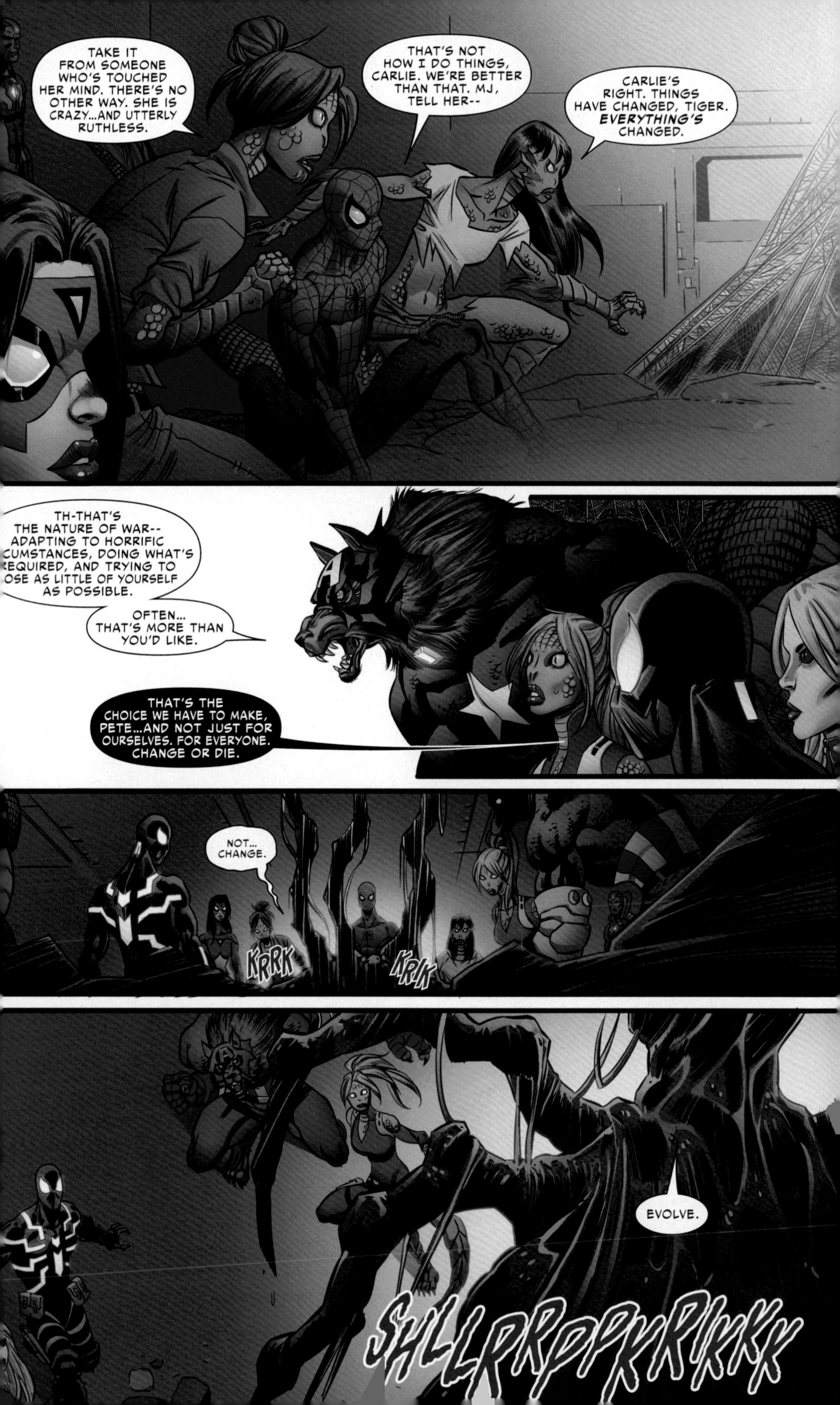

TAKE IT FROM SOMEONE WHO'S TOUCHED HER MIND. THERE'S NO OTHER WAY. SHE IS CRAZY...AND UTTERLY RUTHLESS.
THAT'S NOT HOW I DO THINGS, CARLIE. WE'RE BETTER THAN THAT. MJ, TELL HER--
CARLIE'S RIGHT. THINGS HAVE CHANGED, TIGER. EVERYTHING'S CHANGED.
TH-THAT'S THE NATURE OF WAR-- ADAPTING TO HORRIFIC CUMSTANCES, DOING WHAT'S REQUIRED, AND TRYING TO OSE AS LITTLE OF YOURSELF AS POSSIBLE.
OFTEN... THAT'S MORE THAN YOU'D LIKE.
THAT'S THE CHOICE WE HAVE TO MAKE, PETE...AND NOT JUST FOR OURSELVES. FOR EVERYONE. CHANGE OR DIE.
NOT... CHANGE.
KRRK
KRIK
EVOLVE.
SHLLRRDPKRKKK

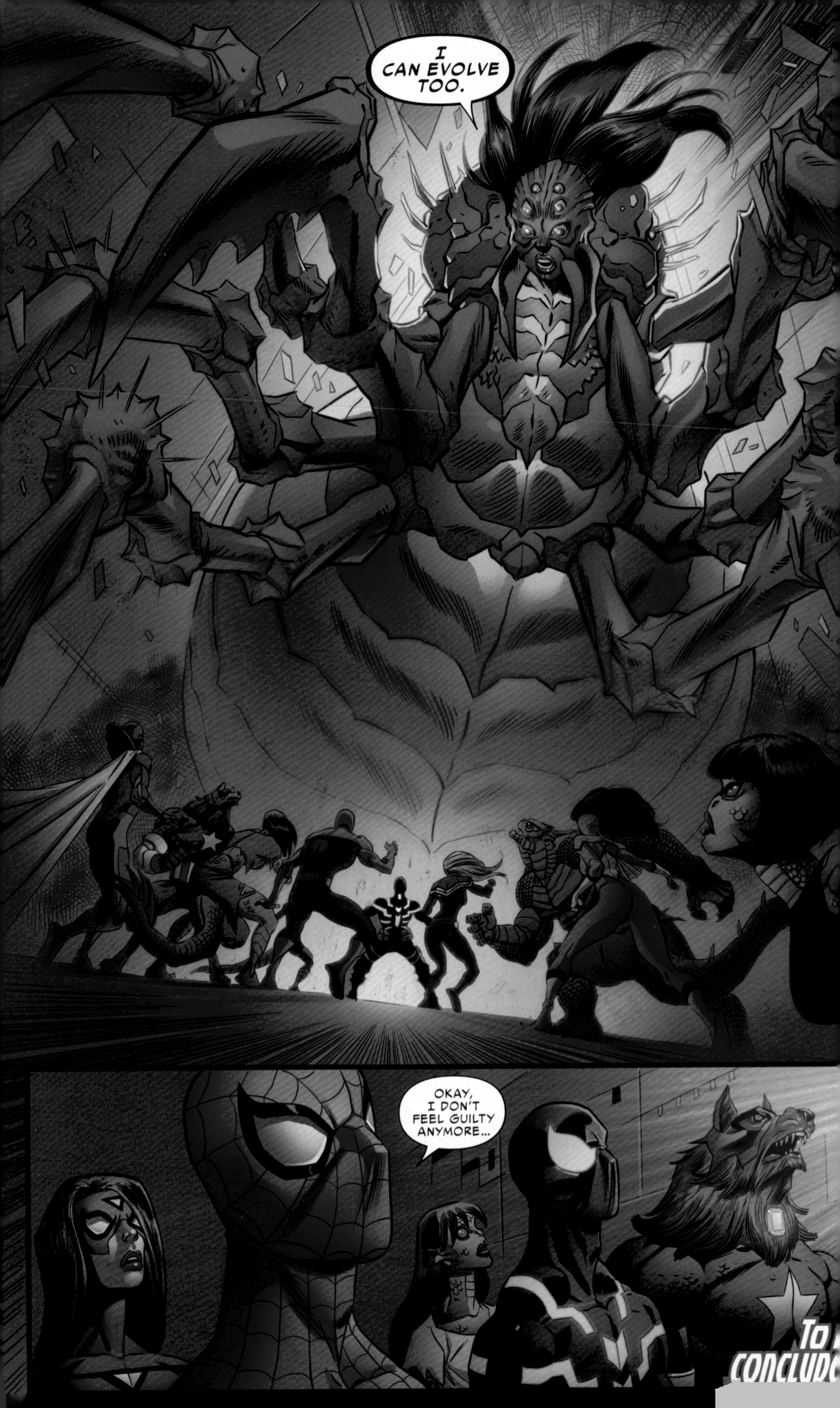
I CAN EVOLVE TOO.
OKAY, I DON'T FEEL GUILTY ANYMORE...

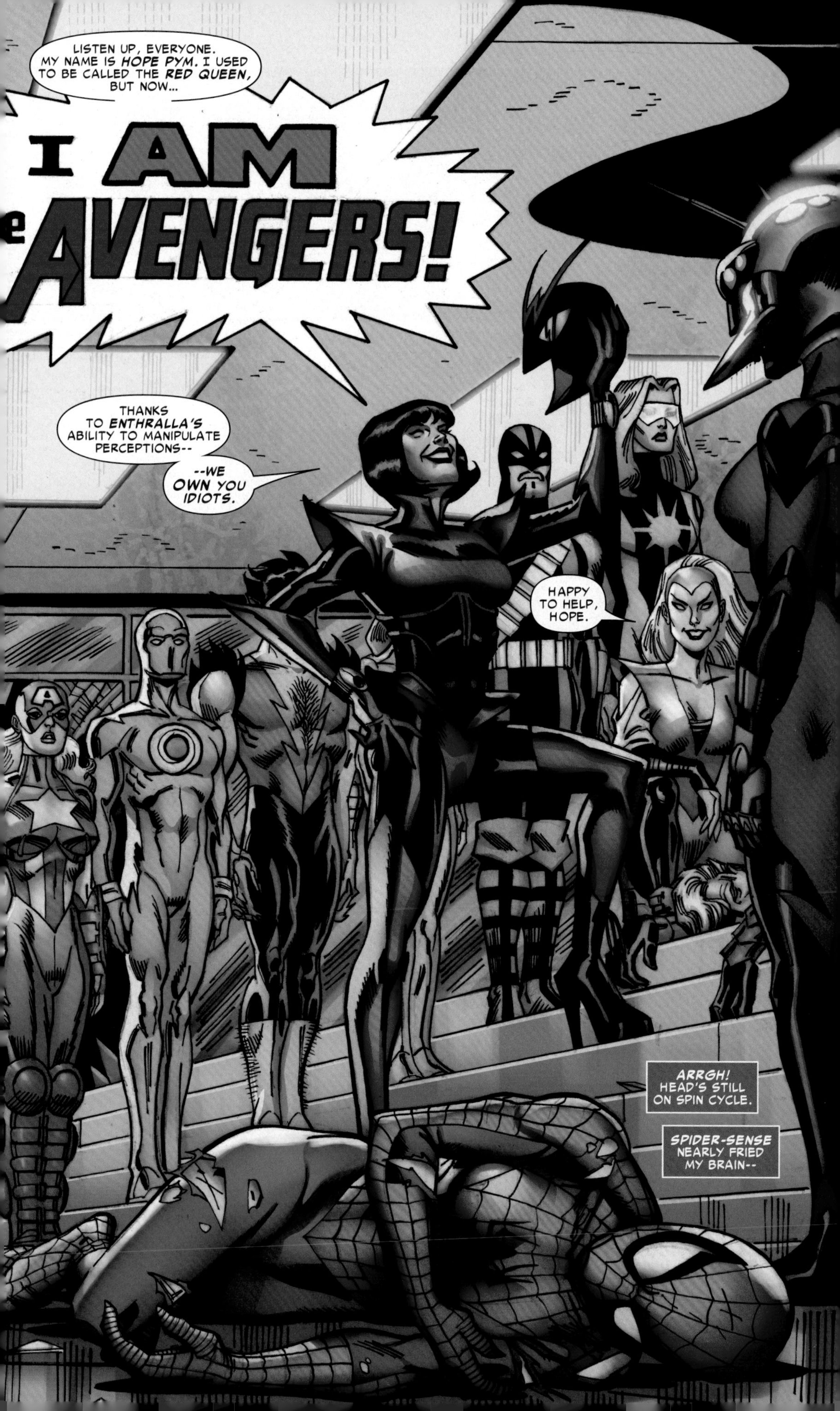

LISTEN UP, EVERYONE. MY NAME IS HOPE PYM. I USED TO BE CALLED THE RED QUEEN, BUT NOW...
I AM
AVENGERS!
THANKS TO ENTHRALLA'S ABILITY TO MANIPULATE PERCEPTIONS--
--WE OWN YOU IDIOTS.
HAPPY TO HELP, HOPE.
ARRGH! HEAD'S STILL ON SPIN CYCLE.
SPIDER-SENSE NEARLY FRIED MY BRAIN--

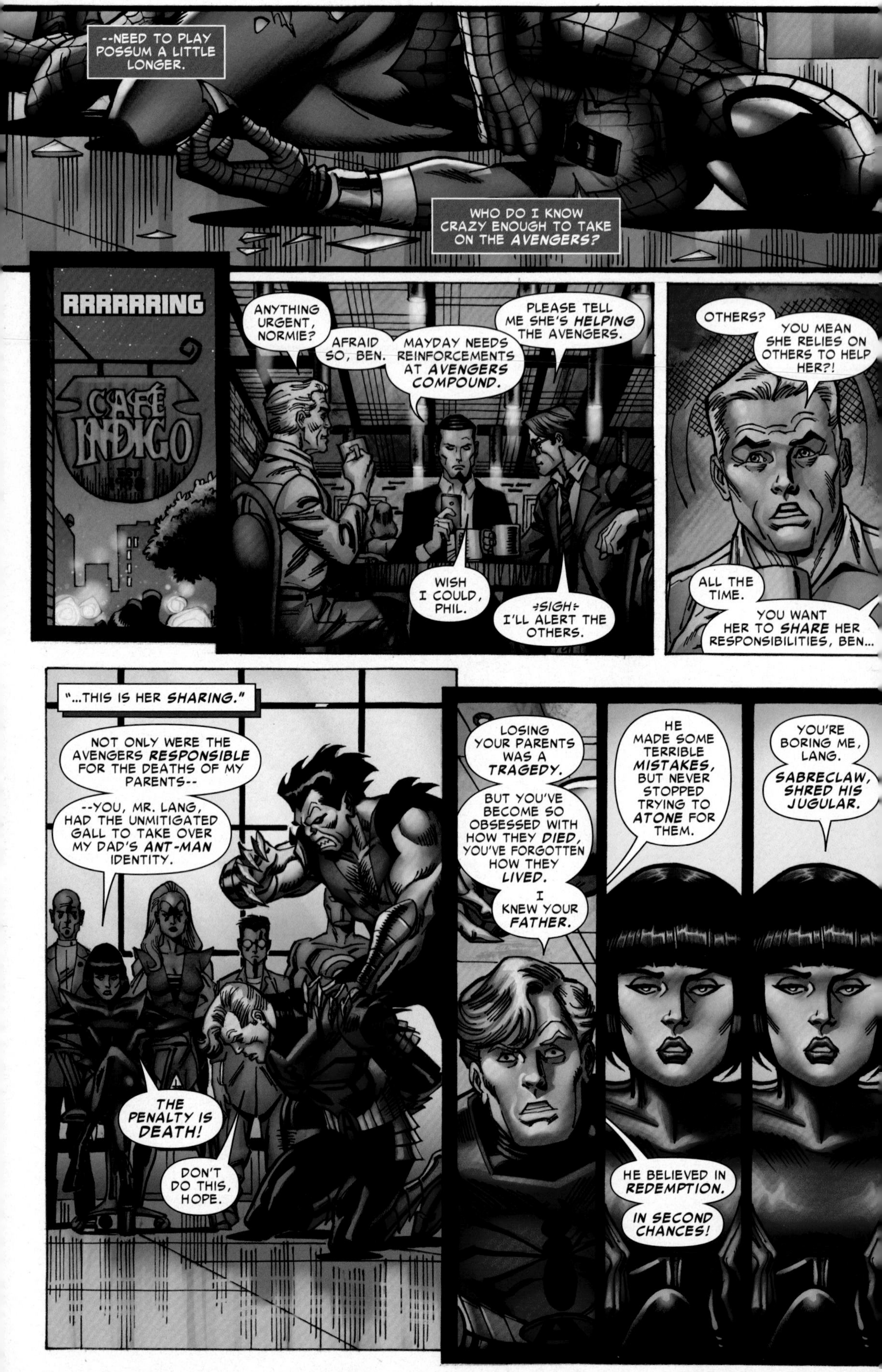
--NEED TO PLAY POSSUM A LITTLE LONGER.
WHO DO I KNOW CRAZY ENOUGH TO TAKE ON THE AVENGERS?
RRRRRRING
CAFÉ INDIGO
ANYTHING URGENT, NORMIE?
AFRAID SO, BEN.
MAYDAY NEEDS REINFORCEMENTS AT AVENGERS COMPOUND.
PLEASE TELL ME SHE'S HELPING THE AVENGERS.
WISH I COULD, PHIL.
SIGH
I'LL ALERT THE OTHERS.
OTHERS?
YOU MEAN SHE RELIES ON OTHERS TO HELP HER?!
ALL THE TIME.
YOU WANT HER TO SHARE HER RESPONSIBILITIES, BEN...
"...THIS IS HER SHARING."
NOT ONLY WERE THE AVENGERS RESPONSIBLE FOR THE DEATHS OF MY PARENTS--
--YOU, MR. LANG, HAD THE UNMITIGATED GALL TO TAKE OVER MY DAD'S ANT-MAN IDENTITY.
THE PENALTY IS DEATH!
DON'T DO THIS, HOPE.
LOSING YOUR PARENTS WAS A TRAGEDY.
BUT YOU'VE BECOME SO OBSESSED WITH HOW THEY DIED, YOU'VE FORGOTTEN HOW THEY LIVED.
I KNEW YOUR FATHER.
HE MADE SOME TERRIBLE MISTAKES, BUT NEVER STOPPED TRYING TO ATONE FOR THEM.
HE BELIEVED IN REDEMPTION.
IN SECOND CHANCES!
YOU'RE BORING ME, LANG.
SABRECLAW, SHRED HIS JUGULAR.

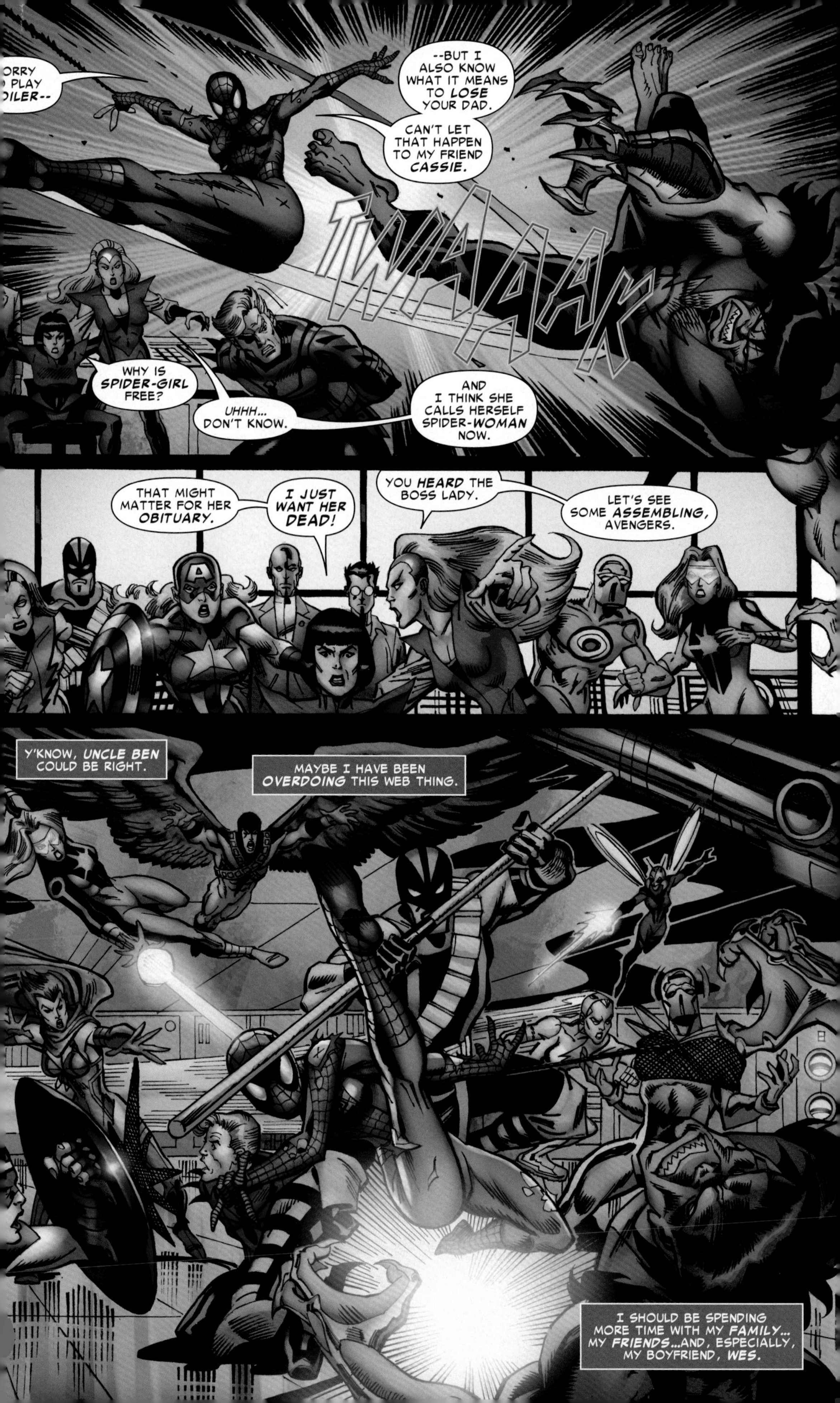

ORRY
O PLAY
OILER--
--BUT I ALSO KNOW WHAT IT MEANS TO LOSE YOUR DAD.
CAN'T LET THAT HAPPEN TO MY FRIEND CASSIE.
TWAAAK
WHY IS SPIDER-GIRL FREE?
UHHH... DON'T KNOW.
AND I THINK SHE CALLS HERSELF SPIDER-WOMAN NOW.
THAT MIGHT MATTER FOR HER OBITUARY.
I JUST WANT HER DEAD!
YOU HEARD THE BOSS LADY.
LET'S SEE SOME ASSEMBLING, AVENGERS.
Y'KNOW, UNCLE BEN COULD BE RIGHT.
MAYBE I HAVE BEEN OVERDOING THIS WEB THING.
I SHOULD BE SPENDING MORE TIME WITH MY FAMILY... MY FRIENDS...AND, ESPECIALLY, MY BOYFRIEND, WES.

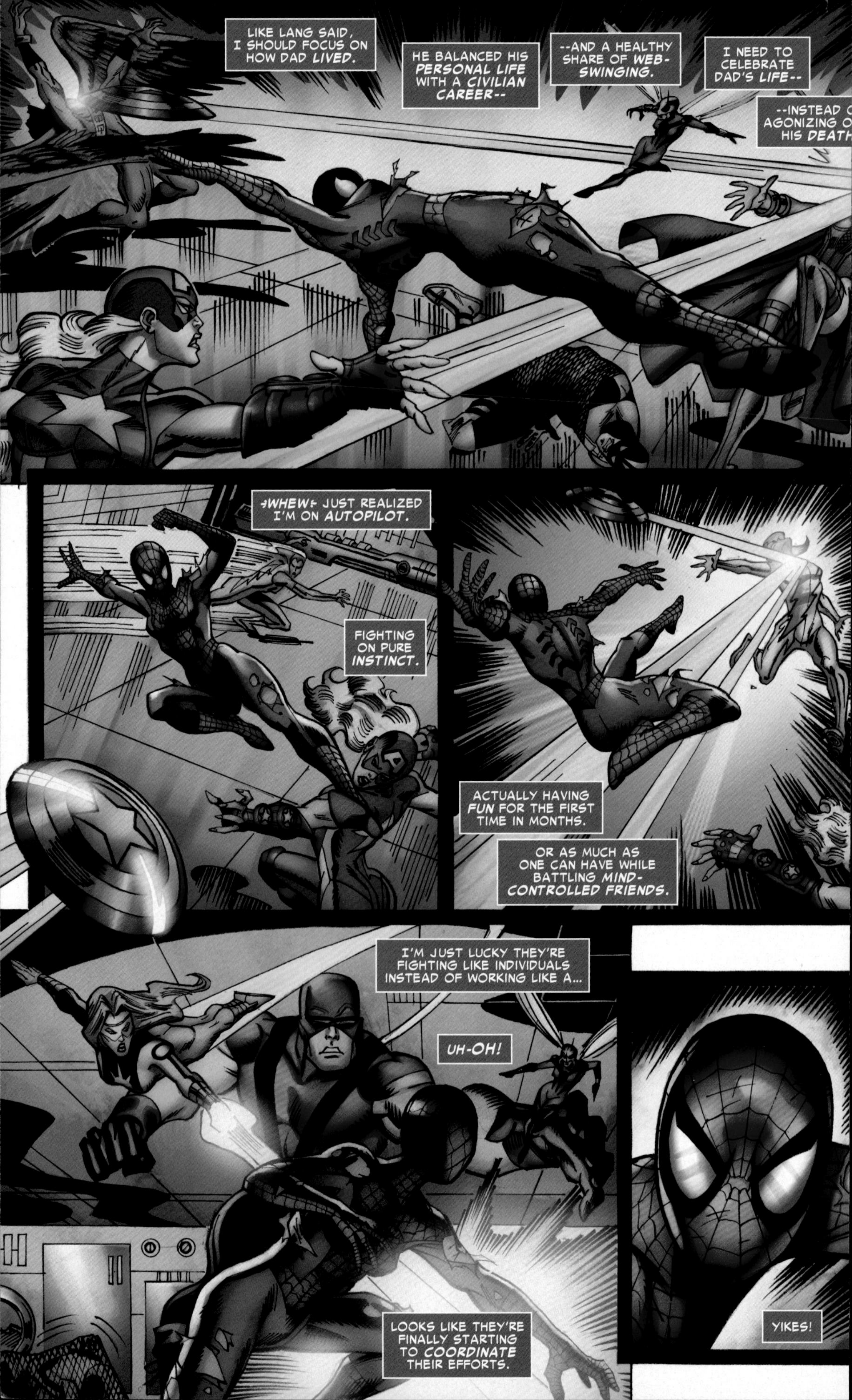
LIKE LANG SAID, I SHOULD FOCUS ON HOW DAD LIVED.
HE BALANCED HIS PERSONAL LIFE WITH A CIVILIAN CAREER--
--AND A HEALTHY SHARE OF WEB-SWINGING.
I NEED TO CELEBRATE DAD'S LIFE--
--INSTEAD O AGONIZING O HIS DEATH
-WHEW- JUST REALIZED I'M ON AUTOPILOT.
FIGHTING ON PURE INSTINCT.
ACTUALLY HAVING FUN FOR THE FIRST TIME IN MONTHS.
OR AS MUCH AS ONE CAN HAVE WHILE BATTLING MIND-CONTROLLED FRIENDS.
I'M JUST LUCKY THEY'RE FIGHTING LIKE INDIVIDUALS INSTEAD OF WORKING LIKE A...
UH-OH!
LOOKS LIKE THEY'RE FINALLY STARTING TO COORDINATE THEIR EFFORTS.
YIKES!

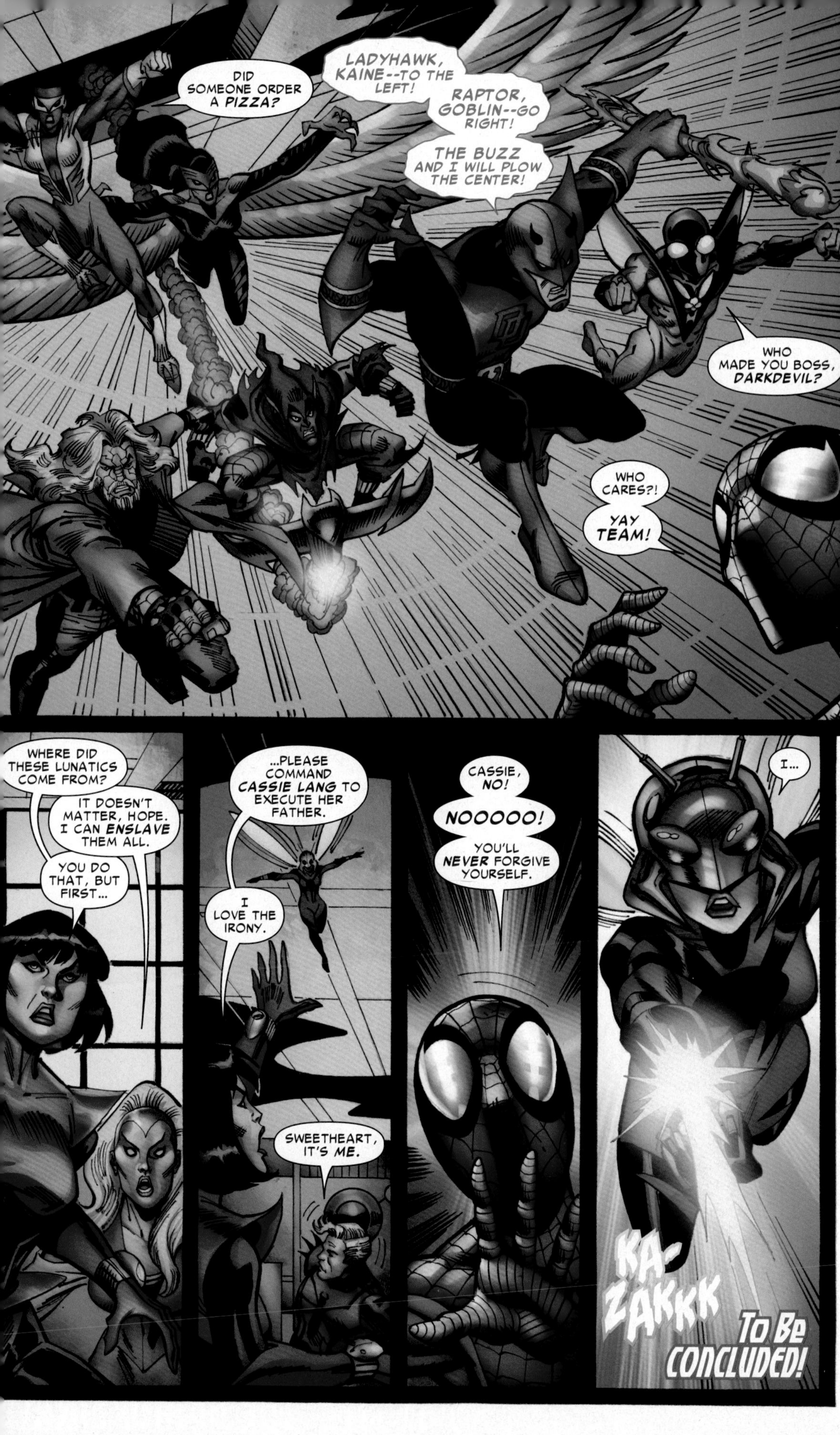
DID SOMEONE ORDER A PIZZA?
LADYHAWK, KAINE--TO THE LEFT!
RAPTOR, GOBLIN--GO RIGHT!
THE BUZZ AND I WILL PLOW THE CENTER!
WHO MADE YOU BOSS, DARKDEVIL?
WHO CARES?!
YAY TEAM!
WHERE DID THESE LUNATICS COME FROM?
IT DOESN'T MATTER, HOPE. I CAN ENSLAVE THEM ALL.
YOU DO THAT, BUT FIRST...
...PLEASE COMMAND CASSIE LANG TO EXECUTE HER FATHER.
I LOVE THE IRONY.
SWEETHEART, IT'S ME.
CASSIE, NO!
NOOOOO!
YOU'LL NEVER FORGIVE YOURSELF.
I...
KA-ZAKKK
To Be CONCLUDED!

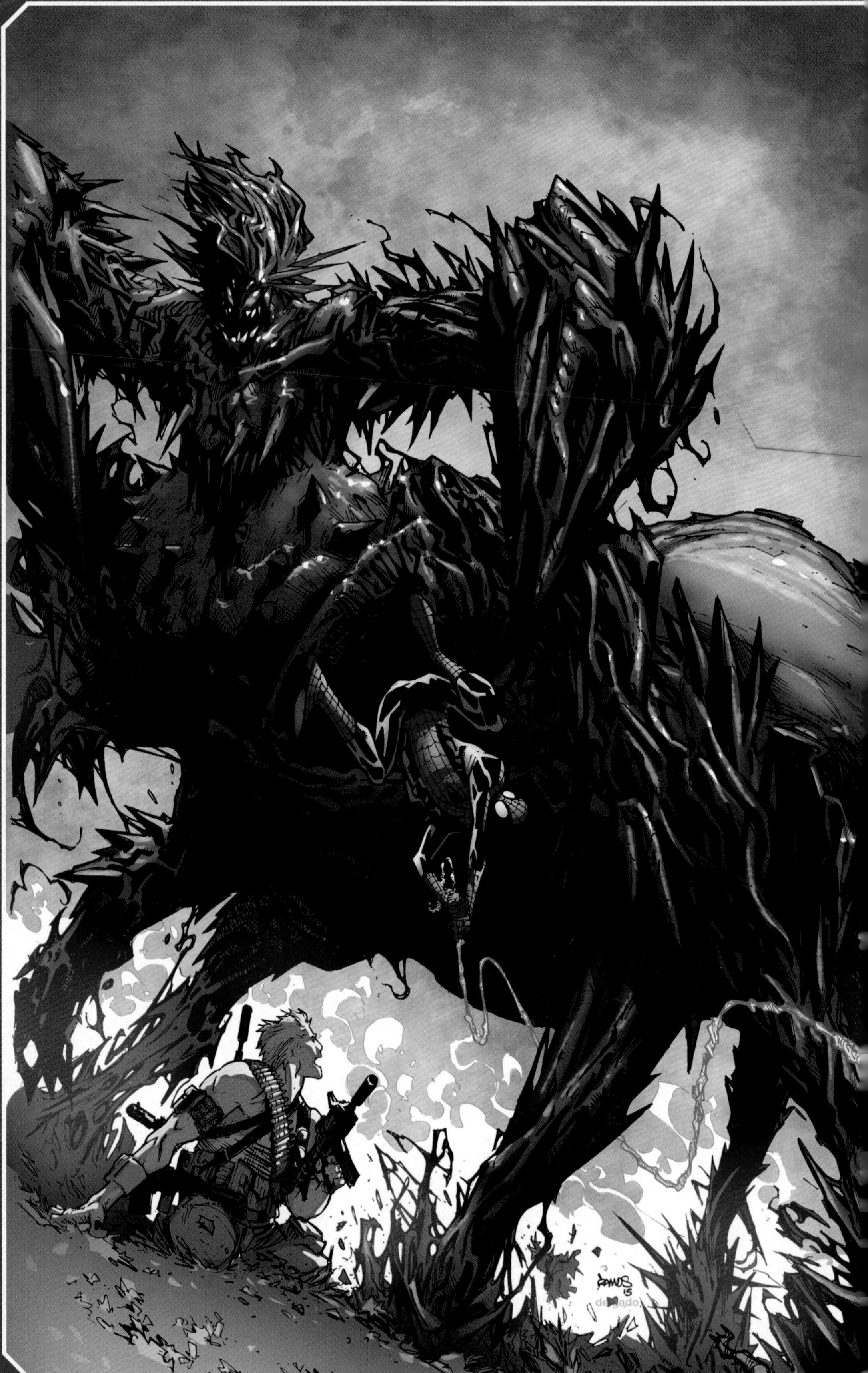
RAMOS 15
delgado

PART FIVE: THE GRAND FINALE

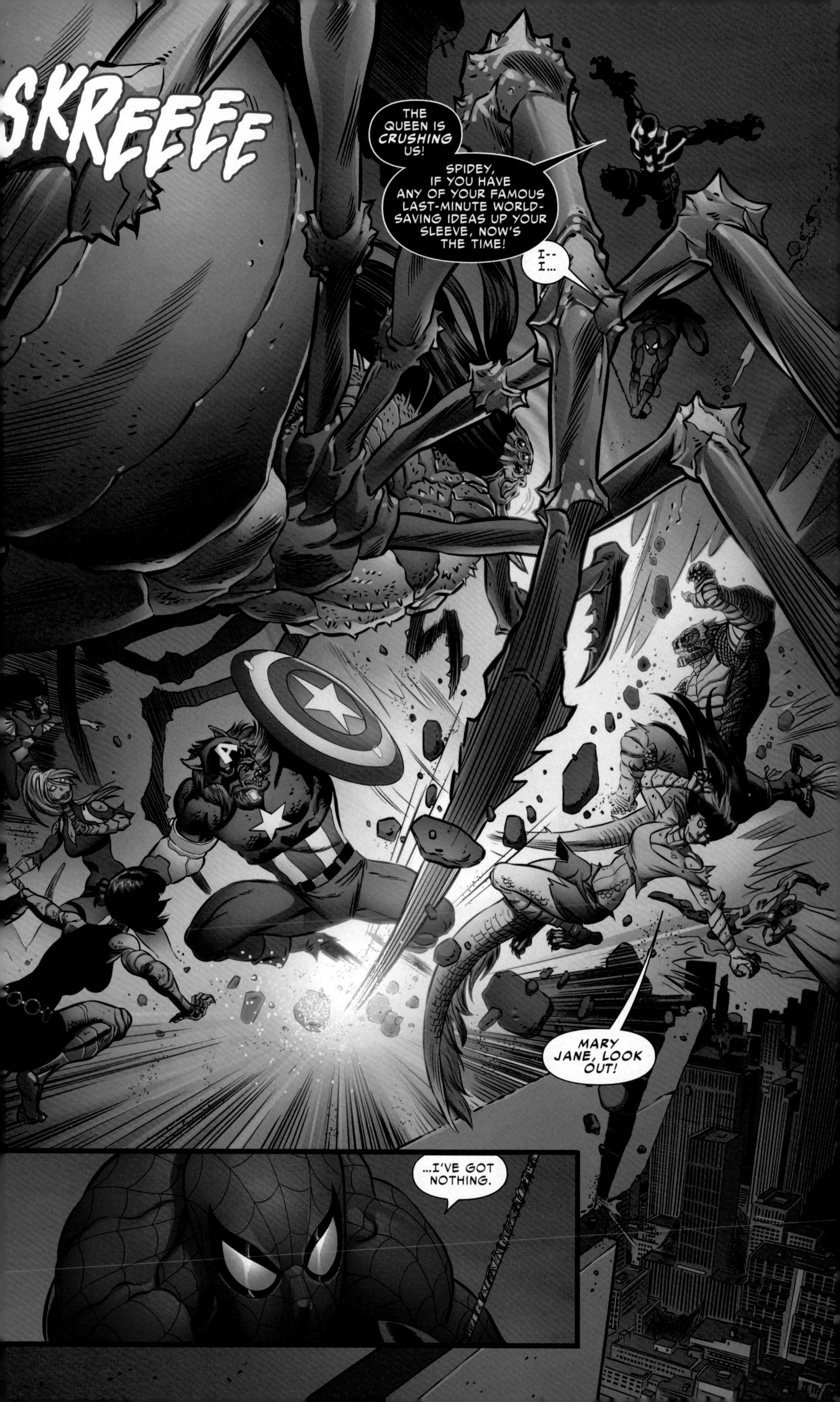
SKREEEE
THE QUEEN IS CRUSHING US!
SPIDEY, IF YOU HAVE ANY OF YOUR FAMOUS LAST-MINUTE WORLD-SAVING IDEAS UP YOUR SLEEVE, NOW'S THE TIME!
I-- I...
MARY JANE, LOOK OUT!
...I'VE GOT NOTHING.

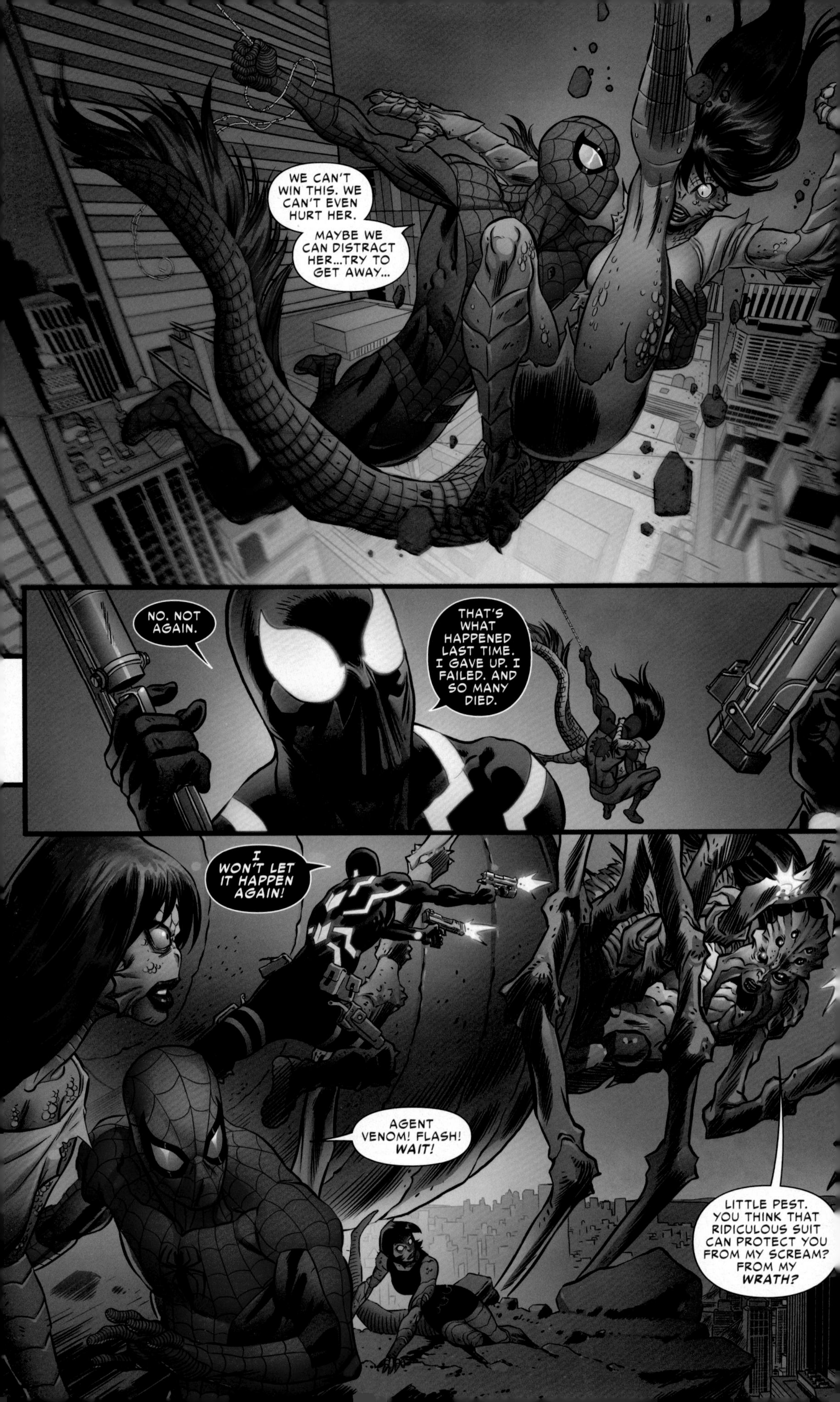
WE CAN'T WIN THIS. WE CAN'T EVEN HURT HER.
MAYBE WE CAN DISTRACT HER...TRY TO GET AWAY...
NO. NOT AGAIN.
THAT'S WHAT HAPPENED LAST TIME. I GAVE UP. I FAILED. AND SO MANY DIED.
I WON'T LET IT HAPPEN AGAIN!
AGENT VENOM! FLASH! *WAIT!*
LITTLE PEST. YOU THINK THAT RIDICULOUS SUIT CAN PROTECT YOU FROM MY SCREAM? FROM MY *WRATH?*

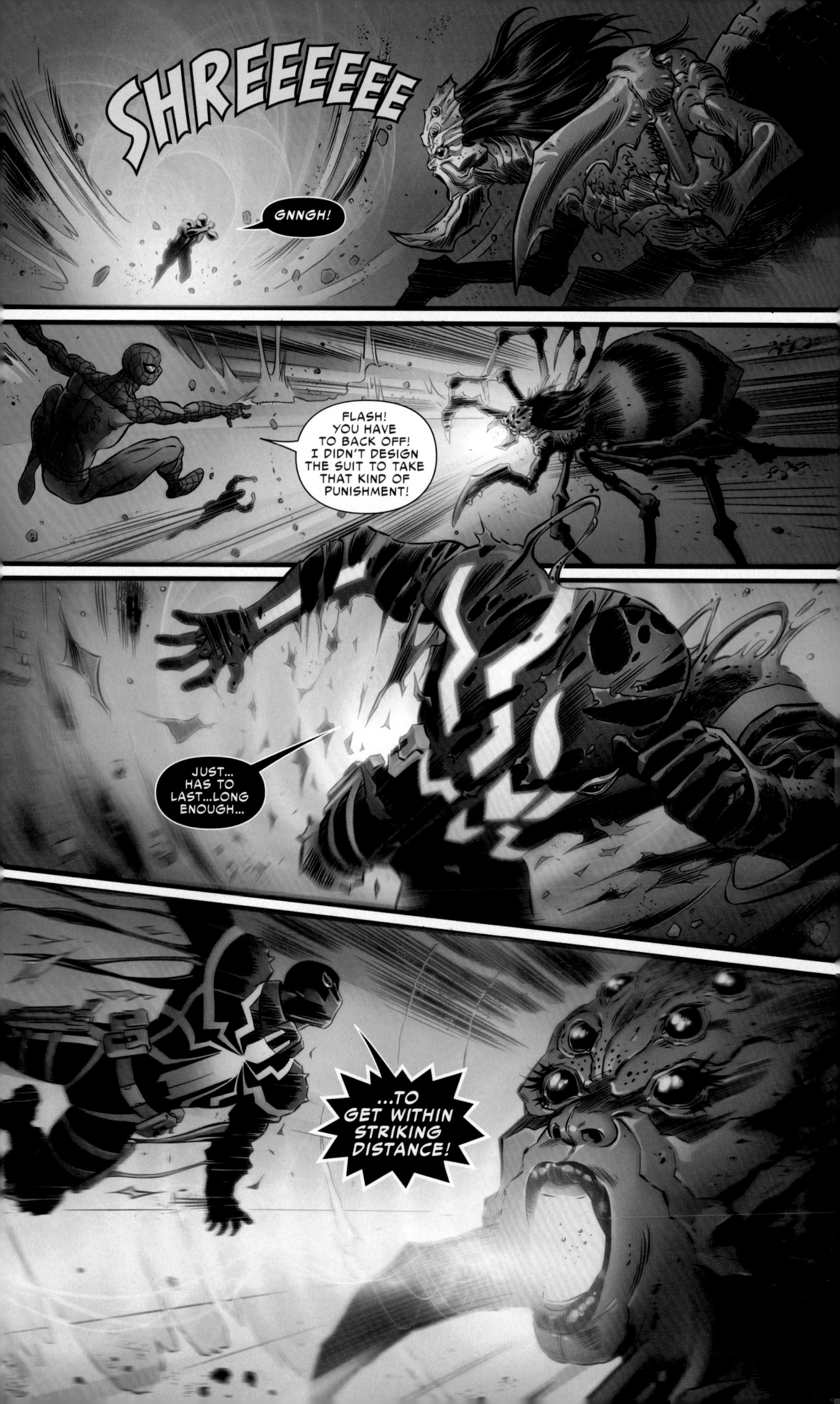
SHREEEEEE
GNNGH!
FLASH! YOU HAVE TO BACK OFF! I DIDN'T DESIGN THE SUIT TO TAKE THAT KIND OF PUNISHMENT!
JUST... HAS TO LAST...LONG ENOUGH...
...TO GET WITHIN STRIKING DISTANCE!

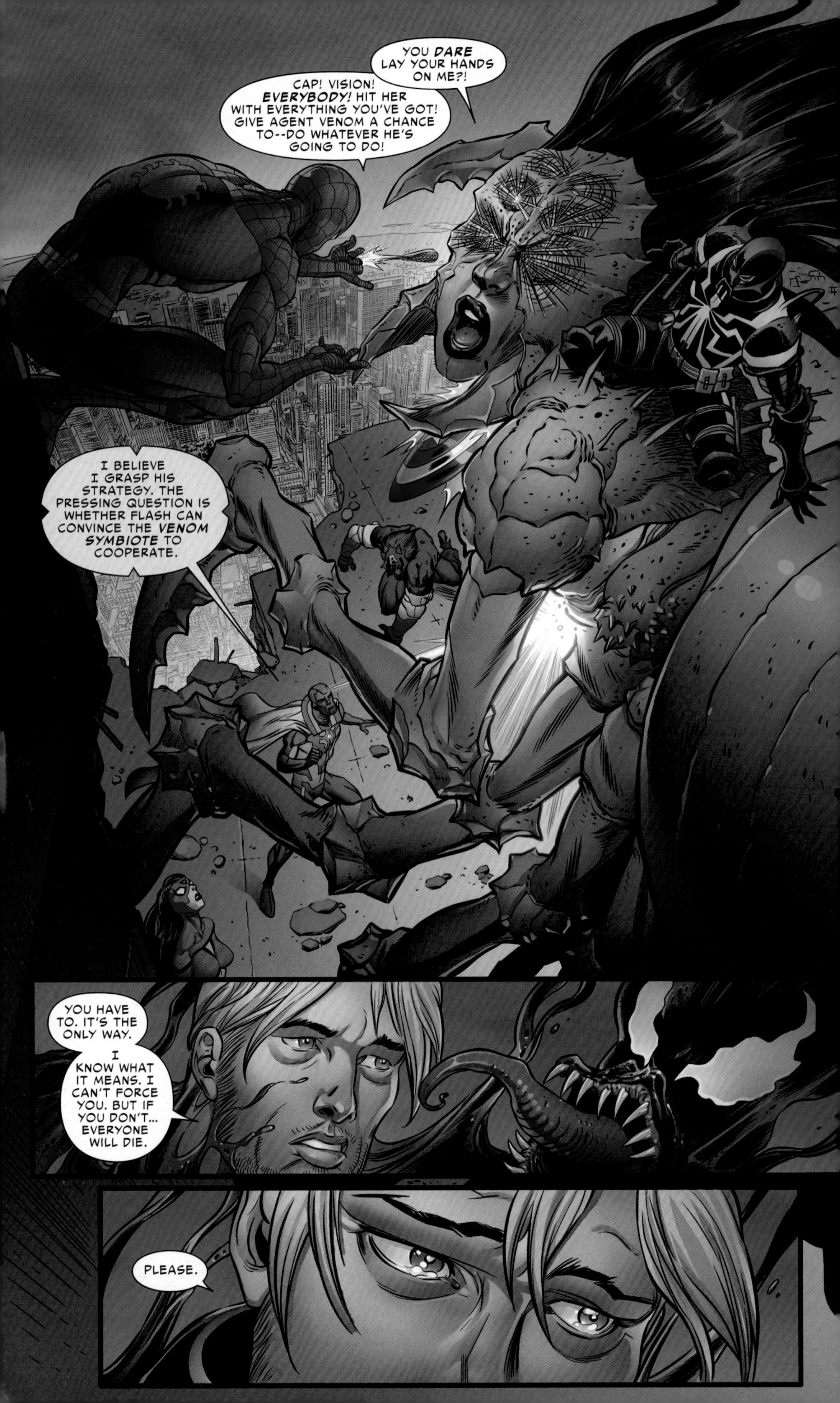
CAP! VISION! EVERYBODY! HIT HER WITH EVERYTHING YOU'VE GOT! GIVE AGENT VENOM A CHANCE TO--DO WHATEVER HE'S GOING TO DO!
YOU DARE LAY YOUR HANDS ON ME?!
I BELIEVE I GRASP HIS STRATEGY. THE PRESSING QUESTION IS WHETHER FLASH CAN CONVINCE THE VENOM SYMBIOTE TO COOPERATE.
YOU HAVE TO. IT'S THE ONLY WAY.
I KNOW WHAT IT MEANS. I CAN'T FORCE YOU. BUT IF YOU DON'T... EVERYONE WILL DIE.
PLEASE.

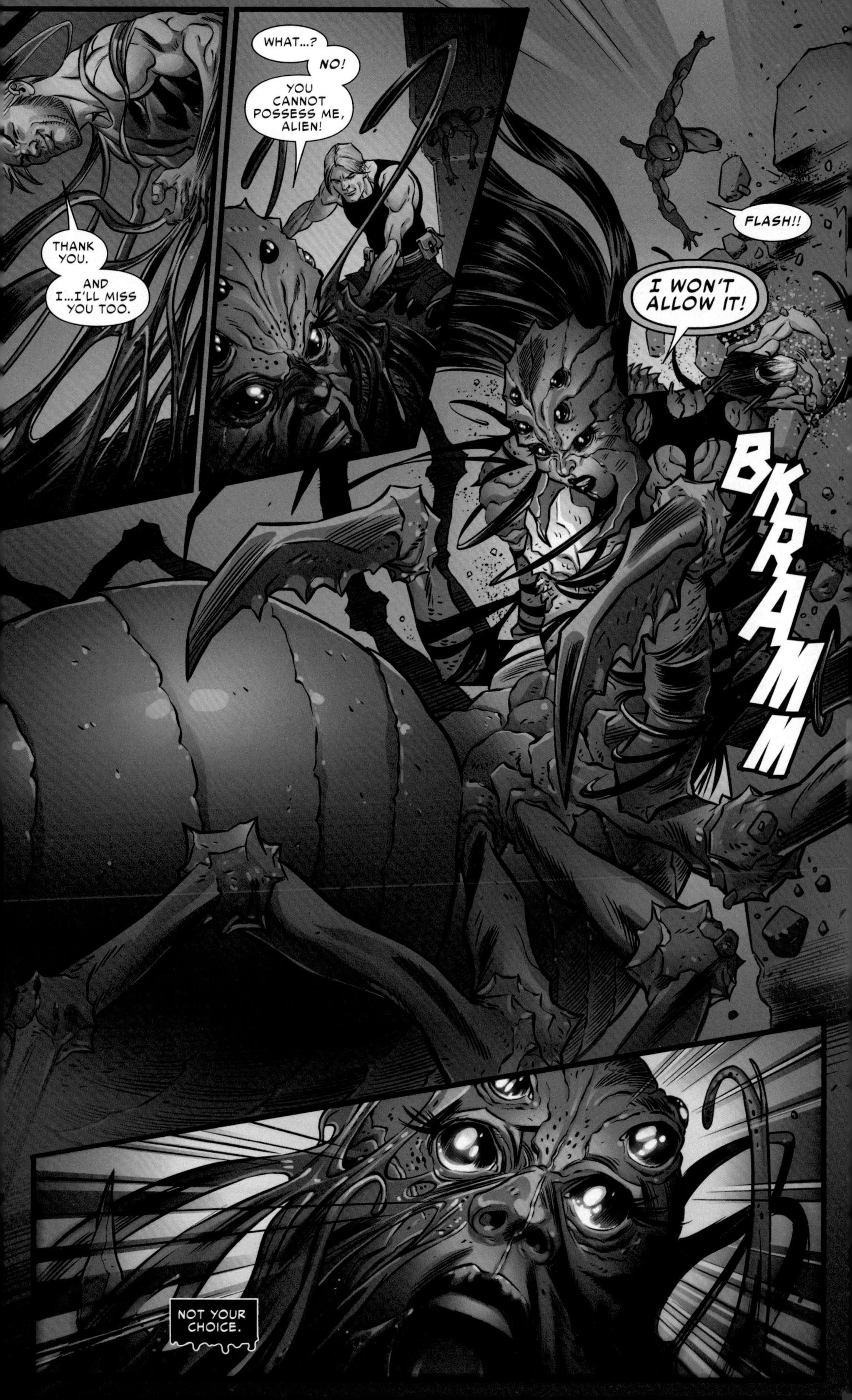
THANK YOU.
AND I...I'LL MISS YOU TOO.
WHAT...?
NO!
YOU CANNOT POSSESS ME, ALIEN!
FLASH!!
I WON'T ALLOW IT!
BKRAMM
NOT YOUR CHOICE.

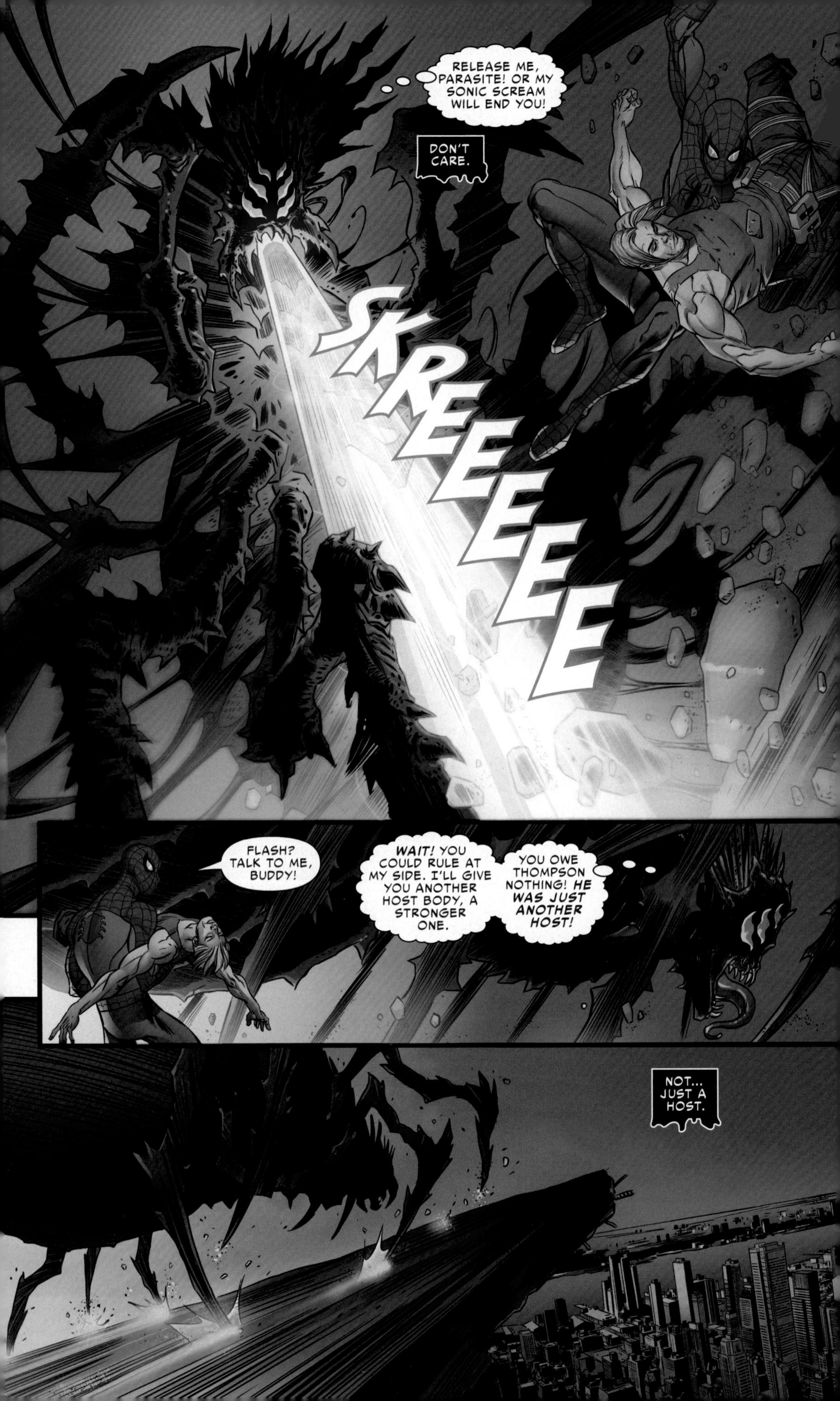
RELEASE ME, PARASITE! OR MY SONIC SCREAM WILL END YOU!
DON'T CARE.
SKREEEEEEE
FLASH? TALK TO ME, BUDDY!
WAIT! YOU COULD RULE AT MY SIDE. I'LL GIVE YOU ANOTHER HOST BODY, A STRONGER ONE.
YOU OWE THOMPSON NOTHING! *HE WAS JUST ANOTHER HOST!*
NOT... JUST A HOST.

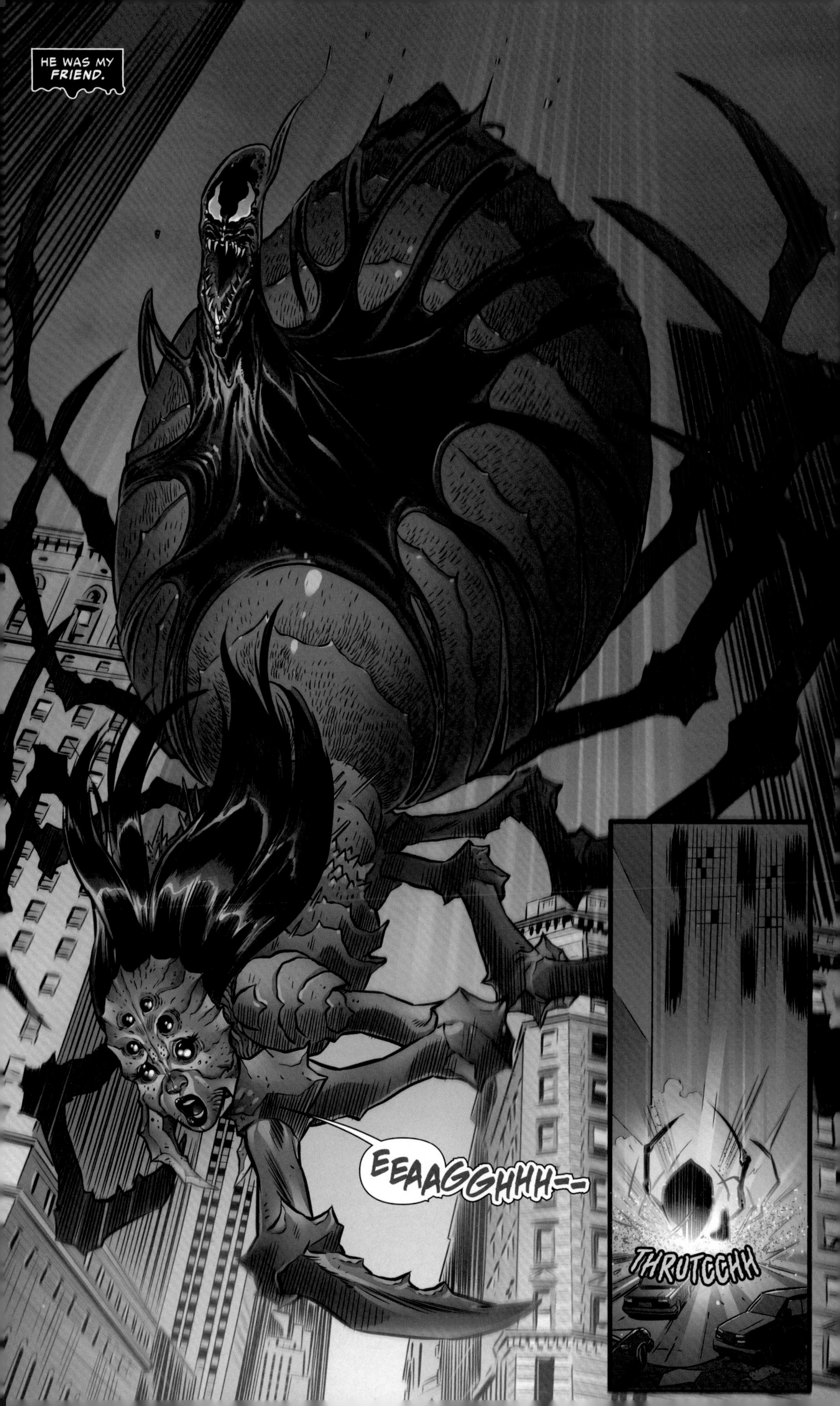

HE WAS MY FRIEND.
EEAAGGHHH--
THRUTCCHH

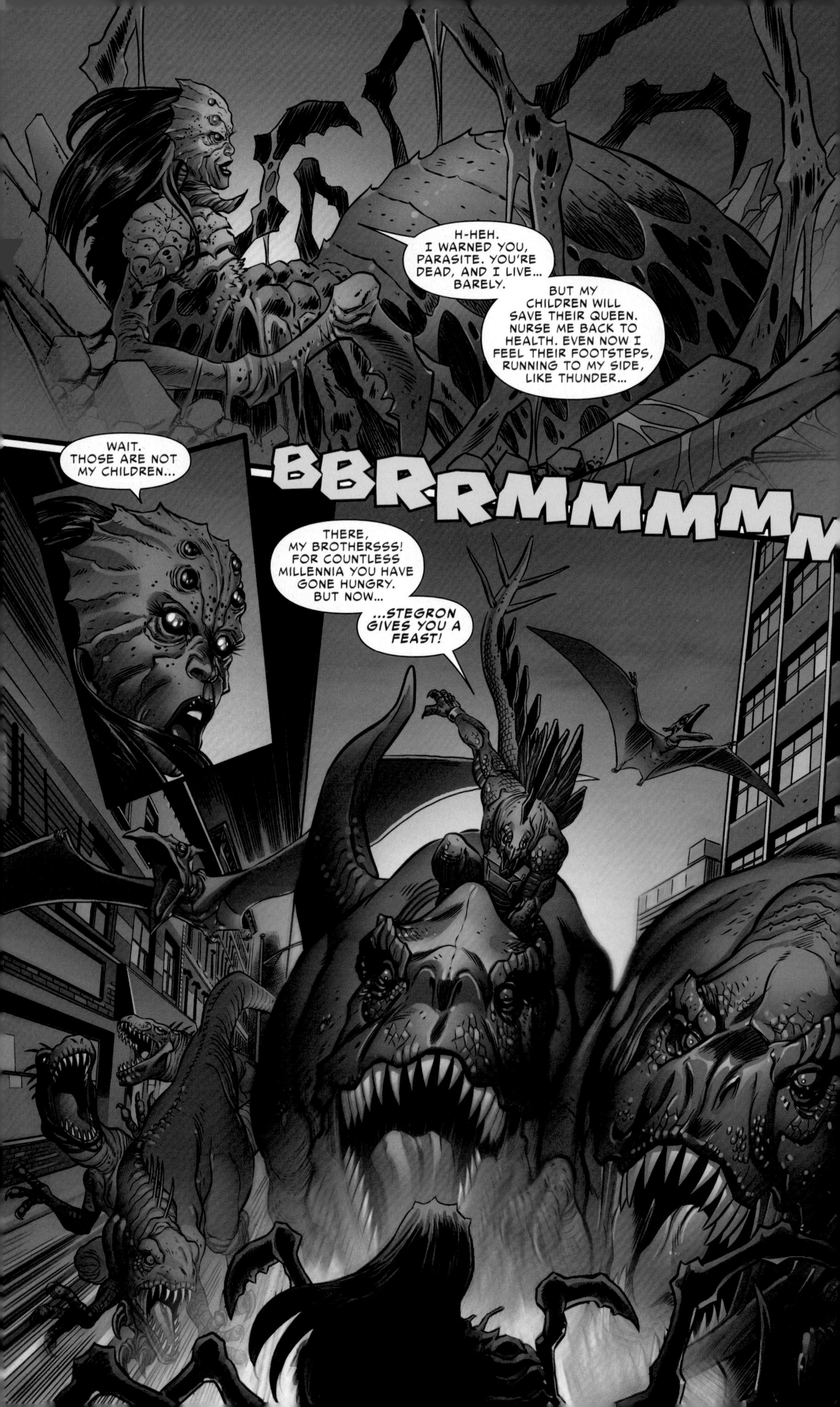

H-HEH. I WARNED YOU, PARASITE. YOU'RE DEAD, AND I LIVE... BARELY.
BUT MY CHILDREN WILL SAVE THEIR QUEEN. NURSE ME BACK TO HEALTH. EVEN NOW I FEEL THEIR FOOTSTEPS, RUNNING TO MY SIDE, LIKE THUNDER...
WAIT. THOSE ARE NOT MY CHILDREN...
BBRRMMMMMMM
THERE, MY BROTHERSSS! FOR COUNTLESS MILLENNIA YOU HAVE GONE HUNGRY. BUT NOW...
...STEGRON GIVES YOU A FEAST!

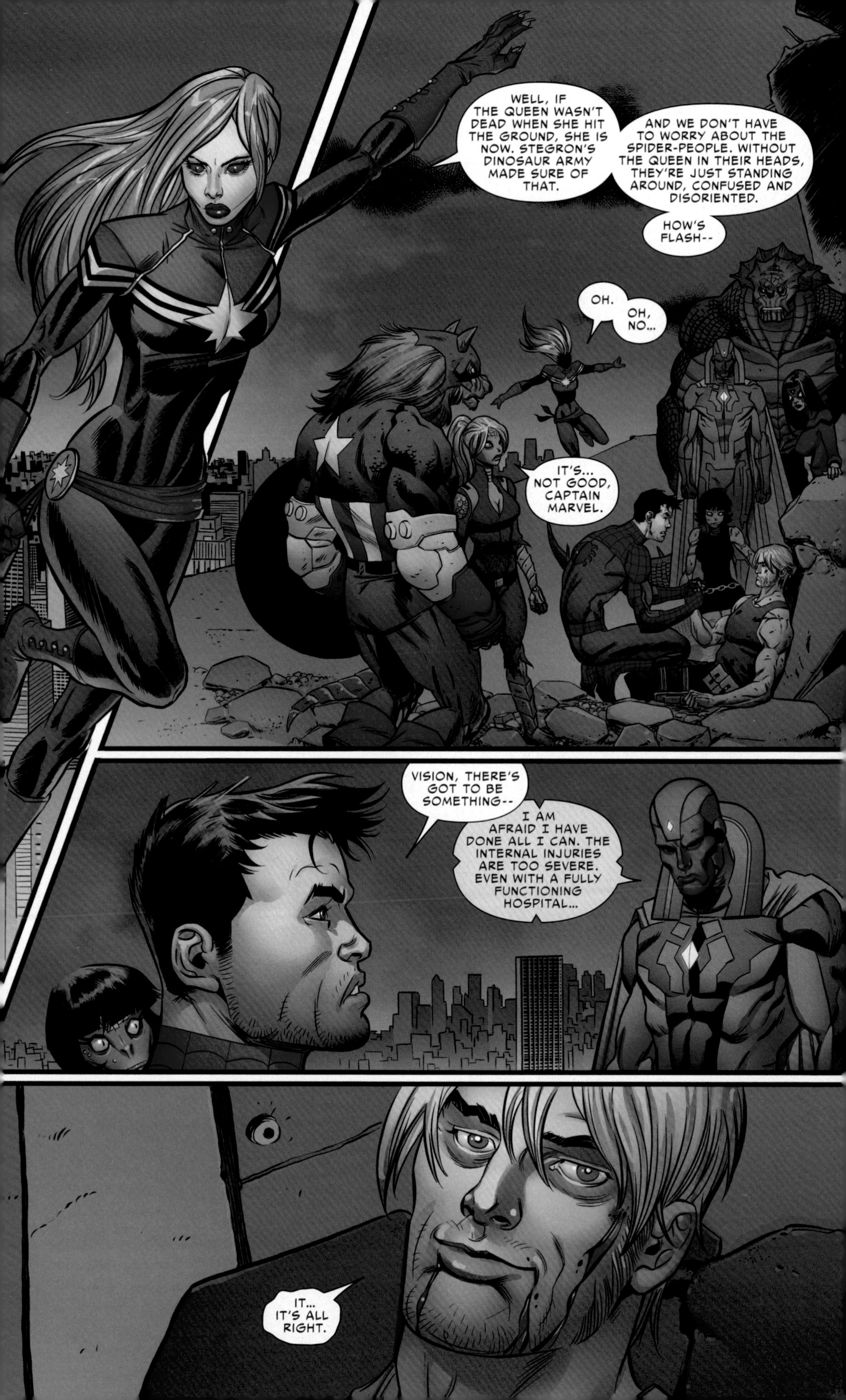
WELL, IF THE QUEEN WASN'T DEAD WHEN SHE HIT THE GROUND, SHE IS NOW. STEGRON'S DINOSAUR ARMY MADE SURE OF THAT.
AND WE DON'T HAVE TO WORRY ABOUT THE SPIDER-PEOPLE. WITHOUT THE QUEEN IN THEIR HEADS, THEY'RE JUST STANDING AROUND, CONFUSED AND DISORIENTED.
HOW'S FLASH--
OH.
OH, NO...
IT'S... NOT GOOD, CAPTAIN MARVEL.
VISION, THERE'S GOT TO BE SOMETHING--
I AM AFRAID I HAVE DONE ALL I CAN. THE INTERNAL INJURIES ARE TOO SEVERE. EVEN WITH A FULLY FUNCTIONING HOSPITAL...
IT... IT'S ALL RIGHT.

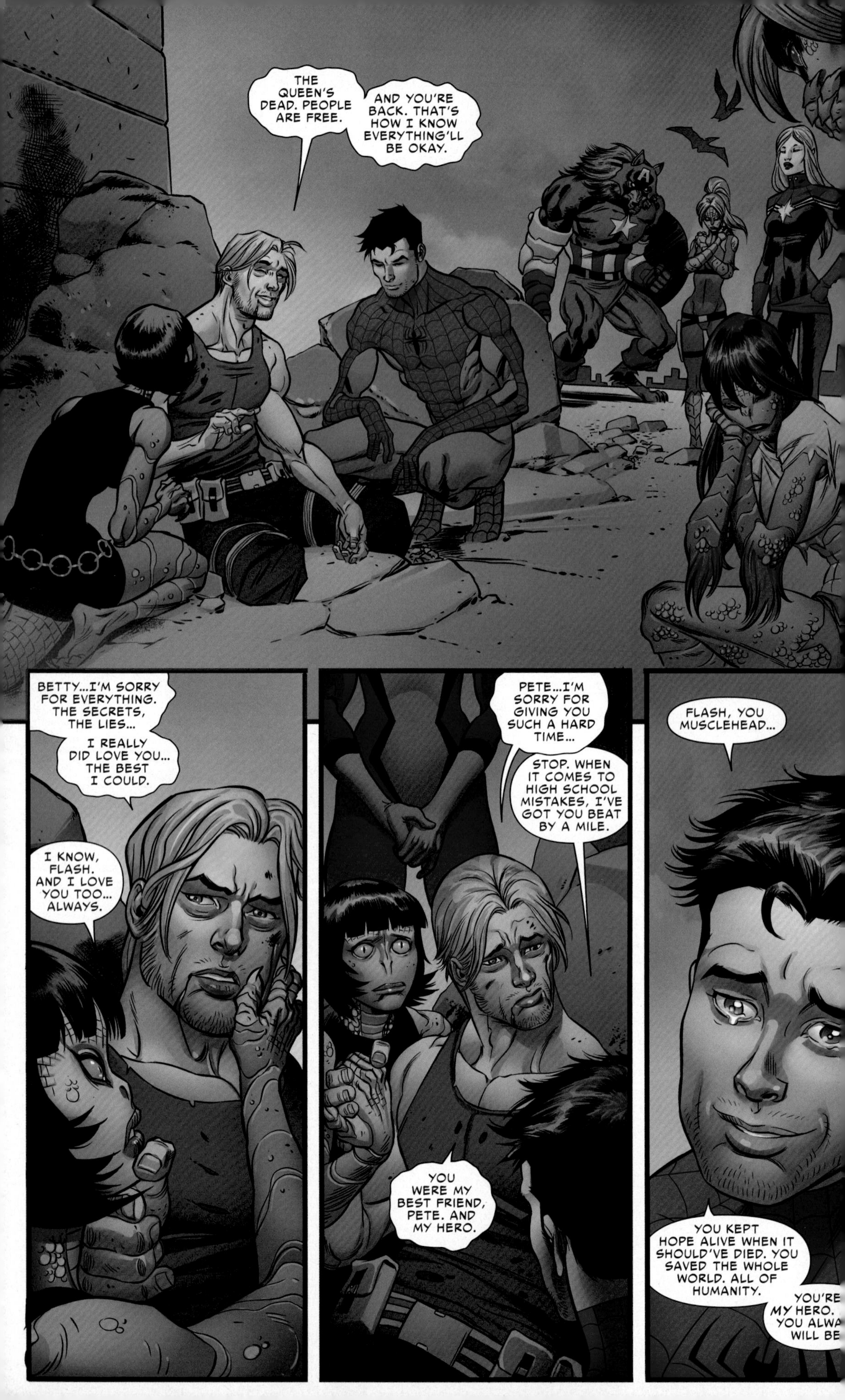
THE QUEEN'S DEAD. PEOPLE ARE FREE.
AND YOU'RE BACK. THAT'S HOW I KNOW EVERYTHING'LL BE OKAY.
BETTY...I'M SORRY FOR EVERYTHING. THE SECRETS, THE LIES...
I REALLY DID LOVE YOU... THE BEST I COULD.
I KNOW, FLASH. AND I LOVE YOU TOO... ALWAYS.
PETE...I'M SORRY FOR GIVING YOU SUCH A HARD TIME...
STOP. WHEN IT COMES TO HIGH SCHOOL MISTAKES, I'VE GOT YOU BEAT BY A MILE.
YOU WERE MY BEST FRIEND, PETE. AND MY HERO.
FLASH, YOU MUSCLEHEAD...
YOU KEPT HOPE ALIVE WHEN IT SHOULD'VE DIED. YOU SAVED THE WHOLE WORLD. ALL OF HUMANITY.
YOU'RE MY HERO.

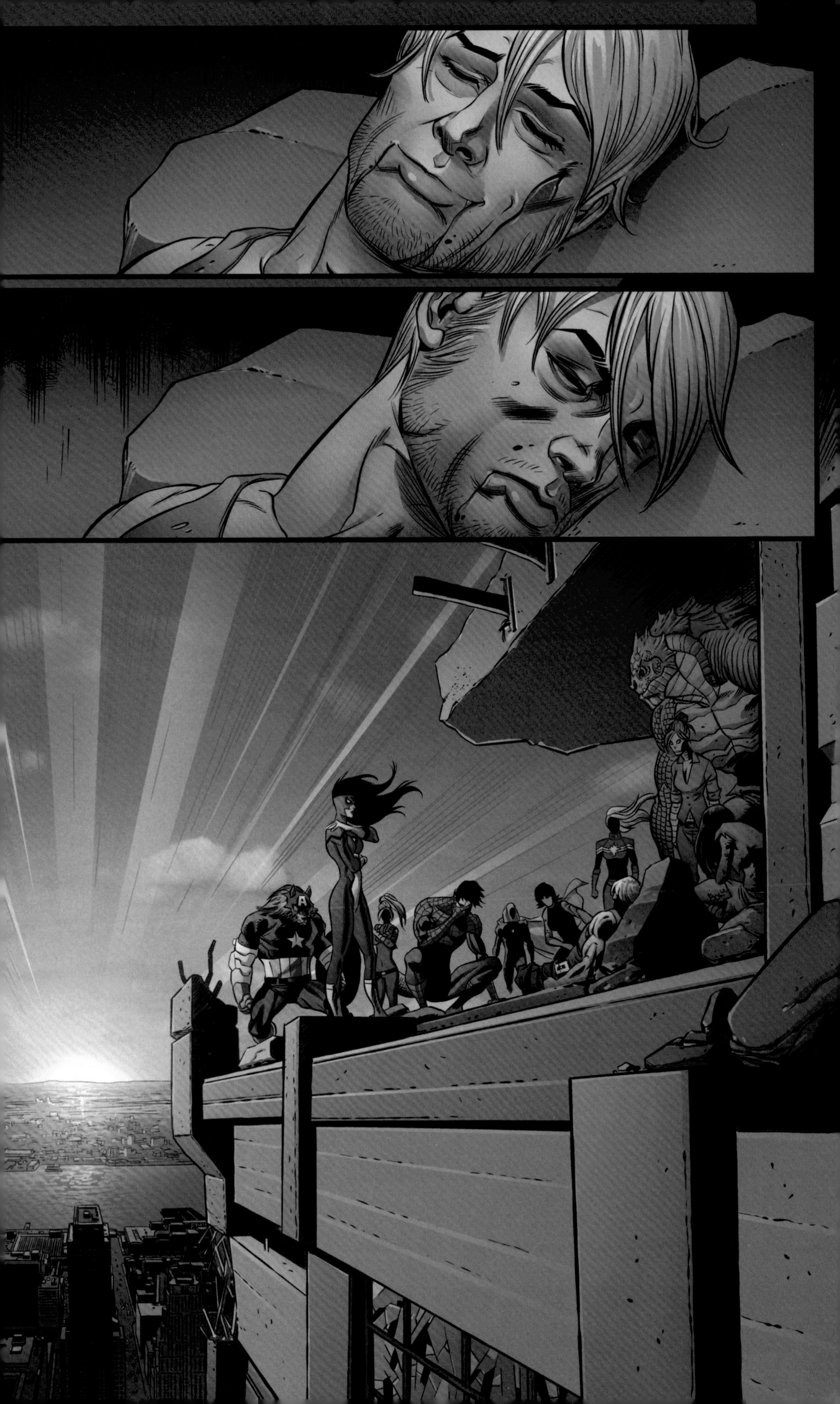

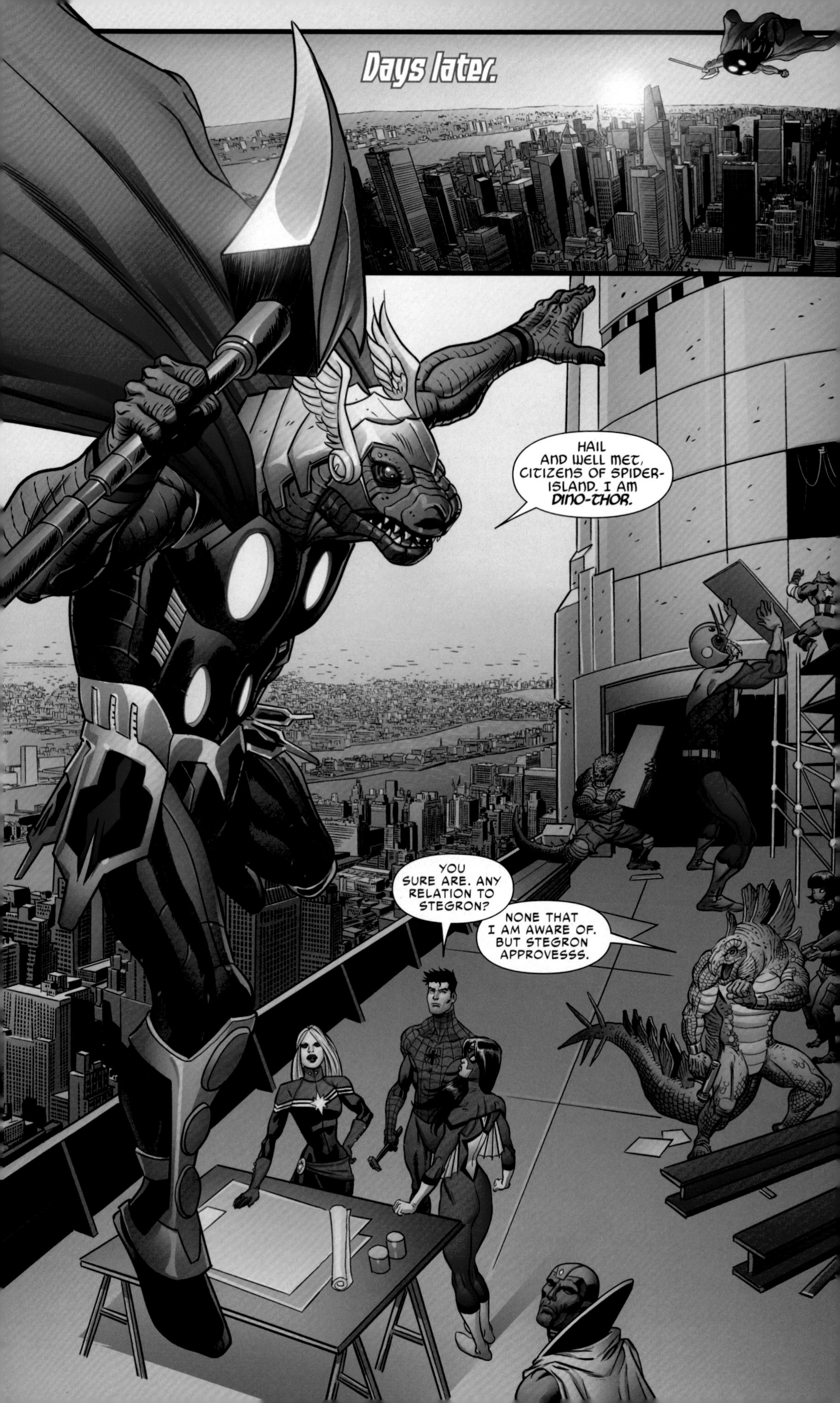
Days later.
HAIL AND WELL MET, CITIZENS OF SPIDER-ISLAND. I AM DINO-THOR.
YOU SURE ARE. ANY RELATION TO STEGRON?
NONE THAT I AM AWARE OF. BUT STEGRON APPROVESSS.

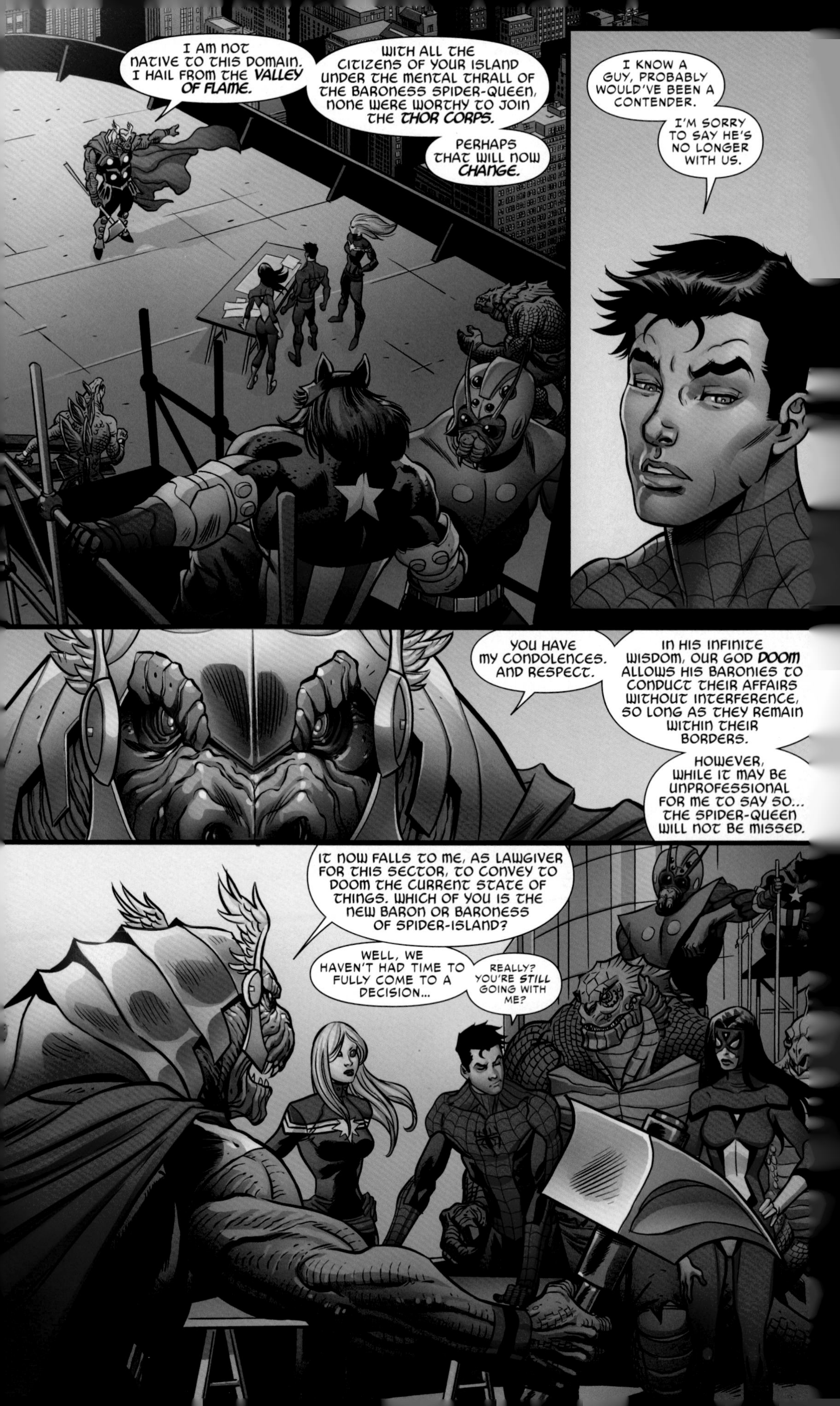
I AM NOT NATIVE TO THIS DOMAIN. I HAIL FROM THE *VALLEY OF FLAME.*
WITH ALL THE CITIZENS OF YOUR ISLAND UNDER THE MENTAL THRALL OF THE BARONESS SPIDER-QUEEN, NONE WERE WORTHY TO JOIN THE *THOR CORPS.*
PERHAPS THAT WILL NOW *CHANGE.*
I KNOW A GUY, PROBABLY WOULD'VE BEEN A CONTENDER.
I'M SORRY TO SAY HE'S NO LONGER WITH US.
YOU HAVE MY CONDOLENCES. AND RESPECT.
IN HIS INFINITE WISDOM, OUR GOD *DOOM* ALLOWS HIS BARONIES TO CONDUCT THEIR AFFAIRS WITHOUT INTERFERENCE, SO LONG AS THEY REMAIN WITHIN THEIR BORDERS.
HOWEVER, WHILE IT MAY BE UNPROFESSIONAL FOR ME TO SAY SO... THE SPIDER-QUEEN WILL NOT BE MISSED.
IT NOW FALLS TO ME, AS LAWGIVER FOR THIS SECTOR, TO CONVEY TO DOOM THE CURRENT STATE OF THINGS. WHICH OF YOU IS THE NEW BARON OR BARONESS OF SPIDER-ISLAND?
WELL, WE HAVEN'T HAD TIME TO FULLY COME TO A DECISION...
REALLY? YOU'RE *STILL* GOING WITH ME?

OKAY. I'M, *UH,* PETER PARKER. SPIDER-MAN.

THEN HAIL, BARON SPIDER-MAN OF SPIDER-ISLAND.

YEAH. *UM,* WE MAY WANT TO RENAME THE PLACE, TOO.

SEE, THE QUEEN MADE EVERYONE INTO SPIDER-PEOPLE. *WITHOUT THEIR CONSENT.*

WE COULDN'T CHANGE THEM BACK. BUT WE COULD AT LEAST GIVE THEM A *CHOICE.*

SOME OF US ELECTED TO REMAIN ARACHNO-HYBRIDS. THE METHODS OF VISUAL PERCEPTION ALONE ARE DOWNRIGHT REVELATORY.

GIANT-MAN ISN'... THE ONLY O... A SURPRIS... NUMBER O... PEOPLE HA... GOTTEN U... TO IT.

OTHERS CHOSE TO BECOME WEREWOLVES, VAMPIRES, LIZARD-PEOPLE, DINOSAUR FOLKS...

WE JUST FOUND OUT *BIRD-PEOPLE* ARE A THING. THE QUEEN HAD A GUY NAMED *RED RAVEN* LOCKED UP IN HER DUNGEONS...

POINT IS, EVERYONE GETS TO DECIDE FOR THEMSELVES. SO MAYBE WE JUST CALL IT "MANHATTAN."

THERE IS ALREADY A MANHATTAN.

REALLY? THAT'S...WEIRD. WELL... MAYBE NAME IT AFTER THE GUY WHO SAVED US. "FLASH CITY"? "THOMPSONVILLE"?

WE OWE HIM EVERYTHING. I WANT TO DO RIGHT BY HIM.

PETER... CAN PROM... YOU THIS...

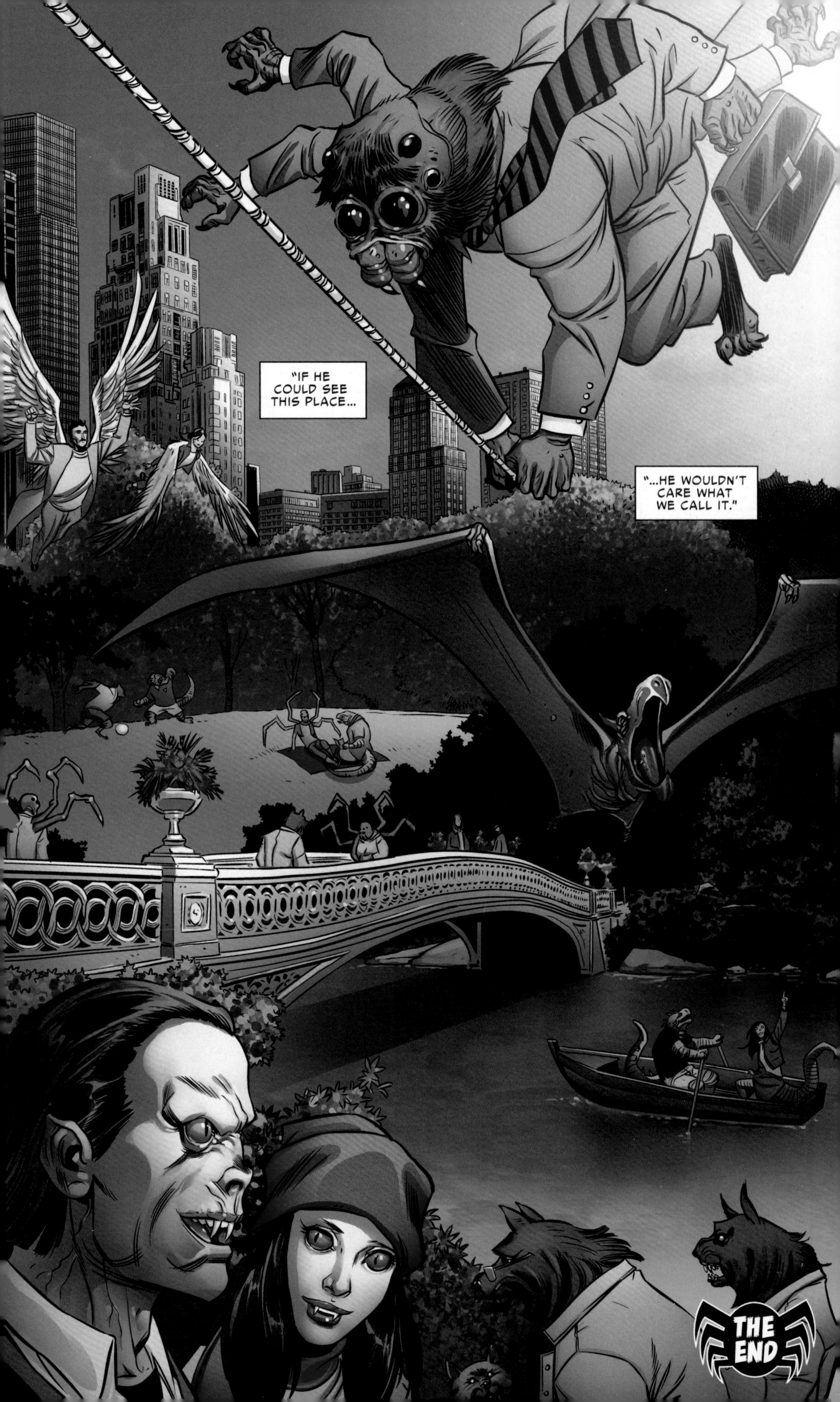
"IF HE COULD SEE THIS PLACE...
"...HE WOULDN'T CARE WHAT WE CALL IT."
THE END

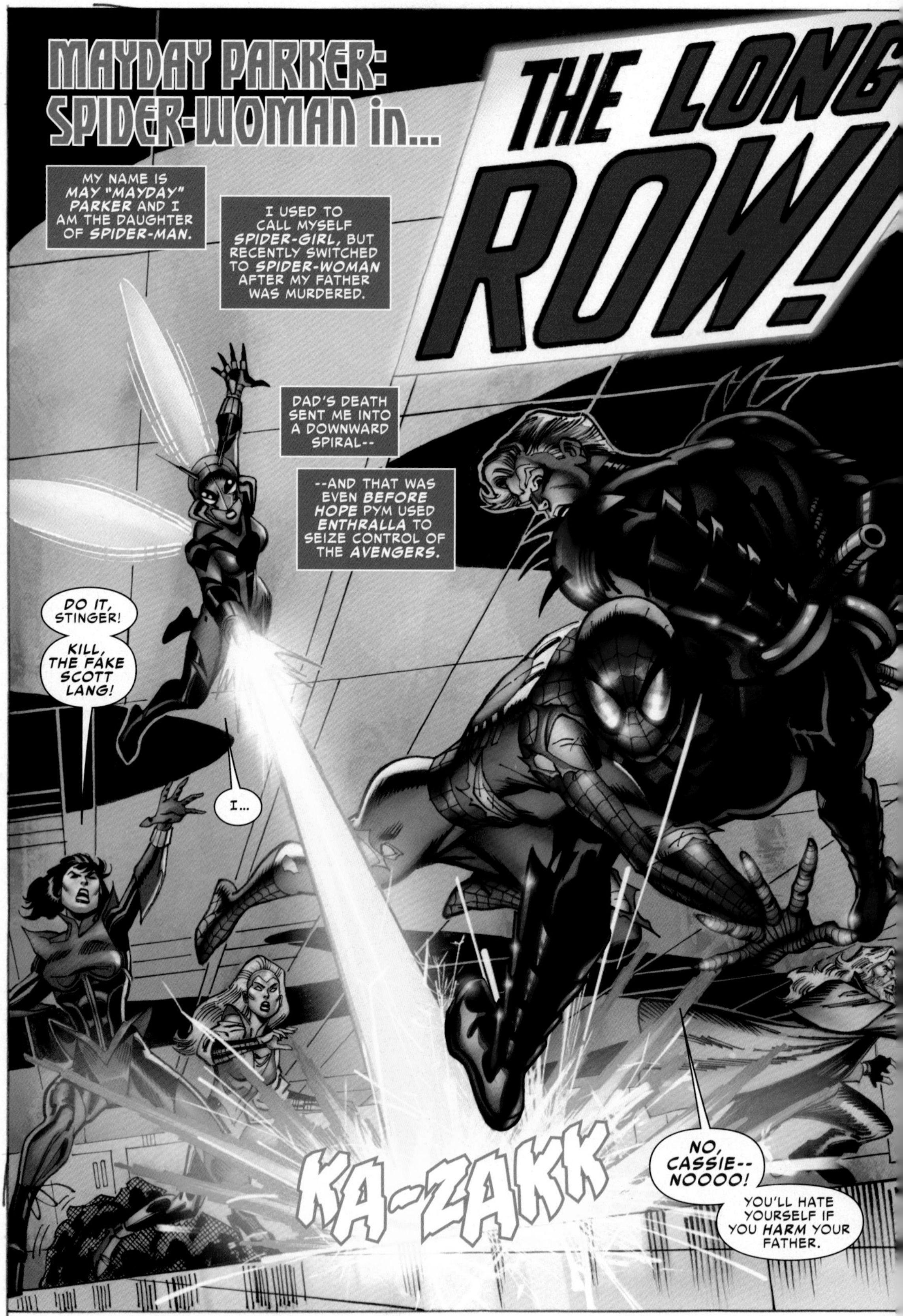
MAYDAY PARKER: SPIDER-WOMAN in...
THE LONG ROW!
MY NAME IS MAY "MAYDAY" PARKER AND I AM THE DAUGHTER OF SPIDER-MAN.
I USED TO CALL MYSELF SPIDER-GIRL, BUT RECENTLY SWITCHED TO SPIDER-WOMAN AFTER MY FATHER WAS MURDERED.
DAD'S DEATH SENT ME INTO A DOWNWARD SPIRAL--
--AND THAT WAS EVEN BEFORE HOPE PYM USED ENTHRALLA TO SEIZE CONTROL OF THE AVENGERS.
DO IT, STINGER!
KILL THE FAKE SCOTT LANG!
I...
KA-ZAKK
NO, CASSIE-- NOOOO!
YOU'LL HATE YOURSELF IF YOU HARM YOUR FATHER.

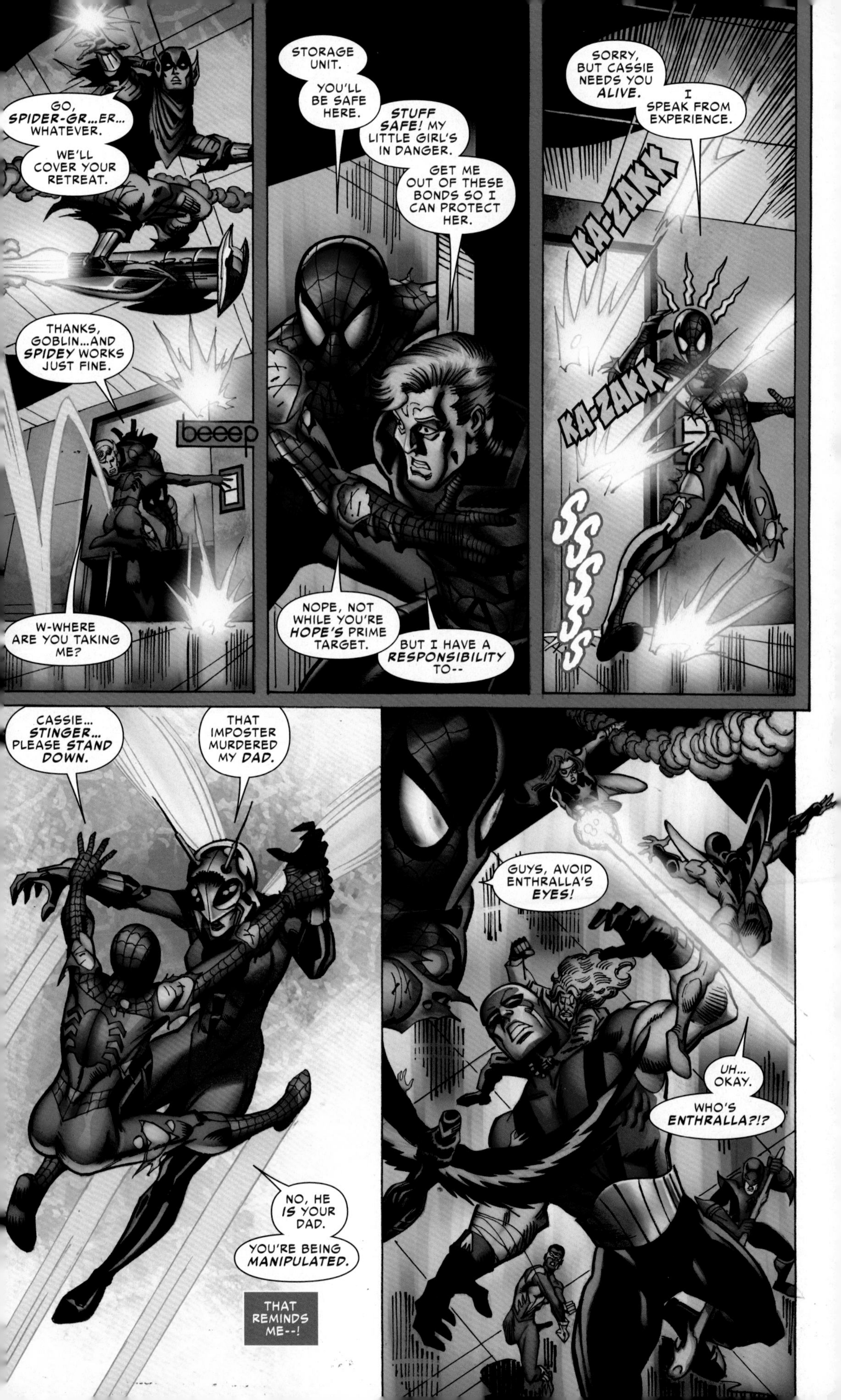
GO, SPIDER-GR...ER... WHATEVER.
WE'LL COVER YOUR RETREAT.
THANKS, GOBLIN...AND SPIDEY WORKS JUST FINE.
beeep
W-WHERE ARE YOU TAKING ME?
STORAGE UNIT.
YOU'LL BE SAFE HERE.
STUFF SAFE! MY LITTLE GIRL'S IN DANGER.
GET ME OUT OF THESE BONDS SO I CAN PROTECT HER.
NOPE, NOT WHILE YOU'RE HOPE'S PRIME TARGET.
BUT I HAVE A RESPONSIBILITY TO--
SORRY, BUT CASSIE NEEDS YOU ALIVE.
I SPEAK FROM EXPERIENCE.
KA-ZAKK
KA-ZAKK
SSSSSS
CASSIE... STINGER... PLEASE STAND DOWN.
THAT IMPOSTER MURDERED MY DAD.
NO, HE IS YOUR DAD.
YOU'RE BEING MANIPULATED.
THAT REMINDS ME--!
GUYS, AVOID ENTHRALLA'S EYES!
UH... OKAY.
WHO'S ENTHRALLA?!?

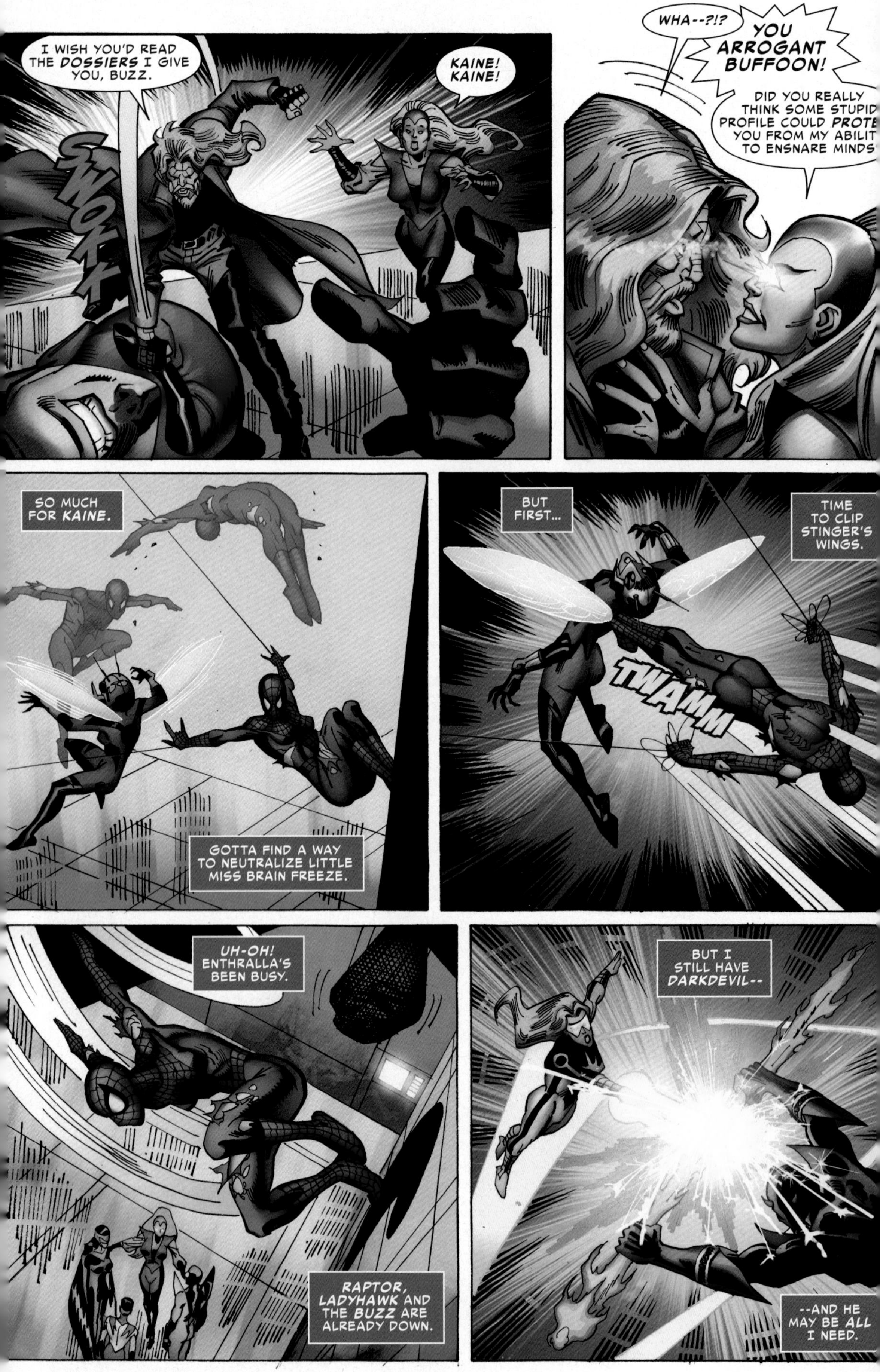

I WISH YOU'D READ THE DOSSIERS I GIVE YOU, BUZZ.
SHOKK
KAINE! KAINE!
WHA--?!?
YOU ARROGANT BUFFOON!
DID YOU REALLY THINK SOME STUPID PROFILE COULD PROTE YOU FROM MY ABILIT TO ENSNARE MINDS
SO MUCH FOR KAINE.
GOTTA FIND A WAY TO NEUTRALIZE LITTLE MISS BRAIN FREEZE.
BUT FIRST...
TIME TO CLIP STINGER'S WINGS.
TWAMM
UH-OH! ENTHRALLA'S BEEN BUSY.
RAPTOR, LADYHAWK AND THE BUZZ ARE ALREADY DOWN.
BUT I STILL HAVE DARKDEVIL--
--AND HE MAY BE ALL I NEED.

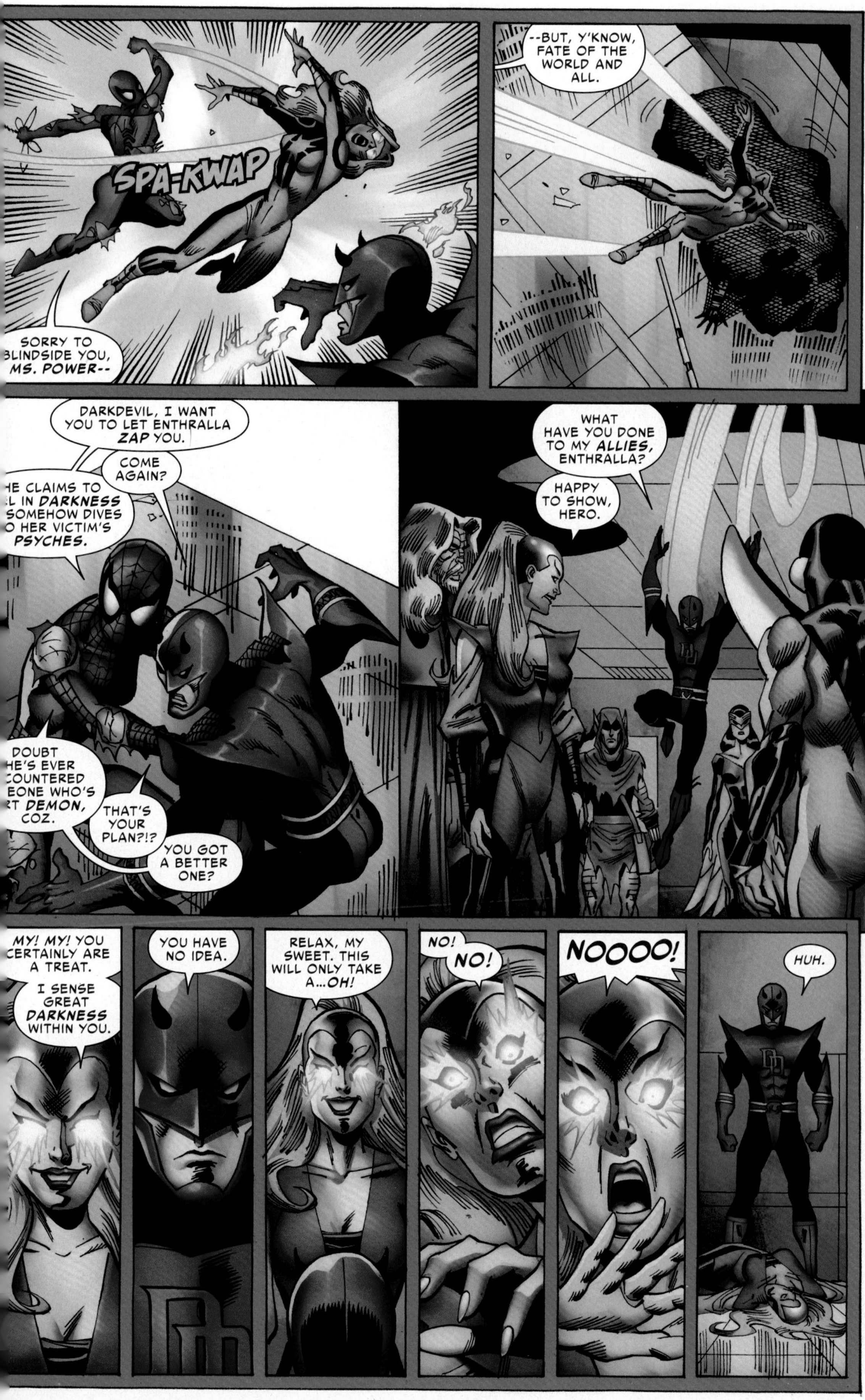
SPA-KWAP
SORRY TO BLINDSIDE YOU, MS. POWER--
--BUT, Y'KNOW, FATE OF THE WORLD AND ALL.
DARKDEVIL, I WANT YOU TO LET ENTHRALLA ZAP YOU.
COME AGAIN?
HE CLAIMS TO ...L IN DARKNESS ...SOMEHOW DIVES ...O HER VICTIM'S PSYCHES.
DOUBT ...HE'S EVER ...COUNTERED ...EONE WHO'S ...T DEMON, COZ.
THAT'S YOUR PLAN?!?
YOU GOT A BETTER ONE?
WHAT HAVE YOU DONE TO MY ALLIES, ENTHRALLA?
HAPPY TO SHOW, HERO.
MY! MY! YOU ...CERTAINLY ARE A TREAT.
I SENSE GREAT DARKNESS WITHIN YOU.
YOU HAVE NO IDEA.
RELAX, MY SWEET. THIS WILL ONLY TAKE A...OH!
NO!
NO!
NOOOO!
HUH.

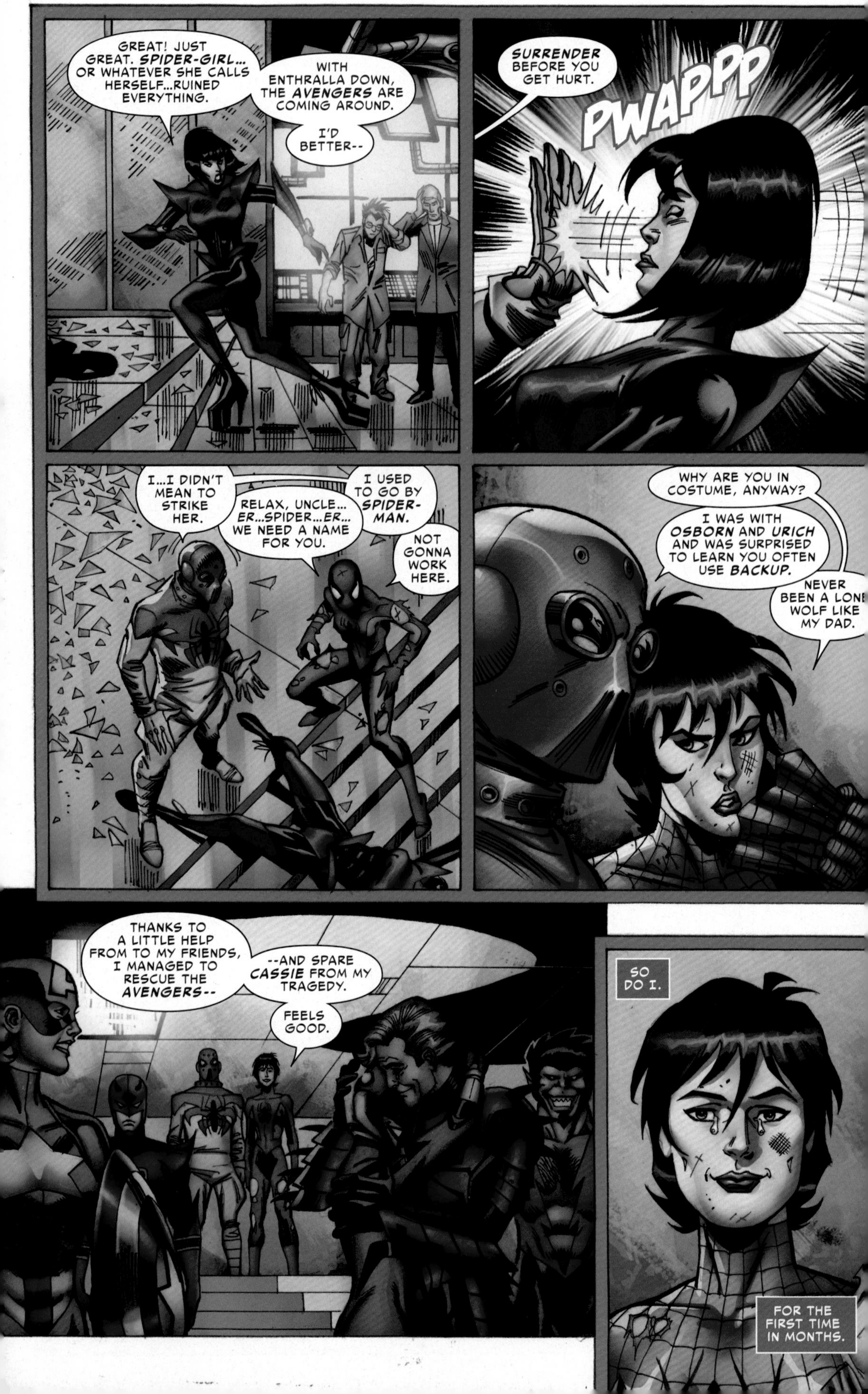

GREAT! JUST GREAT. SPIDER-GIRL... OR WHATEVER SHE CALLS HERSELF...RUINED EVERYTHING.
WITH ENTHRALLA DOWN, THE AVENGERS ARE COMING AROUND.
I'D BETTER--
SURRENDER BEFORE YOU GET HURT.
PWAPPP
I...I DIDN'T MEAN TO STRIKE HER.
RELAX, UNCLE... ER...SPIDER...ER... WE NEED A NAME FOR YOU.
I USED TO GO BY SPIDER-MAN.
NOT GONNA WORK HERE.
WHY ARE YOU IN COSTUME, ANYWAY?
I WAS WITH OSBORN AND URICH AND WAS SURPRISED TO LEARN YOU OFTEN USE BACKUP.
NEVER BEEN A LONE WOLF LIKE MY DAD.
THANKS TO A LITTLE HELP FROM TO MY FRIENDS, I MANAGED TO RESCUE THE AVENGERS--
--AND SPARE CASSIE FROM MY TRAGEDY.
FEELS GOOD.
SO DO I.
FOR THE FIRST TIME IN MONTHS.

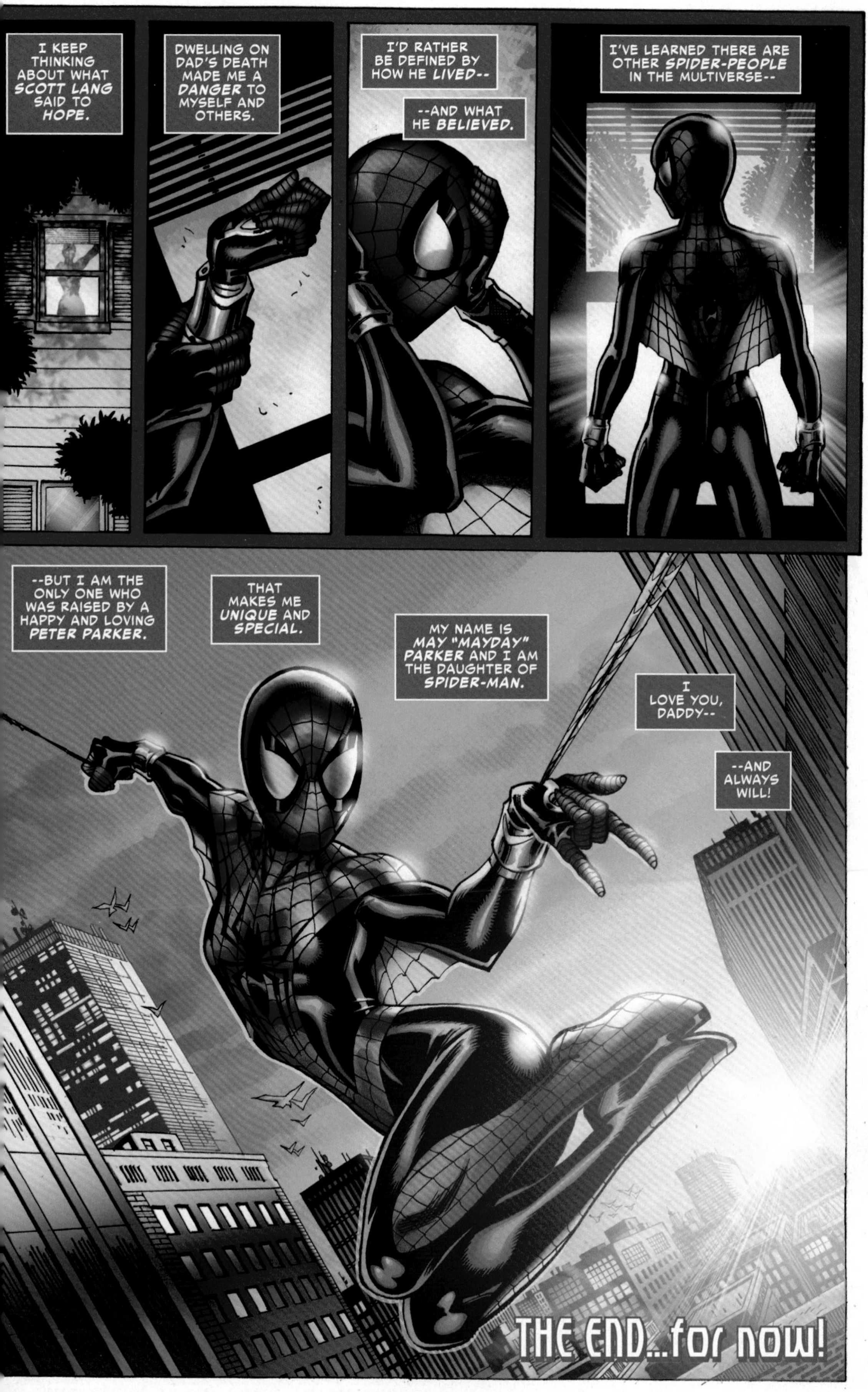
I KEEP THINKING ABOUT WHAT SCOTT LANG SAID TO HOPE.
DWELLING ON DAD'S DEATH MADE ME A DANGER TO MYSELF AND OTHERS.
I'D RATHER BE DEFINED BY HOW HE LIVED--
--AND WHAT HE BELIEVED.
I'VE LEARNED THERE ARE OTHER SPIDER-PEOPLE IN THE MULTIVERSE--
--BUT I AM THE ONLY ONE WHO WAS RAISED BY A HAPPY AND LOVING PETER PARKER.
THAT MAKES ME UNIQUE AND SPECIAL.
MY NAME IS MAY "MAYDAY" PARKER AND I AM THE DAUGHTER OF SPIDER-MAN.
I LOVE YOU, DADDY--
--AND ALWAYS WILL!
THE END...for now!

SPIDER-ISLAND #2 variant by Gabriele Dell'Otto

SPIDER-ISLAND #3 manga variant by Yusuke Murata